SPORT AND HISTORY SERIES

COMBAT SPORTS IN THE ANCIENT WORLD

COMPETITION, VIOLENCE, AND CULTURE

MICHAEL B. POLIAKOFF

YALE UNIVERSITY PRESS   NEW HAVEN AND LONDON

Designed by Sally Harris
and set in Palatino type by
Brevis Press, Bethany, Connecticut.
Printed in the United States of America

Library of Congress Cataloging-in-Publication Data

Poliakoff, Michael.
    Combat sports in ancient world: competition,
violence, and culture.

    (Sport and history series)
    Bibliography: p.
    Includes index.
    1. Hand-to-hand fighting—History.   2. Combat—
History.   3. Sports—History.   I. Title.   II. Series.
GV1111.P65   1987   796.8'15   86–32419
ISBN 0-300-03768-6 (cloth)
        0-300-06312-1 (pbk.)

The paper in this book meets the guidelines for
permanence and durability of the Committee on
Production Guidelines for Book Longevity
of the Council on Library Resources.

10   9   8   7   6   5   4

In memory of my mother,
Clare Poliakoff
In honor of my father,
Ben Poliakoff, MD

CONTENTS

ILLUSTRATIONS

ACKNOWLEDGMENTS

Many colleagues and friends have graciously helped me in the preparation of this book. Professor H. W. Pleket read the manuscript and made many suggestions for strengthening the argument. Professor Frank Nisetich, Dr. Walter Ameling, Lawrence Kenney, and Professor Jon Levenson have read sections of the manuscript and given very helpful advice on all aspects of the book. Dr. Dietrich von Bothmer was most generous in looking over the archaeological parts of the book and making important corrections. The final version is much better for Robert Fitzwilliam's careful reading and learned advice. Delving into the Near Eastern material was a daunting task; indeed, it would have been impossible without the help of Professor Marc Brettler, Professor William Hallo, Dr. Ulla Kasten, and Professor Wolfgang Decker. Amy Grice deserves my thanks for making the best possible prints from negatives of uneven quality. I learned a great deal about the tactics and ethos of wrestling from Yale's superb coach, Bert Waterman. Edward Tripp of Yale University Press has been an unfailing source of encouragement and help: he saw the potential in my undergraduate thesis long before I did.

As in the past, the Institut für Altertumskunde of the University of Cologne proved a most fruitful place for research and writing, and I wish to thank Professor R. Merkelbach both for his hospitality and for the very important advice he offered concerning this project. My thanks are also due Professor Wolfgang Decker and Professor Manfred Lämmer of the Seminar für Sportgeschichte; I gleaned much from the seminar collection and even more from the many discussions I had with Professors Decker and Lämmer about ancient sport; the manuscript is much improved after Professor Decker's careful reading of it.

I am deeply grateful to the organizations whose financial support made this project possible. A National Endowment for the Humanities Summer Stipend allowed me to start the research in Cologne; I did some very fruitful thinking and writing as a Fellow of the Center for Hellenic Studies in 1984–85, and a fellowship from the Alexander von Humboldt

Stiftung allowed me to finish the project shortly thereafter in Cologne. Wellesley College provided financial assistance toward preparing the plates.

My colleagues and friends have helped; I remain responsible of course for the contents and whatever shortcomings it may have. My children Cyrus and Emily shared the travels and the stresses that the book engendered with good nature and patience. I hope it will be worthy of them.

I acknowledge gratefully the following curators, museums, and staffs for their help: The Trustees of the British Museum; Dr. Michael Vickers of the Ashmolean Museum; The Metropolitan Museum of Art; The Toledo Museum of Art; Professor Åke Sjöberg, The University Museum; The Fogg Art Museum; The Museum of Fine Arts, Boston; Mr. John Larson of The Oriental Institute, Chicago; Mr. Kenneth Lohf of the Columbia University Papyrus Collection; Ellen R. Wilson of the Walters Art Gallery; The Cleveland Museum of Art; The Hood Museum of Art; Professor John Pollini of The Johns Hopkins Archaeological Collection; Professor Petros Themelis of the University of Crete for providing photos of the Eretria vases; The Heraklion Museum; The National Archaeological Museum of Athens; Dr. Günther Dankl of the Tirolerlandes Museum Ferdinandeum, Innsbruck; Dr. B. B. Piotrovskij of the Hermitage Museum, Leningrad; Dr. Peter Noelke and Dr. M. Riedel of the Römisch-Germanisches Museum; Dr. G. Platz of the Staatliche Museen Preussischer Kulturbesitz, Berlin; Dr. M. Raumschüssel of the Skulpturensammlung der Staatliche Kunstsammlungen Dresden; Staatliche Antikensammlungen of Munich; Dott. Francesco Nicosia, Soprintendente, Museo Archeologico, Florence; Dr. Fede Berti, Director of the Museo Archeologico Nazionale of Ferrara; Prof. Werner Johannowsky, Soprintendente Archeologico for Salerno, Avellino, and Benevento; Museo di Antichità, Turin; Prof. Ettore de Juliis, Soprintendente Archeologico for Puglia; Dott. Paola Pelagatti, Soprintendente of the Villa Giulia; The Vatican Museum; Christiana Morigi Govi, Direttore, Museo Civico Archeologico, Bologna; Museo Nazionale, Tarquinia; Museo Nazionale delle Terme, Rome; Dr. Caterina Caneva, Vice-Direttore of the Uffizi, Florence; The Louvre; Bibliothèque Nationale, Paris; Stiftsdechant Wolfgang Payrich of the Augustiner-Chorherrenstift Herzogenburg.

INTRODUCTION

You come to the Olympic festival itself and to the finest event in Olympia, for right here is the men's pankration. Arrichion, who has died seeking victory, is taking the crown for it, and this Olympic judge is crowning him. . . . Let's look at Arrichion's deed before it comes to an end, for he seems to have conquered not his opponent alone, but the whole Greek nation. . . . They shout and jump out of their seats and wave their hands and garments. Some spring into the air, others in ecstasy wrestle the man nearby. . . . Though it is indeed a great thing that he already won twice at Olympia, what has just now happened is greater: he has won at the cost of his life and goes to the land of the Blessed with the very dust of the struggle. Don't think this is the result of chance! There were very clever advance plans for this victory. . . . The one strangling Arrichion is depicted as a corpse, and he signals concession with his hand, but Arrichion is depicted as all victors are—indeed his blush is blooming and his sweat is still fresh, and he smiles, as do the living, when they perceive their victory.—Philostratos, Imagines *2.6*

Frenzied crowds at sporting events are familiar enough, but other elements in this third-century description might well cause the modern reader to recoil in horror. The occasion for this wild response (and the clear approbation of the Greek author who wrote about it) is the willing death of the victor, who has quite literally given his all for athletic success. The passage introduces us forcefully to the nature of our topic. The study of games and play is not a trivial pursuit, for it tells a lot about the character, values, and priorities of a society. The combat sports in particular, with their elements of violence and savagery, offer an unusually revealing perspective of different societies. Since modern man regularly has to do some serious thinking about his sports establishments and since the classical past tends to hover in all its venerability over such cogitations, the least we can do is to get our facts about antiquity and its games straight. If we are very fortunate in our search we can benefit from the articulate reflections of our ancient forebears, see what sport did for and to their societies, and look at ourselves with better and clearer vision. This, after all, is one of the best reasons for studying antiquity.

This book will cast its net rather wide, examining combat sport over an area that extends in space from Asia Minor to Italy and in time from 3000 B.C.E. to the twelfth century of our era. This is not for a moment to imply that similar institutions in different locations in time and place necessarily developed the way they did because of contact with each other. I will not impose an evolutionary structure on what calls for none. The unifying thread is combat sport, a common human activity that differs according to its social context—in fact, the most interesting thing about fighting as a sport is the form in which various peoples institutionalize it and what they reveal about themselves in so doing. That Greece receives the greatest number of pages here reflects not a hellenocentric bias but the historical reality that the Greeks pursued athletics to a far greater extent than any other ancient civilization and blessed us with much more information about themselves. Occasional gaps in the narrative about the ancient Near East are due to lack of evidence, not lack of interest.

I have attempted as far as possible to keep the text unencumbered with obscure names, scholarly apparatus, and jargon, either academic or athletic. It serves no purpose to make antiquity inaccessible to the nonspecialist, least of all here, where the subject is one which raises so many issues of general interest. In the sections that describe the nature of the combat sports my reconstruction of these activities often differs substantially from that found in mainstream and traditional works on the subject. The relative lack of polemic or even response to rival theories in the body of my text does not represent disregard for other scholars but an attempt at creating a more readable book. The endnotes offer both documentation and, where appropriate, technical discussion of controversial points; with the few exceptions noted in the text, the translations are my own. Throughout the book, I will use the less sectarian abbreviations B.C.E. (Before the Common Era) and C.E. (Common Era) in place of B.C. and A.D.

A fair question for a reader to ask is, How do we know about the ancient combat sports? Valuable evidence comes from ancient inscriptions on stone and bronze. The kings of the Mesopotamian peoples and the pharaohs of Egypt regularly recorded their exploits on the walls of their temples and tombs; Egyptian carvings are the principal source of knowledge for the athletic interests of the pharaohs. In Greece and Rome the custom of carving inscriptions in honor or in memory of both private and public figures was widespread, and our body of information steadily increases as archaeological excavations bring more inscriptions to light, allowing the values, aspirations, and careers of the ancients to reach us directly. Victors in the festivals had permission to erect statues of themselves with inscriptions celebrating their success; in some cases the proud city or the athlete's fellows might underwrite the cost of the monument.[1] Inscriptions were also an official vehicle for government decrees, and important information on the rules of Greek athletic festivals has survived in this form.

Other, less monumental writings have also come down to us directly from the ancients. The most popular writing surface in the ancient Mediterranean world consisted of thin sections of papyrus reed laid across each other and hammered until the oozing of their natural resins glued the strips into a durable and flexible section of writing material. Thousands of papyrus documents written by Greeks and Romans who lived in Egypt have survived, all preserved by the dry desert sands; among these are a number of decrees and letters concerning athletes as well as an extremely important section of an ancient wrestling manual. Long before the Greeks started to write, Mesopotamia developed a system of cutting letters with a reed in damp clay tablets, then baking them so that they would last indefinitely; the form of the letters has given them the name cuneiform ("wedge-shaped"). Thousands of tablets survive, yielding tax records, law cases, letters, and accounts of rituals. Some tablets clearly offer evidence for sport, though many gaps still exist in the lexica of ancient Near Eastern languages, and both details and at times even the sense of many intriguing texts remain unclear.

We are also fortunate in having, albeit in an indirect form, some of the official records of the Greek national festivals. Since the great festivals were events of religious importance, from early on the Olympic and Delphic officials began to keep registers of victors and notable occurrences.[2] These records have not survived intact—and, compounding the difficulty, they were not above question even in antiquity, especially in regard to the earliest years of Olympia—but many of them appear in ancient reeditions and in the discussions of ancient authors, including some who were extremely astute. Among others, the learned sophist Hippias of Elis composed a list of Olympic victors, and later Aristotle researched the records of Olympic victors from the earliest days of the festival.

Poetry and prose, too, provide important insights. Early Mesopotamian poetry such as the hymns of Shulgi and the epic of Gilgamesh contains references to wrestling: although both texts are incomplete, the fact that the hero or king appears in an athletic role is a significant witness to the importance of sport in the early Near East. The brilliant Greek poet Pindar composed songs in honor of those who won at the great games, giving us insights into the aspirations and values of his society. This body of evidence requires a critical eye, since the author's bias or motive for writing will substantially affect his use of facts. Comedy, for example, is a relatively rich source of sport terms, which appear in the colorful imagery and slapstick buffoonery of this genre. But one cannot be literal-minded: we learn, for instance, from ancient lexica that a wrestling hold called *mesoperdein* or *mesopherdein* appeared on the comic stage, and some discussions of ancient sport duly note it as an unexplained tactic. What the word really denotes, however, is a rude (and hilarious) imitation of the common wrestler's waistlock, *mesolabein*, "to hold around the middle": by replacing *-labein* ("hold") with *-perdein* ("fart") the comedian has created a tactic that surely never appeared in a palaestra: "to squeeze out a fart."[3] The physician Galen (court physician of Marcus Aurelius, second century C.E.) had firsthand knowledge of athletes, their training, diet, and injuries, and has preserved a wealth of information. Doctor and sports trainer, however, were locked at that time in a fierce rivalry for recognition in the world of physical therapy, and Galen's works bristle with polemics against the athletic establishment that sometimes distort the facts. We should be warned against taking at face value such sweeping judgments of his as, "We will dismiss completely from our treatise those who bring about this so-called 'good conditioning,' those who have authored these amazing tomes which are now disseminated by those people with cauliflower ears [that is, former pugilists]."[4] Greek authors of the first and second centuries C.E., particularly Plutarch, Lucian, Philostratos, and Pausanias, give important testimony for the study of ancient sport. But here too caution is in order. Greek authors of this era have a tendency to take a nostalgic trip down memory lane, enjoying the thought of a Golden Age six or seven hundred years before their time. Even the learned and responsible Plutarch includes misinformation, and Philostratos's treatise *On Athletics* is so intent on glorifying Greece's past that the work often has myth, legend, and moralizing where one expects hard facts about athletic practices.[5] On the other hand, excellent information regularly surfaces in unexpected places. The Jewish philosopher Philo of Alexandria offers the largest collection of sport metaphors of any extant Greek author, many of which are so detailed that they help establish the rules and procedures of sporting events. Church Fathers tended to vilify the gymnasia, but usually they knew their enemy intimately, and their writings can be extremely valuable for this study.[6]

Art is the other great source of information. Athletes appear in Mesopotamian sculpture as early as the third millennium B.C.E., and all of the civilizations I discuss here have left an abundance of visual evidence of their sports in their sculpture, carvings, painting, and coinage. Such evidence helps one reconstruct the tactics of the sports. Excavations are constantly bringing new finds to light; in 1969 a dig at Eretria on the

Greek island of Euboea, for example, yielded a series of Panathenaic vases with superbly drawn scenes of wrestling and pankration, including some very rare examples of wrestling on the ground (figs. 31, 32, 42, 59). The multitude of ancient objects poses a substantial challenge to those who study them, for their number far exceeds the cataloguers' resources to record them thoroughly, and they lie scattered in collections public and private all over the world.

Like literature, art is governed by conventions. Greek vase painting, which provides vivid illustrations of ancient sport, was generally a minor art form, rapidly executed for sale at a low price. The vase painter had a tendency to paint conventional, standard poses, and so symmetrical depictions of boxers and wrestlers about to engage are more common than those showing intricate holds, especially on the ground. The painters liked to show boxers' chests, and often at the expense of good perspective they present two pugilists fighting each other but with their chests fully turned toward the viewer. Since the vase paintings rarely come with captions identifying the action and the combat sports had some tactics in common with one another, it is sometimes difficult to decide, for example, whether the vase painter had in mind wrestling or pankration; pankration or boxing. One is guided only by a feeling for

1. Wall painting of wrestling groups, c. 2000 B.C.E., from Beni Hasan, Egypt.

what tactics do or do not make sense in the different events; in such cases dogmatism is quite out of place. Furthermore, time has taken its toll on the objects. The beautifully detailed depictions of Egyptian wrestling from the tombs of Beni Hasan are badly faded, as figure 1 shows, and one must depend on nineteenth-century sketches of them to understand their intricacies. Vases once fired in the kiln tend to survive everything except pulverization, though often their glazes erode, and restorations can be highly misleading. Nor is sculpture immune from the imaginative restorer, and sometimes it is necessary to visualize a fragment stripped of the extremities supplied by artists who lived a millennium or two later.[7]

The information consists of fragments, of course, for time has not left the records of the past intact. But all in all there is a considerable amount of primary information about ancient sport. Although some gaps will remain in the story, and we will have many occasions to use the word *probably,* there is much to tell.

I

GENERAL ASPECTS OF THE ANCIENT COMBAT SPORTS

DEFINITIONS

Boxing, wrestling, and pankration, a sport that allowed a variety of unarmed fighting tactics, were the three important forms of combat sport in the ancient world. Although a minor sport elsewhere in antiquity, stick fighting became a formal competition in Egypt, and it properly falls within the scope of this book. The element of fighting makes combat sports easy to mark off as a group; more difficult is settling on a definition of sport in general. I define sport and athletics in this book as activity in which a person physically competes against another in a contest with established regulations and procedures, with the immediate object of succeeding in that contest under criteria for determining victory that are different from those that mark success in everyday life (warfare, of course, being included as part of everyday life in antiquity). In other words, sport, as opposed to play or recreation, cannot exist without an opponent and a system for measuring the success or failure of the competitors' performances. Jogging alone or in a group is recreation (or training) until someone starts to compare performances, at which point it becomes an athletic contest—a sport. Whether or not the competitor receives money or some other prize is irrelevant, for both professional and amateur have the immediate goal of winning the contest, and what happens afterward does not change the nature of that contest.

This definition of sport excludes a number of forms of combat, such as fencing, armed dueling, and gladiatorial events, activities that fall more properly into categories other than sport. In antiquity, the purpose of fencing (with blunt-tipped weapons) was military training, and these activities did not have a fixed structure or system of competition. A gladiator fighting to kill or disable his opponent and save himself in any manner possible is not participating in a sport but in a form of warfare for spectators. The fact that gladiators (most of whom were slaves or condemned criminals—even the volunteers were bound by a fearsome oath to obey all commands) followed under compulsion the orders of the arena organizers is another strong sign that the arena had a purposefulness in its activities that does not square with the more arbitrary conventions of sport.[1]

SIMILARITIES AMONG THE COMBAT SPORTS

Although boxing, wrestling, and pankration require different skills and tactics—a fact borne out by the careers of modern athletes, who rarely compete at high levels in both boxing and wrestling—the Greeks, at least, considered their combat sports to be closely related. Often the same man excelled in more than one combat sport. Theogenes of Thasos won in his long career approximately thirteen hundred crowns in boxing and pankration, and twice at the Isthmus (see below) he won both events in the same day.[2] The text of the epigram that graced the victory statue of a man who won all three combat sports in one day has come down to us:

> In Kleitomachos' statue, my friend, you see a spirit of brass
> Like the one which was once witnessed by all Hellas.
> For straight from stripping off the boxer's bloody glove,
> He took his stand in the fierce pankration.
> In the third contest on his shoulders came no dust,
> But taking no fall, he won the three trials at the Isthmus.
> Alone of all Greeks in his prize. He crowns in glory
>   seven-gated Thebes,
> And also his father, Hermokrates.[3]

The inscriptions offer many other examples of victories in two different combat events. On the other hand, for obvious reasons combat athletes rarely succeeded in track and field events, and Theogenes made a special point with much fanfare of winning in the *dolichos* (long run) after a series of boxing and pankration victories: he is an exception that demonstrates the rule.[4]

The Greeks called boxing, wrestling, and pankration the heavy events, for there were no weight classes in antiquity, and these events were the domain of the large and strong. Plutarch was blunt and accurate about the chances less muscular men had for success when he wrote that athletes who have developed their bodies eventually crush their opponents and defeat those with good timing and skill. Stories of sport heroes are prone to exaggeration, but they are still instructive in their emphasis on the size of the athletes. The first victor in pankration, Lygdamis of Syracuse, was gigantic—it was said that his foot was a cubit (about eighteen inches) in length. Milo the wrestler reportedly ate twenty pounds of meat, as much bread, and drank eighteen pints of wine each day, and once carried a four-year-old bull around the stadium at Olympia before eating it in the course of one day. He, like Theogenes, is said to have carried on his back a full-size statue and put it in place. Theogenes' appetite also was proverbial, to the extent that it became the subject of an ancient joke: looking at a statue of the athlete with its hand extended, an epigrammatist wrote that Theogenes had already eaten an ox and was beckoning for more food. Marvelous legends about Poulydamas the pankratiast have survived: Pausanias says he was the tallest of his race of men, that once he slew a lion unarmed, held a bull by its hooves, and stopped a speeding chariot by grasping its wheels.[5]

The ideological and ethical terms that describe these sports are also quite similar. Among other things, the athletes' ability to suffer in silence was proverbial. Cicero noted it as an example of fortitude, and according to an ancient anecdote the poet Aeschylus observed while watching the Isthmian games that the boxer's training is such that though the spectators cry out at the force of the punches, the one struck is silent. So Eurydamas of Kyrene in large measure won through his grim determination—his opponent hit him hard enough to break several of his teeth, but Eurydamas preferred to swallow them rather than spit them out and thereby inform his opponent that he had landed such a successful blow. If the punches were not damage enough, the sun also was threatening. The Olympics were held in July or August in a stadium that offered no shade; with the exception of the Isthmian Games, virtually all the important festivals fell in the hottest months, and at least at Olympia the combat sports began at midday. The spectators found the sun uncomfortable—some slaveowners in jest threatened their unruly slaves with the punishment of a trip to Olympia—but for the athletes it was an even greater problem. Cicero observed that often eager but inexperienced boxers who could bear the blows were unable to bear the heat at Olympia. In one Olympic final contest reportedly both boxers were on the verge of giving up, one because of injuries, the other because of thirst; but luckily for the latter a storm broke, and he lapped up the rainwater that the sheepskin rim of his boxing gloves absorbed and went on to win the contest. Given this notorious stress factor, it became a source of mockery for athletes to train indoors with light sparring but to shun the sun and blows of the stadium. These grueling fights, moreover, had no time limit save nightfall, and not surprisingly *kartereia* ("toughness" or "endurance") figures prominently in ancient descriptions of all the combat sports as well as on the victors' monuments. A pankratiast who fought hard in the finals at Olympia after winning taxing preliminary rounds, continuing the match until night interrupted it, gained praise for "toughing it out." One boxer's inscription starts, "I won at boxing thrice by my skill and the endurance of my hands": perseverance was also the particular strength of the boxer Melankomas, who was said to have been able to keep his guard up for two days.[6] An incident that Philo of Alexandria witnessed shows how crucial the will to continue was:

> I already witnessed once in a pankration contest a man who hurled blows with hands and feet, all of them well-directed, leaving nothing undone that might bring him victory, but who gave up, was worn out, and finally left the stadium uncrowned. The man being battered, on the other hand, was compact with solid flesh, mean, tough, exuding the athlete's spirit, and all muscle, like a stone or iron—he didn't give in to the blows and broke the force of his opponent by the toughness and firmness of his endurance until he won the final victory.[7]

As in modern combat sport, athletes were hardly unanimous in reckoning whether skill or strength is more important for victory. Wrestling, because of its tremendous number of leverages and holds, was usually, but not always, called a sport of craft. One of the earliest mentions of wrestling in Western history, an Akkadian tablet from Mari some 3,700 years old, invokes the stratagems of wrestlers as proverbial. The king rebukes his lazy son: "You think of tricks to beat your enemy and to maneuver for position against him; but your enemy similarly tries to think up tricks to maneuver for position against you, just as wrestlers use tricks against each other." The reputation (and the victors' monuments) of pankratiasts and boxers tended to give somewhat more credit to power and toughness, though skill too figures prominently. Ambidexterity, of course, was a decided advantage, since the athlete so gifted could readily exploit his opponent's weaker side.[8]

Boxing was disfiguring, and praise of the pugilist's appearance is quite rare. For pankratiasts and wrestlers, however, mention of the form or beauty of the athlete is rather common.[9] So ran the inscription on the victor's monument of Theognetos of Aegina:

> Recognize when looking at Theognetos, boy victor
> at Olympia, a master of the wrestler's art.
> Most beautiful to see, at contest no less blessed,
> he has crowned the city of his goodly kin.[10]

And that of Ariston of Ephesos, victor in pankration in Olympiad 207 (49 C.E.), "asks" the statue that stood above it:

Who are you who bear the bloom of youth but manhood's force?
Who are you whose beauty and strength we see?
Who then and whence come you, whose son are you, come speak![11]

The Greeks were unique among the ancients in regularly conducting athletic practice and competition in the nude. Homer's boxers and wrestlers wear a loincloth, but shortly after that time, Greek athletes part with all covering on their bodies. The Romans found the practice of public nudity abhorrent, "the wellspring of vice," and not surprisingly, athletes in Roman cities, especially before the Imperial period, generally wore loincloths in their competitions.[12]

TRAINING

The training routines of heavy athletes were fairly similar. They had the same buildings and often the same diets, equipment, and exercises. On one occasion, we hear of wrestlers in training

2. Roman clay lamp, first half of the first century C.E. Unlike Greek athletes, this boxer wears a loincloth.

at Olympia being sent for a round of light boxing as part of their preparation.

Combat athletes practiced at a palaestra. The word derives from the Greek verb *palaio* ("wrestle"): although other activities took place in the palaestra, it was first and foremost a place for the practice of combat — sport. The earliest palaestrae were privately owned facilities, but by the fifth century B.C.E. public ones existed also. At some time, probably in the sixth century, a new type of athletic building arose called a *gymnasion* (Latin, *gymnasium*). This was a large complex, usually, though not always, public, that included a palaestra for the combat sports but also had a covered running track and playing fields, neither of which was a common part of a palaestra. The Roman municipal baths, starting with Nero's reign, generally included all the athletic facilities that the Greeks knew, though often much reduced to give more room to the bathing facilities that Romans so prized.[13]

The core of the palaestra was the wrestling room, which consisted of an area of softened sand (*skamma*) and another area covered with mud. For obvious reasons, a soft surface was essential to the well-being of the wrestlers; the Hippocratic medical writings grimly record the death of a wrestler who fell on a hard surface and died ten days later from the chest injuries he sustained. The athletes themselves prepared the sand surface by chopping the ground with pickaxes: this was considered a valuable exercise, and the pickaxe was one of the identifying signs of the athlete. The custom gave rise to a moralizing ethnic joke. Some people of Sybaris, a city renowned for its self-indulgence and sloth (from which, of course, we get our modern word *sybarite*), saw some athletes of Kroton digging up the palaestra and couldn't reckon how a city of Kroton's stature failed to have hired laborers for such jobs. The sand was hardly ordinary soil, and when local material was not up to standards, special sand was imported at great cost. The sand area in the palaestra was unroofed—in competition the wrestlers and pankratiasts fought on a *skamma* in the stadium, and as noted earlier tolerance of the heat was a crucial factor. The mud pit must have been in the covered part of the palaestra, among other reasons, to avoid evaporation. It provided an important part of the athlete's training, increasing his strength and skill at holding an opponent. Ancient doctors, moreover, thought that contact with the mud had curative properties, and an expensive mixture of mud and oil was sometimes used in the pits.[14]

Presiding particularly over the palaestra was a statue of Hermes (En)agonios, "Hermes of the Contest," usually in the traditional herm form: a sculptured head on a rectangular marble base, unelaborated except for an erect phallus. Hermes was the mythological inventor of

3. Greek palaestra scene, c. 480 B.C.E. On the left, two youths wrestle, watched by a trainer. On the right an athlete starts to wrap his hands with boxing thongs (see chap. 5), and next to him an athlete uses a pickaxe to soften the exercise surfaces.

wrestling and a general patron of the sport; in some stories he is the sire of Palaestra, the personified goddess of wrestling. In simple, schematic depictions of the palaestra, often a herm alone sets the scene for the viewer. Statues of Apollo and Herakles were also common in the palaestra and gymnasium, Herakles being particularly popular because he himself underwent heavy labors.[15]

The palaestra had a number of small rooms where the athletes prepared for the exercises. Since Greek athletics from the eighth century on were done in the nude, the athlete first entered the *apoduterion* (literally, "undressing room"). This was hardly a simple locker room: the vases show that some general physical preparations—oiling and, after the sports, use of the strigil (see below)—might take place there, but the wide benches also provided a place for relaxation and discussion. When Socrates met with the youth of Athens in the palaestra, it was often this room that hosted their conversations. A room called the *aleipterion* in later times maintained the correct temperature for the application of oil, and the palaestra had storage room for the oil (*elaeothesium*).

Oil was a crucial part of all athletes' hygiene, since it kept the skin supple. Massage (for which oil was essential) was so important that two of the ancient names for trainers derive from it, *paidotribes* ("boy rubber") and *aleiptes* ("oiler"). For wrestlers and pankratiasts, of course, oil had the added function of reducing skin abrasion and hindering dirt from becoming packed into the pores of the skin. The oil was quite costly, and in earlier times it was a notable largess for the gymnasiarch, a gymnasium official, sometimes elected, sometimes voluntary, to provide it completely from his own wealth during his office. Many gymnasiarchs were forced to share their offices with others in order to meet the oil expense. At the festivals either the host city or a philanthropist provided free oil for the competitors.[16]

Repeated blows to the ears, even light ones, cause disfiguring cauliflower ears, and many athletes practicing combat sport wore ear protectors (fig. 4). Socrates spoke of one's having cauliflower ears as a sign of pro-Spartan affectation—although the Spartans refused to compete abroad in boxing, it seems that their home variety was traumatic. The bronze statue of the seated boxer (fig. 74) depicts very damaged ears, and Galen considered it a typical feature of athletic personnel. Plutarch, gentle moralist, wondered whether athletes really needed ear coverings as much as children exposed to indecent language around them.

Long hair would have been a liability in wrestling and pankration, and Greek and Roman competitors at least kept their hair short, while Mesopotamian and Egyptian art shows this was not always the case in the Near East. Customary Greek practice is reflected in the line from the Attic stage "your hair is long—you're not a wrestler" (Euripides, *Bacchae*

4. Greek wrestlers watched by a trainer, c. 490 B.C.E. The athlete on the right wears headgear.

455). In later centuries, athletes allowed a tuft of hair on the top of the head to grow longer, a style called in Latin the *cirrus* (figs. 47, 60, 63, 79). It was particularly popular among the combat athletes, though other sportsmen, including trainers, wore it.[17]

With this preparation, the athletes went to the exercises. While the mud pit offered the strength-building exercise of holding on to a slippery opponent, wrestlers working out in the sand coated themselves or each other with a fine layer of sand before engaging: this ensured that they could take firm grips on one another, as they would in formal competitions. Such firm grips may not have been welcome to all participants. A Greek jest tells of a fictional character who feared his opponent and wiped his neck with an oily hand just before the contest in order to be able to slip from his rival's holds. Ancient medical theory held that dust had cooling properties, and others besides the wrestlers applied it on top of the oil for this purported benefit.[18]

To learn tactics, wrestlers sometimes used a cooperative partner who would follow but not resist. Mostly, however, wrestlers practiced by wrestling, and their workouts were notoriously strenuous, while pankratiasts and in particular boxers sparred lightly (*akrocheirismos*) for the obvious purpose of avoiding injury. Boxers were also fond of shadow-boxing (*skiamachia* or *cheironomia*), sometimes with enough of a show to attract a crowd of spectators. The ancients recognized the importance of rhythm in all physical activities, and like soldiers, long jumpers, and discus throwers, boxers and wrestlers sometimes practiced and competed to the accompaniment of the flute.[19]

The heavy athletes had a variety of training routines involving weights, calisthenics, and punching bags. Some reports of their weight lifting feats, like the story of Milo carrying the bull around the stadium and that of Milo meeting a shepherd who carried for fifteen meters a boulder that he himself could hardly move, have the air of folktales, but other sources give us very accurate information about athletic practices. A fourth-century C.E. author describes how athletes in Athens measured their strength by lifting heavy weights and used this criterion to pair themselves for contests; in other words, there were systematic weight gradations. Certain vase paintings show athletes exercising with very light weights, which would develop their muscle tone and quickness. Boxers used small punching bags much like those used by modern boxers (fig. 5), while pankratiasts practiced their kicks and punches against a larger and heavier device filled with sand instead of grain: the swinging weight, in addition to developing their blows, gave them practice at withstanding the opponent's momentum. The palaestra had a special room for these important bag exercises (*korukeion*). Some exercises in-

5. Practice with a punching bag; the athlete is probably Polydeukes from the myth of the Argonautica. Etruscan engraving, under Greek influence, of the late fourth century, B.C.E.

creased strength without weights. The trainers knew the value of rope climbing and hanging by one's arms, and Galen described a series of exercises which he found as a physician to be of benefit to the general public, all of them based on wrestling positions: for example, hugging the exercise partner around the ribs then lifting and tilting him or, conversely, trying to escape from a partner who was holding tightly around the waist. Galen approved of these routines because they strengthened the muscles and were so safe that they could be performed on any surface, rather than requiring a trip to the palaestra. Wrestlers also had their own advanced routines for developing certain muscles, he noted, such as trapping the partner's foot between one's knees, joining hands, and struggling from that position: these were clearly too hazardous to perform without a soft sand surface underneath.[20]

After the sports, the athletes scraped the oil and dirt off their bodies with a curved bronze implement called a strigil and then washed. Before

Roman times, the washing facilities were simple: cold water flowed into basins along the walls or from overhead spouts, and vase paintings show the athletes standing under the faucets or sometimes pouring water over one another. Hot water inside the gymnasium was a luxury of a later era, though some Greek gymnasia did have heated rooms.[21]

Training and coaching the athletes was a highly developed specialty. So Aristotle noted that the Greeks argue more about the navigation of ships (hardly an unfamiliar area to the Greeks!) than about the training of athletes because navigation was less well organized as a science. Since sport was an important part of the military preparations of the ephebes, the eighteen-year-olds in training for military service and citizenship (see chap. 6), in classical times the state provided them with various trainers at public expense. The best coaches, however, those who trained the athletes for competition, commanded high fees. We hear of one in the fourth century B.C.E. receiving a hundred drachmas (close to one-third the annual salary of a day laborer) from a student. These men were sometimes previous victors, and they often accompanied the athlete to the competition, coaching him even during the contest. Sometimes a city or a wealthy patron subsidized a promising athlete or a youth accumulated enough money in local competition to hire a big-time trainer. Medical knowledge was important as well, that is to say, the care and feeding of the athlete to achieve maximum performance. The formulae for victory were not, however, altogether pleasant. Athletes, especially those training for combat sport, had a meat diet, which was quite a rarity in Greece, but this was coupled with a rigid schedule of rest, exercise, and sometimes purging of the body by induced vomiting. At some point before the first century of our era, trainers developed a four-day cycle, the tetrad, beginning with a day of preparatory exercises, then on the next day an intensive workout, followed by a day of relaxation, and finally a day of medium intensity training. As modern coaches have found, such a program can be useful, but under the direction of an incompetent trainer is dangerous, for it encourages mindless adherence to schedule without regard to the condition of the individual. The Olympic wrestling victor Gerenos died when his trainer forced him after a night of celebrating to perform the exercises appointed for that day of the cycle.[22] Despite their exaggerations, Galen's polemics against athletic regimens contain a core of truth:

> The athletes each day labor at their exercises beyond what is suitable: and they take their food under force, often extending their eating until midnight. . . . For when those who live according to nature have come home from their work, needing food, then these athletes are getting up from sleep—so

that their lives are like that of pigs—except for the fact that the pigs do not work beyond measure or eat under force.[23]

Plenty of vase paintings, moreover, show that the trainers used their sticks freely when the athlete did not perform properly. One ancient writer told of a trainer who struck his pupil despite his victory for playing to the crowd instead of wrestling sensibly. The most rigorous of all places was Olympia, where a special rule required the athletes to train there for at least a month under the eye of the local officials, who had the right to flog or dismiss athletes who did not obey.[24]

THE ATHLETIC FESTIVALS

One important difference between the Greek world (along with that of the Romans, who imitated it) and the Near East is the system of athletic festivals. There is no parallel in the rest of the ancient world for the massive Greek system. Egypt shows no trace of regular sport competitions, with the exception of the festival for the Greek hero Perseus at Chemmis, an event which Herodotos explicitly called a rare borrowing of Greek ways. Mesopotamia did have regular occasions for sport, and at some festivals even food subsidies were granted to the athletes, but as best we can tell the number of these events was small and their scope limited. As we shall see, high-level sports abounded in antiquity, particularly in Egypt, but it is culturally significant that outside of the Greek world little attempt was made to provide formal, regular vehicles for athletic competition.[25]

The Greek, and later the Greco-Roman, world was packed with athletic festivals, ranging from small contests that admitted only local citizens to the great national festivals, to which the whole ancient world thronged. In the top rank were the games at Olympia and Delphi (Pythian festival), held every four years, and those at Corinth (Isthmian festival) and Nemea, held every two years. These were the period games, that is, the games of the four-year circuit (*periodos*), also known as sacred crown games, since at the festival sites the victors received only wreaths: of olive leaves at Olympia, of laurel plus a handful of apples at Delphi, of pine or in some eras of celeriac at the Isthmus, and of celeriac at Nemea, and had to wait until they returned to their city-states to receive more practical monetary rewards. A man who won at all four festivals received the special title of *periodonikes*. Other sacred crown games, fully as international as the Big Four of the Period, often gave material prizes as well as a wreath. Among these were the Great Panathenaia of Athens, a prestigious contest that gave valuable olive oil to the victors and runners-up. Other sacred crown games gave cloaks (Pellene), bronze shields (Argos), tripods, that is, three-legged cauldrons (Lykaia), and a variety of other material rewards. Certain games were reorganized as isolympic ("equal to Olympic") or isopythian ("equal to Pythian"), that is, they imitated the organization, events, and even the name of their models: for example, Smyrna in Asia Minor had its own Olympics and Tralles had a Pythian festival. Finally, a category of games existed that did not give crowns at all but only a material prize—sometimes a large amount of money. By the Roman period more than three hundred Greek contests were held all over the Mediterranean, from Asia Minor to Egypt to Italy. The victors' monuments are the most eloquent testimony to the proliferation of festivals. One inscription, for example, boasted that the man it celebrated competed among three nations, Italy, Greece, and Asia.[26] Perhaps the best summary is that of a nineteenth-century scholar who elegantly wrote when reviewing the victories of a pankratiast who lived during the reign of Marcus Aurelius, "Coming from Aphrodisias, he drank from the Euphrates, received a crown from Caesar's hand on the banks of the Tiber, and filled the Arabs with admiration no less than the Athenians!"[27]

To speak of amateurism in Greek sport is an inadmissible though common fiction. H. A. Harris, for example, wrote in his book *Sport in Greece and Rome* that Greek sport began its "decline" between the fourth and second centuries B.C.E., the reason being that "when money comes in at the door, sport flies out the window." But by this reckoning Greek sport flew out the window before the time of Solon (archon in 594 B.C.E.), who gave handsome cash awards to victors in the national festivals. The sixth-century B.C.E. philosopher Xenophanes complained bitterly about the free meals, treasures, and other benefits athletes reaped, and a recently discovered inscription from southern Italy, which records an athlete's donation of a tithe (tenth) of his Olympic reward to erect a building, shows how massive the earnings could be. Purists who refused to mix money with sport did not exist in the ancient world, and victors' monuments boast of success in the cash competitions as openly as they boast of victory in sacred contests.[28]

ORGANIZATION OF COMPETITION

At the festivals the athletes were required to register. According to one second-century author, the athletes swore to stay and attempt the contest, though a few inscriptions show that there were exceptions: the presence of a famous and formidable athlete could make others, even after they had registered, abandon the contest. The officials did, however, enforce the registration deadline strictly, barring tardy athletes from the competition; the only acceptable excuses for late arrival were illness, pirates, or storm. I noted before that the competitions in the combat sports had no weight classes; they did have, however, a division according to age. Some festivals offered as many as five different categories, though usually there were only two. The Greeks had no birth certificates, and arguments sometimes arose over the appropriate category, though certain particularly gifted and ambitious young men of their own will entered more than one age division in the same competition.[29]

At some point before the first century B.C.E., athletes began to organize into guilds, through which they pursued their corporate interests. At first there were two groups, sacred victors and athletes (without further distinction), based, it appears, in Asia Minor. Around the middle of the second century C.E. the two guilds merged, establishing their headquarters in Rome, for naturally the emperors took great interest in the politics and economics of festivals and worked closely with the guilds. The athletes were required to pay a membership fee, but the associations were very advantageous, arranging athletic festivals and the awards, and they seemed to have gained official favors for their members such as tax exemption.[30]

There were further formalities. At Olympia, for example, the athletes, along with their fathers and brothers, and their trainers swore that they would commit no foul play and that they had trained faithfully. Their instructions were, "If you have worked in a manner worthy of coming to Olympia, and have done nothing in an offhand or base way, proceed with good courage; but as for those who have not so exercised, go away wherever you like."[31] Those responsible for adjudicating the age categories swore that they would judge without accepting bribes and would keep all information concerning the athletes confidential. The officials also ensured that the athletes were Greeks of free birth and that they were free from the taint of homicide, even absolved homicide. When the time for competition came, the participants made a formal entry into the stadium and gave their names.

All Greek competitions took place in the stadium, for the palaestra could not accommodate the large numbers of spectators. These structures were simple and remained so throughout Greek history; even in the Roman era they often provided mere mounds of earth for spectators' seats. Athens and Delphi were unusual in having stone seats, the donation of Herodes Atticus in the second century C.E.; Olympia and Epidaurus never had more than earth mounds. In contrast to this apparent unconcern for spectator amenities, the organizers gave considerable care to the competition surfaces, and an inscription from Delphi records the large sum of 145 drachmas for preparing the boxing area.[32]

The heavy athletes competed in tournaments, sometimes with many rounds. The pairing for each round was determined by lot; a second-century account of the process is so complete that it can stand by itself with only a few notes:

> A silver urn is set forth, sacred to the god, in which small inscribed lots have been thrown, the size of a bean. On two lots alpha is inscribed, on two a beta, and on two others the gamma, and so on the same way: if there are more athletes, two lots always have the same letter. Now each athlete coming forth makes a prayer to Zeus and putting his hand down into the urn draws out one of the lots, and after him another athlete, and the whip bearer standing near each one holds his hand, not allowing him to read whatever letter it is he has drawn. When everyone already has a lot, the alutarch, I think, or one of these Hellanodikai . . . walking around looks at the lots of the athletes as they stand in a circle, and thus he joins the one holding the alpha to the other who has drawn the alpha for wrestling or pankration, the one who has the beta to the other with the beta, and the other matching inscribed lots in the same way.[33]

The process was repeated for every round until the finals, which means, of course, that when there was an odd number of competitors, there could be a bye in several rounds with, perhaps, the same man resting twice or even more times. (There may have been a rule that no competitor could draw a bye more than once, but the sources are silent on this question.) The athletes were keenly aware of the effects of this system. The term *anephedros* ("winning without a bye") appears on some inscriptions as a particular sign of honor, testimony to great endurance and stamina. Pindar speaks of an athlete deprived of victory by the draw—probably he had to compete in straight rounds against a fresh and rested opponent. One victor in boys' pankration at Olympia thought it worth recounting in verse all the details of his triumph in such a situation:

> I am the talk of all Asia, I Ariston,
> Who took the olive crown in pankration.
> Whom Hellas called a man, seeing how in boyhood's flower
> I held in my hands manhood's power.
> My crown lay not in kind fortune's hazard, but in fight
> without pause, I won of Olympia and Zeus the prize.
> Of seven boys, alone I had no rest,
> But always paired, the others of the crown I bereft.

So now I make glad my sire Eireinaios
And with immortal garlands my land of Ephesos.[34]

Ariston fought in three rounds, meeting in the finals the boy who drew
the first-round bye. The following scheme represents his progress (A is
Ariston, E the contestant who drew the bye, and the numbers the re-
maining five contestants):

A:2   3:4   5:6   E

A:3   5:E

A:E

A

The tournaments could be extremely large, and several inscriptions and
victory odes speak of the athlete defeating four opponents in a single
contest. In the absence of a rule limiting the number of byes the same
competitor could have in a given tournament, the number of initial entries could be arbitrarily large; even presupposing a ban on multiple
byes, the defeat of four opponents means there were between nine and
thirty-one initial entries. Other inscriptions speak of six, eight, even nine
rounds of contest. Occasionally the athletes managed to get a pause—
in epic descriptions often the boxers back away from each other to catch
their breath, and there are historical instances of this indulgence as well.
An athlete might, for example, show his battered limbs to the judge and
gain some respite: such indulgence was not uncommon, but it was not
a regular or predictable event either. Since the contests were elimination
tournaments, the officials were willing to allow a bout to go on and on
in order to avoid a tie. When no clear winner emerged from the final
round, the victor's wreath became sacred, that is, dedicated to the god,
and was not awarded to a competitor; though if the officials deemed that
the athletes had competed valiantly, they might award the crown notwithstanding, as they did in the case of Claudius Rufus (see chap. 7).[35]

II
WRESTLING

Wrestling appealed deeply to the ancients. Though far from being a gentle sport, it is substantially less violent and injurious than the other two combat sports: it pits one man against another in a close struggle that maximizes the role of skill and science. In a manner that encourages wide participation, it tests an array of martial virtues: cunning, boldness, courage, self-reliance, and perseverance.[1] Not surprisingly some of the earliest figures in the Western tradition, both legendary and historical—Gilgamesh, the Sumerian king Shulgi, the patriarch Jacob—stand their ground as wrestlers, and quite early in their history the Greeks developed special facilities for the practice of the sport. Hellenic society expected that an accomplished and educated man would practice and enjoy wrestling as an adult.

THE FALL

A basic difference between wrestling and the other two combat sports is that rendering the opponent unable or unwilling to continue accounted for a minor number of victories: the normal objective was to score a fall on the opponent. To win a formal competition, a Greek wrestler needed to score three falls against his opponent; thus a maximum of five bouts could occur. Seneca the philosopher used the expression that the wrestler thrice thrown has lost the victory palm, and the third fall was a common Greek metaphor for a decisive defeat. So in Plato's dialogue the *Euthydemus* Socrates described a critical point in a contest of wit as the moment when one pundit attacked his youthful adversary and attempted, as if it were a wrestling match, to throw him for the third time.[2] Although the ancient world never developed a system of awarding points for successful tactics, as is familiar in modern competitions, there were, in fact, several ways of scoring a fall on the opponent.

Throwing a man to his back or shoulders constituted a fall so dramatic that in the Greek world it practically became symbolic of a wrestler's

victory. The epigram praising Kleitomachos, which we saw in the preceding chapter, recorded that after he won the boxing and pankration
at the Isthmian games he did not get dust on his shoulders—that is to
say, he won the wrestling competition at the Isthmus without taking a
fall. Galen used the image of a back fall to describe total defeat when he
compared supporters of rival medical theories to peculiar wrestlers who
have been thrown and lie on their backs but still refuse to recognize the
fall and continue to struggle.[3] Merely touching the back or shoulders to
the ground constituted a fall; the term *pin* from modern wrestling, which
implies holding the opponent to the ground, has no place in the ancient
world. Note in figure 6 how the vase painter has captured this important
moment by portraying the referee as bending forward to see if the shoulders of the wrestler being thrown will in fact touch the ground for a fall.

Completely stretching a man prone was also a fall in Greek and Roman
wrestling, as was tying him up in a controlling hold from which he could
not escape. A wrestler might fight from his knees and even deliberately
take that position, but once stretched out prone or totally tied in a hold,
he lost the match. The Roman poet Statius described a match that ends
with such a fall. There the hero Tydeus lifted and threw his opponent:

> balancing him in the air, deliberately and without warning he let go, threw
> him on his side, followed him as he fell, wrapped his right arm around his
> neck and his legs around the groin. His opponent was overwhelmed, his
> strength failed, and he fought only out of a sense of shame. Finally he is
> stretched out on his chest and stomach on the ground and sadly arises after

6. Referee bends down and watches carefully to see if the wrestler's shoulders touch the
ground for a fall. Greek vase, c. 530 B.C.E.

a long while, leaving his marks of disgrace on the imprinted ground. [*Thebaid* 6.898–904]

The rules also permitted strangling an opponent to force him to concede: in this respect the nature of wrestling and of pankràtion meet for a moment.[4] The idea of a chokehold held to submission may seem strange to us in light of contemporary Western wrestling rules, but there is too much evidence to doubt that it was a feature of Greek wrestling, as it is a part of the ground wrestling in judo today.

Although it did not mean defeat for a wrestler to drop to his knee, it often placed him in a precarious position, and not surprisingly falling to the knee became a metaphor for being at a disadvantage. Herodotos told how the loss of a battle threw the city of Chios to its knee, after which it quickly fell. These words may seem obscure—for a city on its knee would seem to be in defeat already—unless we understand the rules of the palaestra as the Greeks did and see the progression from danger to defeat. The action on the ground in particular could make the determination of whether a valid fall had occurred difficult, and decisions over the scoring of a fall were occasionally a source of dispute.[5]

In ancient Egypt, the fall seems to have been a simpler matter. The tomb paintings of Beni Hasan (c. 2050–1930 B.C.E.) show many scenes of wrestling on the ground, and since one wrestler attempts to turn a prone opponent to his back in some of them (fig. 7), it seems that Egyptian wrestling was remarkably like contemporary wrestling in limiting the fall to a back or shoulder touch, rather than considering the prone position to be a fall, as the Greeks did. In a set of wrestling scenes from the New Kingdom (c. thirteenth/twelfth century B.C.E.) we find two showing the defeated wrestler lying on his back (fig. 8); several others show him prone or on all fours facing in the direction of the pharaoh and kissing the ground (figs. 9, 10). Most likely the criteria for determining the fall remained the same as in the Middle Kingdom depictions at Beni Hasan with only a shoulder/back fall counting; the prone figures are probably in a ritual posture of obeisance to pharaoh.[6]

RULES

A number of wrestling rules pertained in both Greece and Egypt, and certainly they were significantly modified during the long histories of these societies. The Greeks have left us better informed about their regulations than the Egyptians, but for the latter too some vivid traces remain.

A New Kingdom scene, shown in figure 10, depicts a wrestler putting

7. Scenes of wrestling on the ground from Beni Hasan, c. 2000 B.C.E. The offensive wrestler (black) cradles his opponent's neck and leg to rock him backward for a fall.

8. Wrestling and stick fighting from El Amarna, Egypt, c. 1350 B.C.E. Victors raise their hands in the air, two defeated wrestlers lie on their backs.

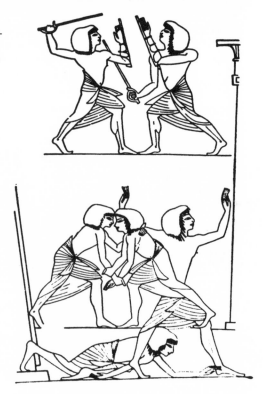

9. Wrestling and stick fighting from Thebes, Egypt, late fourteenth century B.C.E. The stick fighters wear arm guards; their sticks are fitted with hand straps. At the bottom a defeated wrestler lies face down, while his opponent raises his hands in victory.

a chokehold on his opponent, and an inscription accompanying it warns, "Take care! You are in the presence of Pharaoh," which suggests that the referee is cautioning the wrestler against using an illegal stranglehold.[7] This same tactic, however, appears frequently in the paintings at Beni Hasan, made approximately nine hundred years earlier (fig. 11): it may have been illegal in the twelfth century, but it was surely permitted around 2000 B.C.E.

The Greek rules were remarkably tolerant of rough tactics. Striking was forbidden, but some fairly brutal, limb-threatening holds at least at certain times in its history were considered legal. Two literary sources speak of attempts to break an opponent's back or ribs with a waistlock: exaggerated as these accounts are, they still reflect some of the ethos of the sport, as historical sources show. A Sicilian Greek, Leontiskos, won at Olympia in the mid fifth century B.C.E. despite his inability to throw his opponents: his secret was to break his opponent's fingers. The

10. Wrestling and stick fighting in the presence of pharaoh, mid twelfth century B.C.E. An Egyptian wrestler applies a choking neck hold to a Negro opponent; the referee interferes. A defeated wrestler kisses the ground, while his opponent raises his hands in victory. Stick fighters compete using sticks with rounded tips and hand straps. These athletes wear chin straps and some bear arm shields.

11. Offensive wrestler (white) with a choking headlock on his opponent. Beni Hasan, c. 2000 B.C.E.

Greeks had no hesitations about using all forms of neckholds, including, as we have seen, strangling holds. A wrestler will invariably move in the direction in which his head is pulled, and an arm across the larynx is a persuasive addition to the leverage of the hold (figs. 12 and 13). Greek wrestling also appears to have had a rule that throwing an opponent out of the *skamma* counted as a victory: it was not a fall, but it meant defeat for the opponent nonetheless.[8]

Greek wrestling was, to put it simply, a bitter struggle. Appropriately, Pindar notes the "fierce looks" of the wrestling victor in 468 B.C.E. at Olympia: "Offering this victory prize, / Confidently raise the loud cry, / that this man was born, with god's grace, / skillful, of nimble limbs, of fierce looks" (*Olympian* 9.108–12). More appropriate yet is Pindar's praise of Aristomenes, a victor at Delphi, who defeated his four wrestling rivals "with evil intent" (*Pythian* 8.82). References to breaking fingers and strangleholds explode cherished notions about the nobility of ancient Olympic ethics and practice. Modern enthusiasts for sport and scholars alike have been slow to come to terms with the evidence, a failure that has cast more light on the mores of the authors than on Greek sport. "Wrestling, at all events in the early days before it was corrupted by professionalism, was free from all suggestions of that brutality which has often brought discredit on one of the noblest of sports," wrote E. N. Gardiner in the *Journal of Hellenic Studies* in 1905. The fact is that the finger-breaker Leontiskos won his Olympic victories legally in that "noblest of sports," wrestling (not the brutal pankration), in the earlier, "purer" years of Greek athletics, and did so more than once, in 456 and 452 B.C.E. The most recent excavations at Olympia have unearthed a decree passed in the late sixth century B.C.E. forbidding wrestlers to break each other's fingers, and the law empowers the judges to beat the offenders. This startling find shows that Olympic foul play started early, and the story of Leontiskos demonstrates that this early attempt to refine the sport failed. The tactic used by the offensive wrestler in figure 14— gouging the face to persuade the opponent not to resist the leg hold which turns him to his back—may well have violated the rules, but the heat of contest undoubtedly made infractions of this nature a not infrequent occurrence. Most remarkable, however, is what we have already seen to be legal and accepted at Olympia.[9] Gardiner assumed that the Greeks frowned upon finger-breaking in wrestling and furthermore relabels all wrestling bouts in which strangling occurs as pankration. The need to handle the evidence in this manner stems from an ethnocentricity that requires the Greeks to have the same definitions of *sporting* and *fair play* as the nineteenth and twentieth centuries. But the Greek world, with its extreme emphasis on individual success and with the

12. Herakles wrestling Antaios. The hero appears to have his left arm under the throat of Antaios, who is trying to clear the hold with his left hand. Athena and Hermes watch; Athena holds an almost "headless" spear over the wrestlers, as if she were the referee holding his rod. Greek vase, c. 520 B.C.E.

13. Neck lock used to counter opponent's grasp on the leg. On the left stands the trainer, on the right a herm statue, honoring Hermes, god of the palaestra. Greco-Roman carved gem, with a plaster cast to show further detail.

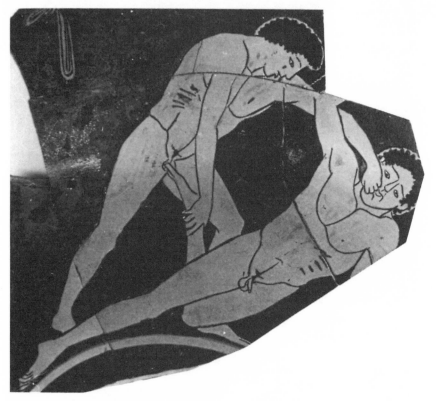

14. Wrestling (or pankration?): offense attempts to turn the opponent to his back by pulling the leg and wrenching the face. The bloody imprint of a hand appears on each athlete. Greek vase, c. 500 B.C.E.

recurring stress and peril of hand-to-hand combat in war, was bound to develop a different athletic ideology. Wrestling was far less injurious than the other combat sports, but expecting the palaestra at any time to correspond to the playing fields of Eton will lead us into deep confusion.

BELT WRESTLING

Certain styles of wrestling, ancient and modern, allow and in some cases require the competitors to grasp each other's clothing: the belt in particular gives excellent leverage for a throw. Belt and/or jacket wrestling has been popular throughout our century in Devonshire and Cornwall, England; in Switzerland; in the Middle and Far

15. Wrestlers grasping the opponent's belt to gain more leverage for their holds and throws. Beni Hasan, c. 2000 B.C.E.

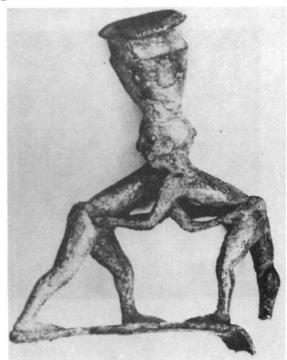

16. Sumerian belt wrestling. The wrestlers (who serve as a base for twin vases) take hold of one another by the belt.

East (both sumo and judo include it); and in the lower Sudan. While the Egyptian Old Kingdom reliefs (c. 2400 B.C.E.) from the tomb of Ptah-hotep and Akhethotep show wrestlers totally naked, as does an early First Dynasty carving (c. 3000), in the tomb paintings of Beni Hasan most of the wrestlers wear belts, and in a few instances the painter shows a wrestler holding onto his opponent's belt (fig. 15). But these belt-wrestling scenes are uncommon, which suggests that at least in the wrestling of the Middle Kingdom belt holds were less important than grasps on the limbs. Mesopotamian art always shows the wrestlers wear-

17. Old Babylonian wrestling scene. A hero and a bull-man, both wearing belts around their middles, take hold of each other's wrists.

18. Sumerian wrestling scene. On the right, a pair prepares to engage; in the middle group, the offensive wrestler tips his opponent backward with a grasp on his knee and neck; on the right, a wrestler reaches behind and takes hold of his opponent's ankle. The wrestlers all wear belts around their middles, but they take hold on the limbs.

ing a belt and often shows them grasping the opponent by it (fig. 16), but it also shows them ignoring the belt and taking holds on the limbs (figs. 17, 18). Cuneiform texts from Mesopotamia similarly tell of holds both on the limbs and belt.[10]

It is remarkable to see how steadily the Mesopotamian wrestling belt has persisted in the Middle East, even into our own day. In Firdausi's eleventh-century epic *The Book of the Kings (Shanamah)* all wrestlers, whether fighting on the ground or on horseback, put on a leather girdle before the contest, and in the eighteenth century, Carsten Niebuhr saw Egyptian wrestlers wearing leather trunks; they are still a wrestler's standard equipment in the popular contests that take place in modern Turkey. Even before Islam, the Persians abhorred displaying themselves naked, and Greek wrestling with its full nudity had little impact on the folk custom of the Near East, despite the Hellenization of the area.[11]

WRESTLING TECHNIQUES

Ancient wrestling reached a level of technical sophistication every bit as high as that of the tactics described in modern coaching manuals. We can tell from the precise athletic imagery used in Greek literature that the general public understood wrestling well, and there were books with systematic drills of different tactics; a fragment of one of these has survived (see fig. 52). In addition, Greek vase painting and sculpture show a variety of complex maneuvers, and ancient Egypt offers almost four hundred representations of wrestling in art, showing the widest possible range of tactics.

The overwhelming majority of the wrestling scenes in Greek art depict the standing part of the bout, primarily because of the conventional nature of vase painting, which makes up the largest body of the visual evidence. Ground wrestling scenes require solid masses of coloring, fill the space less efficiently, and pose problems in perspective. (Significantly, they are less common for pankration than we might expect, given the importance of ground action in that sport.) The aesthetics of the sport may also underlie this preference for depicting the wrestlers upright. Standing wrestling probably represented the purest form of the sport, the execution of a clean, decisive throw without recourse to scrambling on the ground—this was the element of wrestling that so obviously impressed Plato (see chap. 6). (A similar preference appears, in a greatly exaggerated form, in the nineteenth-century Badminton Library handbook of British wrestling, where the author argues even for the banning of ground wrestling.)[12] But as we have seen, fighting on the ground does have a classical Greek pedigree, even if less exalted than that of upright wrestling, and the relative frequency of ground scenes from Egypt makes it clear that there ground wrestling was generally a part of competition.

The key to successful standing wrestling is posture and stance: the wrestler needs to protect himself from being tripped backward or from being pulled forward, and therefore he stands with his weight on the balls of the feet, not the heels, with one or both knees flexed. He thrusts out his hands, looking for opportunities to attack while fending off his opponent's initiatives (figs. 19, 20, 21).[13]

Wrestlers commonly seek to control the opponent's wrists or his neck as a start for a more ambitious offensive. This is everywhere apparent in ancient art (figs. 20, 21). Holding the wrist could be prelude to a controlling drag on the opponent's arm, allowing the wrestler to slip behind and lift his opponent for a throw (cf. figs. 22, 33). A grasp on a man's collar could end in a headlock, shown in figures 23 and 24, or it could permit the offensive wrestler to step in, turning his hip for a side headlock and hipthrow (figs. 25, 26). These were basic, well-known tactics, standard fare in the palaestra. A third-century B.C.E. caricature of a parvenu showed him performing the hipthrow in the baths on imaginary opponents, pathetically trying to prove culture and breeding thereby, and a poem about Herakles' youth cited the hipthrow as the trademark of ancient wrestling, a trick which the young hero learned. Pulling down on the head is a particularly good way to cause an opponent to brace all his weight on one foot, allowing trips executed with the hands (fig. 27) or the leg (figs. 28, 29). This combination of headlock and leg trip appears as a vivid wrestling metaphor in a religious text of the first century C.E. "Those who have no wholesome intent in either speech or thought consider it good to take by the neck and headlock, tripping and dashing to the ground in their wily and twisting wrestling, all those [thoughts] which steer the upright, straight path of life" (Philo, *Dreams* 2.134). Executing the leg trip could cause the offensive wrestler some distress, since he could wrench his own ankle in the process. This occupational hazard was apparently a familiar one, and in an ancient satire concerning a man who tries to conceal his gout-induced lameness, the victim claims that he received a leg injury while trying to work a leg trip (see fig. 29).[14]

Another means of engaging was to take a hold under an opponent's shoulder, in modern terms, an underhook (fig. 30). An ancient commentary on the *Iliad* describes how wrestlers fight from this position, seeking to control first one shoulder then the other:

This is an ancient and rustic manner [of wrestling]. Each wrestler throws his

19. Wrestlers about to take hold
of one another. Greek vase, c.
430 B.C.E.

20. Wrestler on the left secures a
hold on his opponent's wrist
and elbow. Greek coin, fourth
century B.C.E.

21. Wrestlers struggling for control of wrist and neck; on the neck of the vase are boxers, bleeding from the nose. Greek vase, c. 540 B.C.E.

22. Wrestling lesson: watched by a trainer, two wrestlers on the left attempt to slip behind one another to gain a waistlock. On the right, a wrestler has succeeded in lifting
his opponent with a waistlock. Greek vase, c. 525 B.C.E.

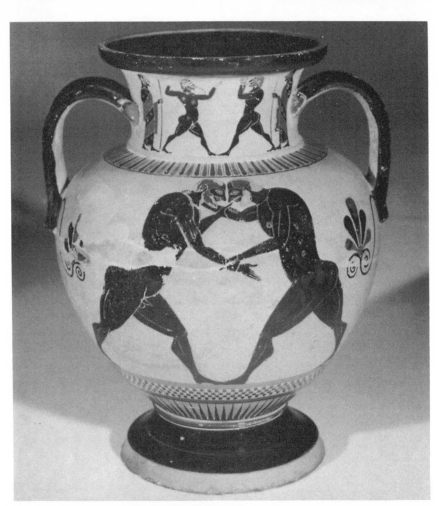

23. Theseus and Kerkyon wrestle: the hero has a
headlock on Kerkyon, who appears to have attempted to grasp Theseus's foot. Greek vase, c.
510 B.C.E.

24. Pressured headlock: the kneeling wrestler twists
his opponent over his back using a headlock, and
with his other hand hoists his hips into the air.
Egypt, c. 1950 B.C.E.

left hand under the rib cage of his opponent, and controlling with his right
the hand thrown onto his own side each man (thus) takes hold of the opponent's left underhook, and with their foreheads they press against each other.
Sometimes "underhook" signifies an encirclement with the hands.[15]

25. Headlock and hipthrow: offensive wrestler seeks to use the
pressure on his opponent's neck
and shoulder to throw him over
his hip and onto his back. Greek
vase, c. 425 B.C.E.

26. Hipthrow foiled by a waistlock: the upright wrestler attempts to throw his opponent
over his hip, but the opponent's
stance is too solid, and he has
secured a tight waistlock. On
the (apparent) use of the loincloth, see chap. 1. Greek vase,
c. 520 B.C.E.

27. Herakles trips Antaios backward by pressing down on the head and lifting the ankle out from under him. Greek vase, c. 515–500 B.C.E.

28. Wristhold and leg trip: wrestler on the left has trapped his opponent's foot between his feet and pulls on his arm to upset his balance. Greek coin, fourth century B.C.E.

29. Wrestler on the right holds his opponent's shoulder and upper arm while attempting to trip his leg. The opponent twists violently away. Greek vase, c. 480 B.C.E.

Gaining control of both shoulders was a means of taking an extremely effective hold, the waistlock. The hold could be applied from the front (our bearhug) or back of the opponent (figs. 22, 31). Being caught in a waistlock was a sign of serious disadvantage, and some victors' inscriptions boast that the wrestler won the event without taking a fall and without being caught in a waistlock, that is to say, he is so good he never was close to losing. The claim of the mythographer Apollodorus that Herakles broke the ribs of an opponent with this hold is heroic exaggeration, but a strong grasp around the abdomen or ribs is difficult to counter and allows the wrestler to lift his opponent for the throw (fig. 32) or pressure him to the ground (fig. 33). In *Iliad* 23.730–31 Odysseus combines the waistlock with a leg trip, lifting the massive Ajax and using a trip to finish the attack: "He moved him a little from the ground but still was not lifting him, then he hooked his knee." This tactic of hooking the leg can also be used defensively against a waistlock, as figure 22 shows. Earlier in the same match (725–26), Odysseus had used this maneuver to block Ajax's attempt to lift him: "[Ajax] lifted him. Odysseus did not forget his trickery. He struck him behind, hitting on the knee, unstrung his limbs, and threw Ajax backwards." It is a particularly effective countermove if the defensive wrestler can manage to slip one of his shoulders under his opponent's bearhug: when combined with a leg hook this allows the hunted to turn into the hunter. Greek art sometimes shows a wrestler facing his opponent and reaching over his back for a waistlock rather than encircling his body directly from the front (figs. 34, 35). The advantage of this hold is that it allows the wrestler to hoist his opponent's hips into the air and render him unable to prevent an immediate fall to his own back (fig. 36).[16]

Some Greek vases show a shoulder throw, a tactic which had tremendous potential for causing an immediate fall (fig. 37), and a drill to teach

30. Wrestler on the right holds his opponent's wrist and underhooks his left shoulder. Greek vase, 367/366 B.C.E.

31. Waistlock from behind: defensive wrestler seeks to break the hold by pushing away his opponent's head and tearing at the encircling arm. Greek vase, 360/359 B.C.E.

32. (BELOW) Wrestler lifting his opponent with a waist-lock. Greek bronze, Hellenistic era.

33. (RIGHT) Using a waistlock from behind, the offensive wrestler pressures his opponent to the ground. Greek vase, 360/359 B.C.E.

34. Reverse waistlock: the offensive wrestler is in position to hoist his opponent feet first into the air. Greek vase, c. 525–510 B.C.E.

35. Theseus counters Kerkyon's attack with a reverse waistlock and begins to lift him from the ground. Greek vase, c. 500 B.C.E.

36. Reverse waistlock, completed throw. Greek bronze figurine, Hellenistic era.

this move appears in the papyrus wrestling manual mentioned earlier (fig. 52). In an even more sophisticated throw, the offensive wrestler puts his knee against the opponent's stomach, and while pulling him forward on top of himself, turns in midair to achieve a fall. In the following passage, the god Dionysos uses this tactic on a female challenger:

> Dionysos took control of Pallene's midsection using a merciless rolling shove with his knee, and greatly desiring to roll the girl on the ground with a throw to one side changed his grasp, wrapping his hands around her sides and bending his neck across his shoulder. Then he encircled the middle of her back, interlocking his fingers behind, planning to snatch an ankle, or leg, or knee.[17]

This description might seem to be a piece of epic fantasy, but the tactic has perfectly good credentials in contemporary international competitions, as an illustration from a modern manual of Olympic wrestling (fig. 38) shows.

A number of vase paintings show attempts at tackling the opponent's legs (figs. 13, 23, 39, 40). The problem with the tactic is that it is not likely to lead to an immediate fall for the attacking wrestler but will leave him open to effective counterthrows. The defensive wrestler can sprawl his weight on top of the attacker and reach over to hoist his hips into

37. Wrestling, shoulder throw: the referee or trainer looks on in alarm. Greek vase, c. 500 B.C.E.

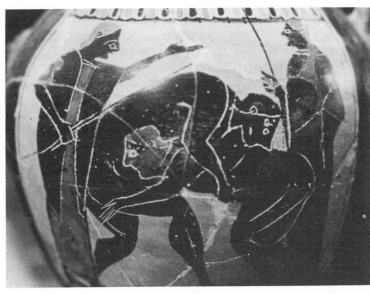

39. Wrestler on the left counters his opponent's attempt at tackling his legs by throwing his weight forward and down. He reaches over the back, attempting, it seems, to hoist the hips into the air (compare fig. 35). Greek vase, sixth century B.C.E.

40. Theseus counters Kerkyon's leg tackle by catching him under the arms and throwing his weight forward. He is in an excellent position to take a headlock on Kerkyon. (On the right, Theseus punishes the villain Prokrustes.) Greek vase, c. 460–450 B.C.E.

ketches of modern wres-
: the wrestler in the black
ks pulls his opponent on
f him, turning him in mid-
 throw him onto his
lders for a fall.

the air, or he can apply a neck hold. A Roman epic includes a description of this sort of situation: "Tydeus drove on the attack and feinting towards his neck attacked the legs. His short arms labored in vain and could not finish what they started, but his opponent came down on him from high above and overwhelmed him, crushed with the vast falling weight" (Statius, *Thebaid* 6.876 ff.). The Greek outlaw Kerkyon commonly used this tactic, as an ancient commentary recounts: "Theseus invented the wrestling with hands, and Kerkyon the wrestling with feet. . . . Theseus lifted him into the air and threw him down, killing him,"[18] and vase paintings of Theseus's exploits show this episode (figs. 23, 35, 40). Kerkyon is most often seen in Greek art trapped under Theseus, who is lifting him off his feet. Usually he has his arm over Theseus's back, perhaps in a futile attempt, as an afterthought, to work a waistlock from underneath his opponent.

41. Standing throws leading to a fall. In *a*, white turns his opponent in midair with a three-quarter Nelson from the front; in *b*, black catches white's neck while tripping him backward, and similarly in *c*, black points white toward his shoulders while tripping him backward. In *d*, white has lifted black from the ground and secures a half Nelson hold on his neck in order to turn him immediately to his shoulders. Beni Hasan, c. 2000 B.C.E.

42. Wrestling on the ground. The top wrestler attempts to draw his opponent's arm back by pushing his head against his upper arm whle pulling backward on the lower arm. If successful, the offensive wrestler will be able to apply a hold like the one in figure 43. Greek vase, 360/359 B.C.E.

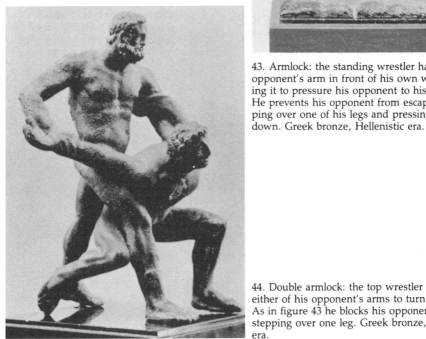

43. Armlock: the standing wrestler has pulled his opponent's arm in front of his own waist and is using it to pressure his opponent to his back for a fall. He prevents his opponent from escaping by stepping over one of his legs and pressing his head down. Greek bronze, Hellenistic era.

44. Double armlock: the top wrestler can now force either of his opponent's arms to turn him for a fall. As in figure 43 he blocks his opponent's escape by stepping over one leg. Greek bronze, Hellenistic era.

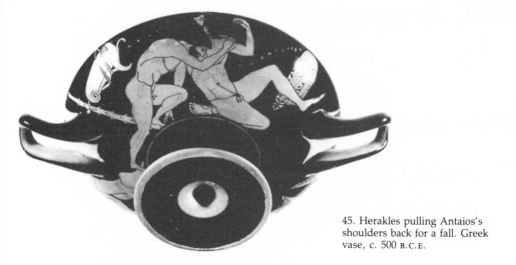

45. Herakles pulling Antaios's shoulders back for a fall. Greek vase, c. 500 B.C.E.

46. Top wrestler uses a leg hook to pull his opponent's hips over, thus turning him to his shoulders for a fall. The clenched fist of the top wrestler is a restoration—the whole upper arm was lost. The piece lacks the pugilism that typifies ground pankration scenes; rather it illustrates a high point of wrestling technique.

The standing tactics depicted in Egyptian art are exceedingly varied. Figure 24 shows one wrestler throwing his opponent over his shoulder, using his left arm to hoist his hips. Also noteworthy are those tactics in which the offensive wrestler secures the head or shoulder along with the legs in order to make the throw a decisive fall (fig. 41).

If a fall did not follow from a standing throw, both Egyptian and Greek wrestling, of course, continued on the ground in a fight that was usually taxing for both parties. Greek vase paintings and sculpture show a variety of tactics for turning a man onto his back. A vase of the fourth century B.C.E. shows a wrestler trying to pull his opponent's arm back, using his head to put pressure on the triceps (fig. 42). This tactic, if successful, gives the wrestler leverage to turn his opponent over: he can control his opponent's leg with his own and wrench one or both arms back for the fall (figs. 43, 44).[19] Another vase shows Herakles pulling Antaios's shoulders back to the ground while Antaios sits on his hips resisting the backward pressure (fig. 45). The well-known Hellenistic wrestling group from the Uffizi Gallery in Florence shows a tight lock on the leg (fig. 46), a hold designed to allow the offensive wrestler to pull his opponent's hips over, thus turning the man toward his shoulders for a fall. Possible sequels to this hold can be seen in the Egyptian Middle

47. Top wrestler has wrapped his legs around his opponent's abdomen and presses his head down to the sand: he is now in position to twist the shoulders over for a fall. Both athletes have their hair bound in the *cirrus*. The same leg hold was popular in pankration; compare figure 63. Roman clay lamp, first century C.E.

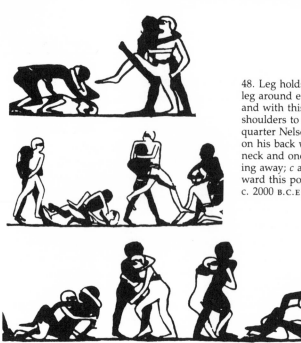

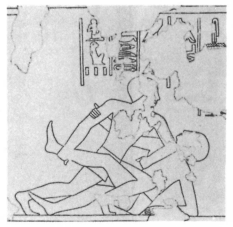

48. Leg holds. In *a*, black has wrapped a leg around each of his opponent's legs, and with this control, starts to turn his shoulders to the ground with a three-quarter Nelson. In *b*, black holds white on his back with a Nelson hold on the neck and one leg to keep him from turning away; *c* and *d* show the progress toward this position. Beni Hasan, c. 2000 B.C.E.

49. Leg holds. In *a*, the top wrestler begins to entwine his opponent's leg; in *b*, the hold on the leg allows him to control his opponent's motion while leaving his own hands free. Egyptian carving, late twentieth century B.C.E.

Kingdom paintings in figure 48. A hold called the *klimax* ("ladder") consisted of climbing onto the opponent's back and wrapping one's legs around his waist or lacing them around each of his legs, a tactic which had applications in pankration (see chap. 3) as well as in wrestling (fig. 47).[20] It was a controlling hold that would stop the opponent's motion, leaving both of the offensive wrestler's hands free to apply a neck hold or to knock the defensive man's supporting arms out from under him.

Egyptian illustrations of ground wrestling are much more varied than those found in Greek art. There are excellent examples of the use of leg holds both for control and as initiatives toward the fall (figs. 48, 49). Ground offensive tactics also include armlocks and Nelson levers (fig. 50). Some scenes seem to depict the wrestler in the position of disadvantage underneath trying to reverse the situation (fig. 51).

A papyrus fragment of a wrestling training manual of the first or second century C.E. gives vivid evidence of the widespread interest in and practice of complicated wrestling sequences (fig. 52). Its elegant

50. Leverage on the arm: in *a*, black applies a half Nelson from standing; in *b*, he uses a hammerlock on white's arm (along with a grasp on his belt). Beni Hasan, c. 2000 B.C.E.

51. Bottom wrestler reversing his position. In *a*, white struggles to get control of black's arm in order to roll him underneath himself; in *b*, white forces black's shoulder down and will be able to get the superior position. Beni Hasan, c. 2000 B.C.E.

52. A fragment of Greek wrestling manual (see description in text). The careful handwriting shows that this was a book intended for sale, rather than private notes. First/
second century C.E.

handwriting shows that the fragment represents a book intended for
sale, not personal notes. The distribution of such manuals must have
served to create a standardized and widely known palaestra vocabulary,
which explains how Greek authors could meaningfully use complicated
wrestling terminology in literary imagery. What follows is a literal translation of this fragmentary text, of which quite large portions are missing.
The drills are intended for a pair of athletes, and this ancient manual
separates the different sequences of holds into paragraphs.

You stand up to his side, attack with your foot and fight it out.

You throw him. You stand up and turn around. You fight it out.

You throw him. You sweep and knock his foot out.

Stand to the side of your opponent and with your right arm take a headlock
and fight it out.

You take a hold around him. You get under his hold. You step through and fight it out.

You underhook with your right arm. You wrap your arm around his, where he has taken the underhook, and attack the side with your left foot. You push away with your left hand. You force the hold and fight it out.—You turn around. You fight it out with a grip on both sides.

You throw your foot forward. You take a hold around his body. You step forward and force his head back. You face him and bend back and throw yourself into him, bracing your foot.

The papyrus prescribes a remarkably sophisticated series of moves, the most elaborate of which is the next to last: one wrestler moves from a frustrated attempt at a trip to a shoulder throw (cf. fig. 37), which his opponent is to counter with a body lock from behind (cf. fig. 31).[21]

III

PANKRATION

Pankration (or in Latin spelling, pancratium) is a Greek word that means "complete strength" or "complete victory." It has a synonym, possibly even an older word, in the name *pammachon*, which means "total fight." These terms reveal a lot about the sport: pankration allowed boxing, kicking, wrestling throws, strangleholds, and pressure locks. The bout ended when a competitor signaled unwillingness or inability to continue the fight.[1]

The idea of an all-out fight must be as old as the human race, but the formalization of that activity into a sport is quite a different and significant matter. Although later Greeks gave the sport a mythological origin, that does not reflect history, and in reality pankration was practically the last athletic event to appear in the ancient Olympics, with the men's contest starting in the 33d Olympiad (648 B.C.E.) and the boys' competitions in the 145th (200 B.C.E.). Pankration does not appear in Homer or in any other literature before the fifth century. It was, moreover, a sport of the Greek and Roman worlds with no counterpart in the ancient Near East. Clearly, as archaic Greek society developed, the need for expression in violent sport increased, and pankration filled a niche of total contest that neither boxing or wrestling could.

RULES

Only two tactics are explicitly prohibited in pankration: biting and gouging. The Spartans allowed even these, but they restricted the activity to intracity competition and did not participate in pankration at the national festivals. One vase (fig. 53) shows a referee or trainer flogging the athletes for gouging, but in other cases these infractions seem not to have provoked sanctions (fig. 54). Although Greek authors often made the contest between Herakles and Antaios into the confrontation of a Greek hero clearing the world of evil and a barbarian ogre, one vase painter in the late sixth century B.C.E. felt no inhibitions about showing the noble Herakles grabbing the beard and

53. Pankratiasts gouging each other's faces. The trainer on the right flogs them with his stick for this foul. Greek vase, c. 480 B.C.E.

54. Pankratiast gouging and pummeling his opponent. In this scene, unlike the preceding one, the referee does not interfere. Greek vase, c. 480 B.C.E.

55. Herakles holds Antaios's beard and gouges his eyes: the hero employs some remarkably irregular tactics in his struggle against the barbarian ogre. Greek vase, c. 515–500 B.C.E.

gouging the eye of the giant (fig. 55).[2] A Greek comedy that describes an erotic encounter in terms of pankration, advising the man to strike and gouge his partner with fist and phallus, is perhaps a case of comic license, but the philosopher Epiktetos (first century C.E.) listed being gouged as one of the hazards of a career in pankration, and a second-century C.E. author remarked sardonically that the fan name Lion for pankratiasts was appropriate because of the way they broke the rules and bit each other. Galen also took note of the damage gouging caused. Thus, the fourth-century C.E. definition of the sport which claims that every licence was granted to the competitors is perhaps an overstatement, but good testimony to the reputation of the sport.[3]

TECHNIQUES

Striking with hand and foot was a main part of the sport—sometimes the only one.[4] As figures 54, 56, 57, and 58 show, punching was effective for weakening an opponent or for clearing a hold, and the pankratiasts occasionally wore light boxing thongs (figs. 56, 59) which allowed them to hit harder without fear of damaging their knuckles.[5] Kicking was practically the identifying sign of the sport. In a satire on professional athletes, Galen awarded the prize in pankration to a donkey because of its excellence in kicking, and there is a small bronze statue that shows an athlete poised to give a kick (fig. 60). One victor boasted on his monument of having "a broad foot" as well as undefeated hands. The genitals were in no way off limits: art of the sixth century B.C.E. and the second century shows this tactic (figs. 61, 62). The following second-century C.E. description of a pankration bout suggests that the upright work was foremost in people's idea of the sport: "These folk standing up, who also have been coated with dust, punch and kick each other in their attacks. And now this poor wretch looks like he is going to spit out even his teeth—his mouth is so full of blood and sand, having just taken a blow on the jaw, as you see."[6] Pankration also featured, of course, plenty of wrestling—it is easier to force a man on the ground into submission than one who is standing. Hence we see in figure 59 an ankle and head trip, very much like the wrestling tactic shown in figure 27. In figure 53, the athlete on the left has wound his left leg around his opponent's to hold him while he gouges (illegally) at his eyes. Figure 57 shows a pankratiast about to tip his opponent backward by hoisting his leg in the air. Not surprisingly, pankratiasts became proverbial for people who were ready for all events. They assumed a stance that allowed both good offense and good defense, and a philosopher compared the hazards of a busy man to those of the pankratiast: "just as they stand when called to the contest with their arms thrust out high and protect their head and face with their hands, blocking like a rampart, and before the fight all their limbs are ready to ward off blows and give them—so should a prudent man's sense and intellect be." They kept their fingers curled, midway between making a fist and leaving the hand open, and in this way they were quick to punch or grab as the situation demanded.[7]

The tactic of the wrestler Leontiskos of bending back his opponent's fingers had obvious applications for pankration, and in the fourth century B.C.E., Sostratos of Sikyon won twelve crowns at Nemea and Corinth, two at Delphi, and three at Olympia with this trick. An ancient inscription records that, not surprisingly, he usually conquered his opponents without a fight.

Since touching the shoulders to the ground meant nothing in this sport, the pankratiast was free to use any trick that ultimately put him in control, and he knew a variety of throws which involved grabbing the opponent and falling backward with him. A pankratiast once asked the oracle how he could defeat his opponents and was told to his surprise, "By being trampled." He understood the god's riddle only after

56. Pankratiasts fighting. On side *a*, both pankratiasts wear thongs (compare fig. 59); the bottom athlete has a tight headlock on his opponent, who punches at his face. Side *b* shows a pankratiast holding and pummeling his opponent into submission. On the left stands an athlete with a bundle of thongs. Greek vase, c. 500 B.C.E.

57. A pankratiast lifts his opponent's leg to trip him backward: the defensive athlete attempts to break the hold by punching him. Greek vase, c. 490 B.C.E.

58. A pankratiast holding his opponent on the ground with his legs and punching him. Roman clay lamp, first half of the first century, C.E.

59. A pankratiast wearing thongs (see fig. 56) has tripped his opponent backward by catching his heel and pressing against his head. Greek vase, 360/359 B.C.E.

60. Pankratiast kicking and punching. Imperial Roman bronze from Autun.

61. Roman pankratiasts and boxers. The pankratiast on the right holds his opponent's wrist and drives his knee into his genitals; to the right a boxer wearing a spiked *caestus* stands over a fallen opponent. Marble relief from Rome, second/third century C.E.

62. Pankratiast kicking his opponent's genitals; the opponent seems to be signaling submission by raising his finger. Greek vase, c. 520 B.C.E.

developing in the contest the tactic of clinging to his opponent's heel and not letting go. Pindar appropriately praises a pankratiast by noting, "One must wipe out his rival by doing everything."[8]

Scissors holds around the waist were extremely effective in this sport. A Roman mosaic (fig. 63) shows this hold being applied to opponents both on the ground and standing. The scissors can exert an enormous amount of pressure on the abdomen, but more important, it leaves both hands free for choking the opponent. This hold cost the two-time returning Olympic victor Arrichion his life in the 54th Olympiad (564 B.C.E.). A Greek rhetorician some eight hundred years later described a painting of this match, giving excellent details of the scissors and Arrichion's counter:

> Having already grabbed Arrichion around the waist, the opponent had in mind killing him and rammed an arm against his throat, cutting off his breath, while with his legs fastened around Arrichion's groin, he pressed his feet against the back of both his knees. He got ahead of Arrichion with this stranglehold since the sleep of death was from that point creeping over his senses, but in relaxing his grip, he did not get past Arrichion's stratagem. For Arrichion kicked away his heel, which put his opponent's right side into an

63. Pankratiasts and boxers. In two of the groups, the pankratiast on top has a scissors hold around his opponent's waist and has wrapped his arms around his throat. Elsewhere we see a pankratiast kicking and boxing with his opponent and boxers wearing the spiked *caestus*. On the right stands a prize table and underneath it an urn, which probably held the lots the competitors drew to determine pairing for the fights. Imperial Roman mosaic.

unfavorable position, since now the knee was dangling. Then Arrichion held his opponent—who was not really an opponent any more—to his groin and leaning to his left he trapped the tip of his opponent's (right) foot in the bend of his (right) knee and pulled the ankle out of joint with the violence of his twist in the other direction.

Pankration was a heated contest, and the competitor had to be prepared for considerable discomfort—kicks, punches, sand in the mouth, wrenched limbs, chokeholds. In addition to Arrichion, we learn from an inscription of another pankratiast who died in the contest, and the trainer of one pankratiast is said to have written to the athlete's mother, "If you should hear that your son has died, believe it, but if you hear he has been defeated, do not believe it." But the Greeks did not consider it as dangerous as boxing: a man who wanted to compete in both events at Olympia requested that the pankration come before the boxing, so he would not come to his second contest already wounded. Dreaming of pankration, according to a Greek book on dream interpretation, was a bad omen, but a dream about boxing was worse, for it portended bodily harm.[9]

IV
STICK FIGHTING

Stick fighting has been a common and popular contest from early antiquity to our own day. Although it was never a formal event in Greek athletic festivals, Alexander the Great, at least, advocated stick fighting competitions over the traditional combat sports (see chap. 6). The Egyptians were particularly enthusiastic participants: they had formal contests and often their artwork shows crowds of spectators watching the fighters.

The earliest visual evidence of stick fighting appears on a mid-fourteenth-century B.C.E. tomb at El Amarna, and in this instance the contest takes place along with other combat sports in the presence of the pha-

64. Egyptian boxers and stick fighters. The boxers are barefisted; the stick fighters seem to be using thick papyrus stalks as their weapons. c. 1350 B.C.E.

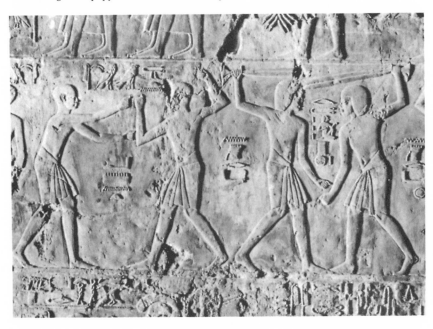

raoh (fig. 8). A tomb relief from Egyptian Thebes of the same era (fig. 64) similarly depicts stick fighters performing next to boxers at a state occasion in pharaoh's presence: here, interestingly, the contestants seem to be using thick papyrus stalks as their weapons. A century later, we find stick fighters sporting elaborate equipment when they compete before Ramses III (fig. 10). Some wear a shield on the left arm; and in his right hand each holds a stick with a knob on the striking end and a loop on the other end to ensure a tighter grip. A chin strap adds further protection to the face. Other Egyptian depictions show participants using two sticks, one in each hand (fig. 65). It remains unclear, unfortunately, what determined victory. Concession of the loser would be an obvious possibility, but the hieroglyphic "captions" on the Theban tomb (fig. 64) record the "hits": perhaps there was a scoring system.[1]

The military value of such a strike-and-parry game is obvious, but there was (and still is) a considerable amount of popular interest and pleasure in stick fighting. A recently discovered fourteenth-century B.C.E. carving shows a country scene of Nubians wrestling while other men wait nearby holding their sticks; clearly they are about to engage recreationally as the wrestlers do in a stick fighting contest (fig. 66). On this occasion not pharaoh, but a woman and a dog are the spectators. Carsten Niebuhr saw Egyptian peasants practicing both single and dou-

65. Stick fighters; one uses two sticks, the other a stick and a shield. Egypt, twelfth century B.C.E.

66. Nubian wrestlers and stick fighters. Here the contests seem recreational and informal: the setting is clearly countryside rather than city. The balls on the Nubians' skirts bring to mind the gourds which decorate the wrestling costumes of the modern-day Nuba. Egypt, c. 1350 B.C.E.

67. An eighteenth-century scene of stick fighting in Egypt.

ble stick fighting on his eighteenth-century journey to the Middle East (fig. 67), and the Egyptian tradition of stick fighting has continued to this day. So also the practices of nearby African nations suggest a continuum of athletics spanning the millennia. The Nuba of the lower Sudan still actively wrestle and stick fight, and the remarkable decorations they wear on their loincloths today may well be developments of the balls the Nubian athletes wear in the carving in figure 66.[2]

The sport had at least on some occasions great cultic significance. It already finds mention in the Old Kingdom Pyramid Texts (c. 2300 B.C.E.) in the context of the cult of the dead; the Ramesseum Papyrus

(c. 1991 B.C.E.) appears to describe how certain priests held a two-stick contest, and how the offspring of the god Horus tell the offspring of Seth (who killed Horus's father, Osiris), "Lift to the sky your sticks, by which your backs are like those of wandering goats"—in other words, within this ritual the representatives of Horus are to beat them.[3] What remains clear is that the stick fight was an integral part of the ritual and mythology of Osiris, a central figure in Egyptian religion and probably has even older roots in the Onuris rituals, the cult of the celestial eye. Many centuries later Herodotus on his travels watched Egyptian priests accompany a cult statue of a god whom he called Ares (but who seems much like Horus) into its temple with a vigorous stick fight, so vigorous that the Greek observer conjectured that many died from their wounds, an interpretation which Herodotos' hosts insisted was untrue.[4]

V —— *BOXING*

"A boxer's victory is gained in blood," begins an inscription of the first century B.C.E. praising a tough and successful boxer from the island of Thera.[1] To say that victory in ancient boxing depended on brutality alone would be a great exaggeration, for the sport required a high degree of skill and strategy in addition to courage and fortitude. But trauma has always simply been a given, an essential part of the sport, and the Greeks quite accurately viewed boxing as the most physically punishing and damaging of all athletic contests.

THONGS AND GLOVES

The most revealing information about ancient boxing is what the boxer wears on his fists, for that readily indicates the level of injury tolerated (or expected). Fighting with some sort of equipment on the hands is in general typical of the Greek and Roman worlds, and this equipment runs the range from padded practice gloves to the Roman *caestus,* which had lumps of metal and spikes sewn into it. The earliest depiction of gloves appears around 1500 B.C.E. in the Minoan civilization of Crete, where the pugilists carved on stone drinking vessels wear devices that cover the whole hand with what seems to be a stiff plate (fig. 68); the fact that some of the boxers wear war helmets and an armguard is a strong sign of the glove's destructive potential.[2]

In contrast to normal Greek usage, the few extant Near Eastern and Egyptian depictions are unanimous in *not* using any hand covering outside of a simple band supporting the wrist, as we see in figure 69. Even in the depiction of formal boxing in Theban Tomb 192 (fig. 64), which shows spectators and even includes captions offering the familiar ringside exclamation, "Hit," the boxers wear no gloves or thongs.[3] Barefisted boxing also plays a small but colorful part in Greek sport; it appears on occasion in Greek art and forms the subject of a magnificent piece of poetry. Homer's *Odyssey* 18:1–107 tells how the suitors in Odysseus's halls arranged a fight between the bullying court beggar Iros and an

68. Minoan boxer. A wrist strap secures the plate under the boxer's fist: the helmet suggests that these boxing gloves were damaging. Stone vase from Crete, c. 1500 B.C.E.

69. Mesopotamian boxers. The athletes wear a small wrist band, but there is no covering on the fist. Early second millennium.

aged traveler who later turns out to be the hero himself, home after twenty years. Neither wore anything on his fists, and the only preparation for the fight involved wrapping their beggar's rags around the groin: Odysseus does this for himself, while Iros is so frozen with fear at the sight of his opponent's muscles that others must gird him for the fight. His fear was not unreasonable, for although he threw the first punch, it landed without effect on Odysseus's right shoulder, and the hero responded with a blow under the ear that shattered the bones— "straightway red blood came from his mouth, and he fell in the dust bellowing, gnashed his teeth together, and kicked the ground with his feet." This is, of course, a street fight that happens to involve a very skillful athlete in disguise; in the athletic competition at the funeral of Patroklos in Homer's *Iliad* 23, the boxers wear the typical Greek boxing thongs (see below), and it is not exaggeration to say that barefisted boxing played only a very minor role in the history of ancient sport.

The Greeks used light rawhide thongs in most of their boxing matches from the beginning of their history until the fourth century B.C.E. These thongs were no doubt popular for so long because of their simplicity and flexibility. The boxers apparently had their choice about how to wear them, for on the vases we find some who wrapped themselves almost to the fingertips and others who stopped at the wrist, using the thong merely as a wrist brace; every possible variation in between also shows up on vase paintings (figs. 70, 71, 72). Occasionally a boxer would even leave one hand completely uncovered. The fact that the boxers did not always wear them over the knuckles shows that the thongs were intended primarily for the comfort of the man wearing them, protecting the wrist from sprain and the fingers from fracture—they were not enough of an offensive weapon to encourage boxers to use them in a consistent manner.[4] These light thongs are an identifying feature of boxers in the classical era. Socrates caricatures Athenians who act like Spartans as sporting cauliflower ears, wrapping on boxing thongs, and being excessively in love with athletics. Boxers on their way to the fight carry them (fig. 73), and a statue of the Olympic boxing victor Akousilaos (now lost) (see chap. 7) portrayed him holding his bundle of thongs in his outstretched left hand. The many loops show that they were long and very supple.[5]

In the fourth century B.C.E. Greek boxers started using much heavier, more damaging equipment known as sharp thongs. Unlike the earlier thongs, which the boxers wound around their hands, these devices had gloves on the inside with holes cut out for the fingertips, and over the gloves were wrapped leather thongs. The most distinctive feature was a heavy pad of leather over the knuckles. One modern sport historian

70. Boxer wearing light thongs.
Greek vase, c. 440–430 B.C.E.

71. Boxer raises a finger in submission. Both athletes wear light thongs but wrap them only as far as the wrist. Greek vase, c. 515–500 B.C.E.

72. Boxer using an open hand to block his opponent's blows. He wears a thong on his right hand but not his left. Greek vase, c. 550 B.C.E.

73. Boxers carrying their bundles of thongs. A pickaxe for softening the *skamma* stands on the right. Greek vase, c. 480 B.C.E.

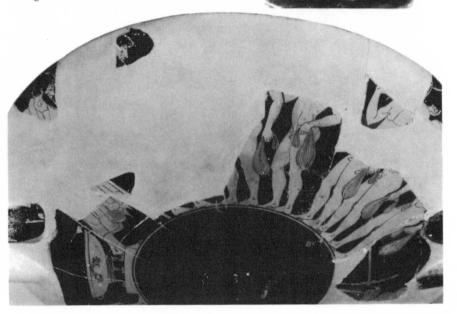

fondly saw in this knuckle pad a humanitarian attempt to soften the blow, but in fact it provided the boxer's fist with a cutting edge. The ancients often described these gloves as hard or dry: the knuckle pad was probably made of inflexible and hardened leather, and the name sharp thongs meant just what it said, referring to the glove's potential for cutting the opponent's face. These gloves were laced high on the forearm and sometimes had a piece of sheepskin at the top, no doubt to protect the boxer's arms against being broken by his opponent's heavy punches. The life-size bronze boxer found in Rome (fig. 74) shows clearly the high knuckle pad, and one sees in his face and ears that sharp thongs were anything but protection against injury. These became the boxer's regular equipment for the rest of the history of Greek athletics, and they appear very often in art.[6]

Practice sparring with the earlier light thongs was undoubtedly painful: the sharp thongs must have inflicted even more pain. Not surprisingly the Greeks had practice gloves called *sphairai* or *episphairai* ("balls") (fig. 75). The first time we hear of them is in Plato, who lists them with other practice devices. Describing what pugilists do when preparing for a boxing match, he notes that *sphairai* rather than thongs are appropriate because they encourage people to practice vigorously: that is to say, *sphairai* are in the realm of the safe and nonthreatening and promote vigorous and fearless training. Plutarch exaggerates a little when he says that the glove makes the battle harmless and gives a soft and painless blow, but something padded like our modern gloves must have seemed marvelously gentle to those used to abrasive strips of leather over the knuckles. One Latin author wrote of boxers wearing softer gloves of some sort and said that they weren't really boxing: the "real" sport was a much tougher affair.[7]

A popular name for boxing thongs both light and sharp—*myrmex*—means "ant." Ants, then as now, were known for their ability to bite, and *myrmex* lends itself to boxers' gallows humor.[8] Here is an example from an ancient joke book: "A man from Kyme saw a boxer with many wounds and asked where he got them. The boxer answered, 'From the *myrmex*.' The other said, 'Why do you sleep on the ground?'"[9] A medieval commentator on Homer gives in passing another example of this wit: "A man who wasn't good at boxing and who took many blows bought a piece of land in which he learned there were ants (*myrmekes*). At once he put it up for sale, stunned by the name ants (*myrmekes*) just as if he had actually been hit."[10] The theme makes its way into verse. What follows is a little poem from the first century c.e.:

> A sieve, Apollophanes, is what you've got for a head.
> much like what moths leave on a book's edge:

74. Greek boxer wearing the sharp thongs. The fighter bears the signs of trauma on his face: a cauliflower ear and a broken nose. Bronze statue, first century B.C.E.

75. Caricature of a boxer wearing *sphairai*, padded practice gloves. His ears and nose show exaggerated signs of trauma. Greco-Roman terra-cotta.

Surely we see the drillings of the ant,
and some tracks go straight, some at a slant—
like harpist's scales for Lydian or Phrygian cant!
Come on and box, have no fear—
for if you get gouged some more up there,
What you'll get is what's been before—
Now with so many scars, you can't get more![11]

In the whole history of Greek athletics, we find no other equipment than the two types of thongs, light and sharp, and the padded practice gloves. Illyria and Italy introduced two other types: a puzzling horseshoe shaped device and the notorious weighted and spiked Roman *caestus*.

Horseshoe shaped gloves (figs. 76, 77) show up at least eighteen times in Illyrian and Italic art of the seventh to third centuries B.C.E.—whatever it was, it was not an artist's error or fantasy. Almost always a strap secures the device to the boxer's hand, though one example from Rome is a full glove with projections from the sides. Provided that the horseshoe was made of a soft substance, it would have dampened the blow—but here we have only the ancient pictures to guide us.

Rome's contribution to boxing was a glove that reached almost to the shoulder and was reinforced at the striking end with lumps and spikes. When Vergil claims that a pair of these gloves were "seven vast oxens'

76. Boxers with dumbbell-shaped gloves. Roman marble sarcophagus.

77. Boxers with dumbbell-shaped gloves. Illyrian Bronze engraving, fifth century B.C.E.

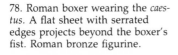

78. Roman boxer wearing the *caestus*. A flat sheet with serrated edges projects beyond the boxer's fist. Roman bronze figurine.

79. Roman boxers wearing the *caestus*. Two types are evident: in *a* two spiked projections extend beyond the fist; in *b*, lumps of metal have been sewn into the leather strapping. Roman mosaic, second century C.E.

huge hides, stiff with lead and iron sewn in" (*Aen*. 5.404–05), the only exaggeration lies in the amount of leather—a glance at figures 78, 79, 80 confirms the poet's description of the metal work involved. The variety that appears most often in Roman art is that shown here in figures 61, 63, and 78. To wear this glove, the boxer curves his fingers around a cylinder in the palm: the fingers are protected by a stiff casing. From the knuckles extends a flat sheet about the length and width of the three middle fingers, with a toothed edge. The projection (and probably also the finger guard) must have been made of metal. Another type (fig. 80) resembles the Greeks sharp thongs in every way except that the ridges on the knuckle pad show that it is not a leather pad like the one Greek boxers used, but a molded piece of metal. Figure 79a shows another variation of the glove: the whole fist fits inside a spherical case and the two finger-length spikes project from the end. Another variety (fig. 79b) has lumps of metal studding the thongs; it is almost exactly the glove

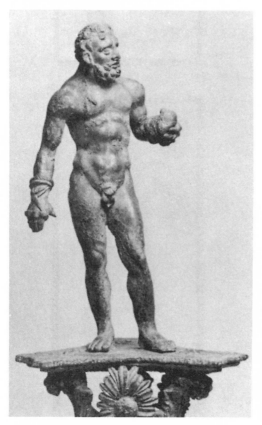

80. Roman boxer wearing the *caestus*: a plate of ridged material, probably metal, covers the boxer's knuckles in this style of *caestus*. His face shows damage to the ears and nose. Bronze figurine, first century C.E.

Vergil describes. These gloves were lined to the shoulder with heavy sheepskin and strapped with thongs, for without this protection, the *caestus* boxer could not use his arms to deflect his opponent's blows. Needless to say, the very appearance of these deadly gloves removes any skepticism about another detail Vergil gives—that they were stained with blood and spattered brains.

THE RING

The boxing competition area was not a standard size, but the officials in Greek boxing, at least, did take precautions to see that the boxers stayed within striking distance of each other. An ancient lexicon explained: "a ladder was placed for the boxers whenever they were wasting time, so that they would remain in the same place."

81. Boxers confined behind a barrier. A referee stands to their right. Italic art under Greek influence, sixth century B.C.E.

82. Boxers being confined to a smaller space. A referee watches as two men hold a long stick in front of the pugilists. Greek vase, sixth century B.C.E.

In other words, the Greeks did not bother erecting ropes and posts, as in modern boxing, but rather, as figures 81 and 82 illustrate, they put a barrier on one side, either a ladderlike object with cross-slats or a simple stick, and in this way reduced the size of the fighting area until evasive footwork became impossible.[12]

THE CONTEST AND ITS RULES

The Greeks had a tradition that already in the 23rd Olympiad (688 B.C.E.) a man called Onomastos from Smyrna drew up the rules for Olympic boxing. No description of his system has come down to us, but we do know a fair amount about Greek and Roman practice in later centuries.[13]

Greek and Roman contests had no rounds: they continued until one man either acknowledged defeat by holding up a finger (fig. 71), as the vase paintings show, or was knocked cold. The latter is what happens in the match in *Iliad* 23.689–97, when Epeios defeats Euryalos:

> Godlike Epeios rushed at him and hit him on the cheek as he glanced up. He didn't stay standing very long, for there his fine limbs collapsed. Just as a fish leaps out of the water rippling with the North Wind on to the sea weed strand and the dark wave covers it, so did Euryalos leap when punched. But great hearted Epeios took him with his hands and set him upright, and his companions gathered around him and led him through the playing ground dragging his feet, spitting thick blood, tossing his head to one side.

Although the fighters sometimes paused to catch their breaths, clinching was strictly forbidden. Vases show a trainer or referee vigorously using his stick on a boxer who has caught his opponent's neck or arm in some manner (figs. 83, 84), confirming what Plutarch says: "The referees don't allow boxers to clinch, although they greatly want to do so."[14]

TECHNIQUES

According to tradition, Pythagoras of Samos (not the mathematician) brought scientific boxing to the 48th Olympiad (588 B.C.E.) and won. His victory was particularly impressive: he arrived looking dashing and perhaps a little decadent "with long hair and wearing purple" and applied to box in the boys' division, only to be mocked and adjudged too old. So he entered the men's division and won. An epigram boasting of this feat adorned his victor's statue:

> Wayfarer, if you recall a certain Pythagoras,
> Long-haired far sung boxer of Samos,

83. Official striking a boxer for clinching with his opponent. Greek vase, c. 510 B.C.E.

84. Official striking a boxer for grasping his opponent's arm. Greek vase, c. 425 B.C.E.

Here am I. Go ask some Elean about my deed,
Though nothing he says will you believe.[15]

The two founding fathers of Greek boxing, the rule-giver Onomastos of Smyrna and the first technician, Pythagoras, were both Ionians, Greeks from the coast of Asia Minor and the islands nearby. Ionians were often

85. Boxer striking with half-closed fist; his opponent prepares an uppercut. Greek vase, sixth century B.C.E.

86. Knockout blow with the left; both boxers are barefisted. Greek vase, late sixth century B.C.E.

accused of effeminacy; indeed Philostratos tells that it was something of a surprise that people adopted the system of Onomastos, because of his nationality, and Pythagoras reinforced the stereotype with his appearance.[16] But at the same time this refined Ionian heritage also demonstrates a major element of Greek boxing—the triumph of skill and intelligence over brute violence. When Demosthenes chides Athens for fighting Macedon by relying on superior strength rather than strategy, he maintains that they fight "as barbarians box—when one of them is hit he follows the punch, and if you hit him on the other side, there are his hands. He neither knows how nor cares to put up his guard or watch the opponent."[17] Greek mythology quite interestingly makes Apollo the god of boxing—Apollo who also excelled in music and art. One tradition records that in the first Olympic festival (see chap. 8) he defeated Ares, god of war, in boxing, thus it seems vindicating skill over brutality. Plutarch notes that one of Apollo's cult titles was *Pyktes* ("The Boxer"), and the people of Delphi offered sacrifices to him under that name. In a few exceptions mindless force wins (see below), but there is a decided preference for skill.[18]

A boxer's first trick was to get a favorable position in the fighting area, for the contests were outdoors and sunlight in the eyes was a major disadvantage. So familiar was this scrapping for position that it was used at least once to illuminate courtroom procedure. When Demosthenes and Aeschines wrangled in court, the latter warned the assembly that they must not disturb the order of the inquiry: "So then, just as in the athletic competitions you see boxers fighting each other for position, so also, Athenians, fight with him the whole day for the city's sake over the sequence of argument (Aeschines 3.206)." In Theokritos's vision of the mythological fight between Polydeukes and Amykos, the bout begins with this kind of sparring: "They struggled a lot, vying to see who would get the sunlight on his back. Cunningly you got the better of that massive man, Polydeukes, and all of Amykos's face was struck with the sunlight."[19]

The pugilists usually stood with the left arm extended as a guard, but the fight depended very much on two-handed punching, and vase paintings show the boxer using his guard arm to strike (figs. 85, 86). The guard arm, moreover, as figure 86 demonstrates, was useful for more

87. Boxers and trainers. On the left, boxers wrap their hands in thongs. On the right two boxers spar; both bleed from facial cuts. Greek vase, c. 490 B.C.

than irritating light blows—combined with a lunge it entered into a knockout sequence. Polydeukes, in the account mentioned above, batters his opponent with both hands: "Now appearing on this side and that, he cut him with one hand then the other and stopped him from his attack, arrogant though he was. His opponent stood drunk with blows and spat out red blood."[20]

The back arm was used for a variety of powerful punches, not all of which are legal today. In figure 87 the fist is held at shoulder level for a straight punch. Figure 85 shows the fist at waist level ready for upper-cuts and hooks. The modern ring has banned the chop from above, but it was a favorite in antiquity. In Vergil's *Aeneid* 5.443–48 the veteran Entellus tries this chop unsuccessfully: "Pulling himself up high, he flashed his right fist and raised it high in the air. His opponent saw the blow coming from above and quickly slipped away with nimble body. Entellus poured his strength out on the wind and his heavy frame fell heavily by its own momentum to the ground." Amykos rose up on the tips of his toes trying a downward smash on Polydeukes, "like a man slaughtering an ox."[21] This wild style of fighting is not a poet's fantasy; it appears frequently in ancient art work (fig. 88). Greek boxers seem to have concentrated their blows on the head, though punishing punches

88. Boxer on the right has risen on his toes to deliver a downward chop. Roman clay lamp, second century C.E.

to the trunk were clearly part of the repertoire as well. In his First Letter to the Corinthians 9 : 26–27, Paul insists that in his religious struggles he is a genuine fighter and does not act like a shadow boxer who punches the air: "I bruise my body and bring it into subjugation." In other words, he bears the scars of contest on his frame. One Etruscan vase, at least, suggests that there was no stricture against punching the genitals (fig. 89), and the vases sometimes show a singularly unappealing punch in which the boxer keeps his thumb extended—clearly for its use in damaging the opponent's eyes (fig. 90).[22]

The fights had a lot of movement and action. We hear of feints and setup punches and footwork. One fourth-century author described how the boxers close upon each other on their toes, with small steps, shifting from one knee to the other.[23] Here is a description from the first century c.e.: "The boxer or pankratiast fighting for the victor's crown pushes away the punches coming at him with both hands and bends his neck this way and that, guarding against being struck. Often he stands on tiptoe and draws himself up to his full height, then drawing himself back he forces his opponent to throw idle punches as if he were shadow boxing."[24]

Punching power, even in the absence of skill, could sometimes secure the victory. The young boxer Glaukos of Karystos (see chap. 7) won his first Olympic attempt on the strength of his punch, though he received many injuries in the process at the hands of more skillful opponents. A third-century b.c.e. poem tells, perhaps with more imagination than verisimilitude, of a herdsman who goes to the Olympics with the strength of Herakles but no gymnasium experience.[25] These are unusual instances, and it is worth noting that Glaukos later became famous for his sparring skill; his narrow and painful first Olympic victory must have convinced him to improve his technique.

HAZARDS AND INJURIES

The ancients considered boxing to be the most injurious of their sports. As noted earlier, when Kleitomachos of Thebes wanted to compete in boxing and pankration on the same day, he asked the Olympic officials to change the usual order of the contests and put pankration first, so that he would not be hindered in that contest by the injuries he would receive boxing. He was not the only Greek who felt that the limb-twisting and kicking of pankration was in fact safer than the boxer's punches. The vase paintings often show blood pouring from one or both boxer's noses, as well as from cuts on the face (figs. 21, 90, 91): this was an expected part of the game. A writer of the second

89. Boxer punches his opponent's genitals. Greek vase, sixth century B.C.E.

90. Boxing with the thumb extended; the boxer on the left bleeds from his nose. Greek vase, sixth century B.C.E.

91. Boxers bleeding heavily from the nose. Greek vase, c. 520 B.C.E.

century C.E. said it was a bad omen to dream of boxing—it meant a deformed face and loss of blood. Two ancient texts speak of athletes whose eyes have been struck out, and the manner in which the boxers in figure 90 extend their thumbs suggests that damage to the eyes in that sport was neither rare nor accidental.[26]

The anecdotes we saw earlier in this chapter about the ant tracks on the boxer's face are some of many macabre jokes concerning pugilists, and this humor reveals quite a bit about the ethos of this sport. The same author who wrote the epigram about Apollophanes also produced this poem:

In every boxing fight that the Greeks oversee
I, Androleos the boxer, made sure they enrolled me.
My prize at Olympia was one ear—and at the Plataean fest,
One eyelid. From Delphi they bore me no longer drawing breath:
The herald called for Damoteles my sire, my countrymen too,
And told them get me off the field, whether dead or drilled through.[27]

In another epigram we hear of a boxer whose injuries are such that he will not recognize himself in a mirror; another loses his portion of the estate when no one will acknowledge that this man without facial features is the deceased's son. By Roman times, the spiked *caestus* made boxing little different from gladiatorial combat, but even in its earlier and purer days it was an unusually punishing and injurious sport, and when a successful boxer, questioned how he escaped defeat in a desperate match, replied, "By scorning death," his answer was not purely pugilist bravado.[28]

VI

THE NATURE AND PURPOSE OF COMBAT SPORT

THE PROBLEM OF ATHLETIC VIOLENCE

Modern societies often object strongly to boxing. Critics consider its casualties senseless and the violent spectacle detrimental to the values and mores of the society that tolerates it. Since 1970 Sweden has made prizefighting (though not amateur boxing) a punishable crime, and twentieth-century America has seen heated controversy over the ethics of pugilism. The death of boxer Duk Koo Kim on 13 November 1982 from injuries received in the prize ring coincided with an American Medical Association report that 15 percent of all professional boxers suffer permanent brain damage: two years later the American Medical Association followed the lead of its British colleagues and asked its members to work actively for legislation to abolish all boxing, amateur and professional. Political scientists and sociologists have added their weight to the doctors' case.[1] Here, for example, is what syndicated columnist George Will argued in "Boxing hurts the fans, too":

> It will be said that if two consenting adults want to batter each other for the amusement of paying adults, the essential niceties have been satisfied, "consent" being almost the only nicety of a liberal society. But from Plato on, political philosophers have taken entertainments seriously, and have believed the law should, too. They have because a society is judged by the kind of citizens it produces, and some entertainments are coarsening. Good government and the good life depend on good values and passions, and some entertainments are inimical to these.[2]

Yet more impassioned is the end of historian John Hoberman's newspaper column "Boxing's Cloaked Message": "Unlike Fascist societies, the democracies do not need boxing, or the cult of aggression which sustains it, to preserve a sense of their own vitality. The end of boxing is not the end of manhood. That is the fear, the male hysteria, from which every society deserves emancipation."[3]

Little information exists concerning attitudes toward the hazards of combat sport in the ancient Near East and Egypt, but an abundance of witnesses show that Greek and Roman attitudes could hardly have been farther from our own. An unprejudiced verdict on the nature of these games in the Greco-Roman world must acknowledge a level of officially sanctioned violence and danger that the modern Olympic movement would never tolerate. Roman nonchalance about the behavior and welfare of athletes (whom it generally regarded as disreputable) is, of course, readily predictable—a society used to watching gladiators as well as public executions in the arena would be disinclined to worry about injuries incurred by athletes in combat sport. But Greek society (excepting Sparta) did not encourage gratuitous cruelty, especially toward its own citizens, and it shunned lawlessness. Perikles' words about the quality of life in Athens, as recorded by Thucydides, are not empty rhetoric, given the other possible life-styles for a city-state: "In regard to education, whereas our rivals from their very cradles by a painful discipline seek after manliness, at Athens we live *in a milder way,* and yet are just as ready to encounter every reasonable hazard."[4] Thus the near absence of what we would call humanitarian anxieties about the perils of its combat sports calls out for an explanation.[5]

When Duk Koo Kim died, Leigh Montville, sportswriter for the *Boston Globe,* wrote an imaginary epitaph for him:

> Duk Koo Kim (1959–1982). He gave his life to provide some entertainment on a dull Saturday afternoon in November.[6]

Nothing more clearly shows the gulf between classical and modern values than the contrast between this sportswriter's reaction to Kim's death and an epitaph recently discovered at Olympia for a young boxer who met the same fate about eighteen hundred years ago:

> Agathos Daimon, nicknamed 'the Camel' from Alexandria, a victor at Nemea. He died here, boxing in the stadium, having prayed to Zeus for victory or death. Age 35. Farewell.[7]

The epitaph shows no embarrassment about the boxer's ambitions—on the contrary, it celebrates his demise with the phrase "victory or death," which is a point of honor recorded on the tombs of Greek soldiers. The Camel's sentiments were as common in antiquity as condemnations of the hazards of prizefighting are today; as an orator of that era noted, "You know that the Olympic crown is olive, yet many have honored it above life."[8] About a century before the Camel died, a pankratiast named Tiberius Claudius Rufus (see chap. 7) fought his way through the Olympic tournament, drawing no byes and encountering in the finals an opponent who had drawn a bye; the pair fought until nightfall, but Rufus, as the decree honoring him reads, "considered it better to scorn life than the hope of the crown," and for this brave perseverance he gained high honors despite the fact that the match ended in a tie.[9] The clearest praise for the athlete who scorns death comes in the accounts of Arrichion, who died in the final round of pankration at the Olympic festival of 564 B.C.E. but still won, since his injured opponent signaled submission before the lifeless Arrichion collapsed. Of the three ancient accounts of his victory, one is matter-of-fact and two praise him warmly for refusing to concede to his opponent. The following account, which claims to be a description of a painting of the pankratiast, is highly rhetorical, but at the heart of it lies the popular sentiment that Arrichion's decision was sensible and praiseworthy: already quoted above on page 1, it is worth looking at again here:

> You come to the Olympic festival itself and to the finest event in Olympia, for right here is the men's pankration. Arrichion, who has died seeking victory, is taking the crown for it, and this Olympic judge is crowning him. . . . Let's look at Arrichion's deed before it comes to an end, for he seems to have conquered not his opponent alone, but the whole Greek nation. . . . They shout and jump out of their seats and wave their hands and garments. Some spring into the air, others in ecstasy wrestle the man nearby. . . . Though it is indeed a great thing that he already won twice at Olympia, what has just now happened is greater: he has won at the cost of his life and goes to the land of the Blessed with the very dust of the struggle. Don't think this is the result of chance! There were very clever advance plans for this victory. . . . The one strangling Arrichion is depicted like a corpse, and he signals concession with his hand, but Arrichion is depicted as all victors are—indeed his blush is blooming and his sweat is still fresh, and he smiles, as do the living, when they perceive their victory.[10]

Another account tells how Arrichion had been on the point of giving up when his trainer made him actually desire death by shouting, "What a noble epitaph, not to have conceded at Olympia!" The death-scorning perseverance of athletes in combat sport practically became a byword, and Philo the Jewish philosopher wrote, "I know wrestlers and pankratiasts often persevere out of love for honor and zeal for victory to the point of death, when their bodies are giving up and they keep drawing breath and struggling on spirit alone, a spirit which they have accustomed to reject fear scornfully. . . . Among these competitors, death for the sake of an olive or celery crown is glorious."[11]

Reform with a view to safer contests was well within Greek capabilities: it is, for example, remarkable that the Greeks used padded practice gloves, *sphairai* (see chap. 5), but shunned such inoffensive devices in competition. The disregard for the safety of the participants is deliberate and must be explained as such.[12]

It is at first even more surprising that at the same time the Greeks cultivated such brutal athletic contests, they abhorred and strictly punished violence in civic life. A man guilty of assault (*hybris*) commonly faced a serious lawsuit, but it was also possible to summon a jury which had the power to impose any sentence it deemed appropriate, including the death penalty, upon such malefactors. This law, the *graphe hybreos*, protected slaves as well as free citizens. Any citizen could act on the city's behalf and bring criminal charges against the alleged assailant, as Demosthenes explained: "The lawgiver considered every deed one commits with violence to be a public wrong and directed also against those unconcerned with the affair. . . . For he thought that one who commits *hybris* wrongs the city, and not only his victim."[13] Although punishing those who injure others was the practical substance of the law, both court orators and philosophers recognized that *hybris* and the *graphe hybreos* referred to the arrogant state of mind that seeks to dishonor another person, what one scholar called "self-indulgent egotism." The Athenians felt that acts of physical violence betrayed attitudes inadmissible in a democracy: it was the tyrannical oligarchs who behaved in such a fashion. Observe how the plaintiff in the following fourth-century B.C.E. suit vividly (and opportunely) describes the sinister threats that assault could represent:[14]

> For you will find that the other wrongdoings injure some part of our lives, but that *hybris* ravages all of our interests, and many houses have been destroyed by it, many cities overthrown. Now then why must I waste time telling the misfortunes of others? For we ourselves have already twice seen our democracy dissolved, twice lost our freedom not because of those guilty of other crimes, but because of those who despise the laws and wish to be slaves to our enemies—those who commit acts of outrage (*hybrizein*) against citizens. The accused is one of this sort. . . . For this is the same nature that betrayed our strength to the enemy, overthrew the walls of our homeland and killed fifteen hundred citizens without trial.[15]

It did not escape at least one Greek author, Lucian, that the violence required in their combat sports seemed to be contrary to the values of civic life. This paradox becomes the subject of his imaginary dialogue between Solon, the lawgiver of Athens in 590 B.C.E., and a visitor from barbaric Scythia named Anacharsis. The Scythian recoiled in horror as he watched the sports, especially appalled that the referee praised a man for striking his opponent in the jaw and filling his mouth with blood. In fine irony, Lucian describes how the traveler argues that the Scythians would call such an event *hybris* and prosecute: "Solon, if anyone among us Scythians strikes another or rushes upon him and throws him over or tears his cloak, the elders lay heavy fines on him—and that even if the victim suffers this with only a few witnesses, to say nothing of it happening in such great theaters as you describe at the Isthmus and Olympia."[16] As we shall see in this chapter and the following one, it is not by accident that such words are placed in a barbarian's mouth.

THE NATURE OF ANCIENT CRITICISM

The grounds for the Scythian's aversion to sport may be remarkably similar to modern sentiments, but they are in general foreign to the Greek world. Considerable criticism of sport was voiced in classical antiquity, but its focus was nothing at all like the modern criticism of "blood sports," which decries their danger and cruelty and the corruption they work on society at large: ancient objections were much more often practical than humanitarian (see also the section entitled "Military Considerations," below), the only noteworthy exception being the doctors. Medical texts do indeed deplore the injuries of the palaestra, but even their discussions of combat sports lose much of their potential force, since they always appear in the context of general condemnation for athletes and athletics and do not single the palaestra out from other more or less harmless activities. The doctors' agenda is in fact a study of social class as much as health. Galen cited with approval a Hippocratic saying, "A healthy condition is better than the unnatural state of athletes"[17] and thundered about the invalids of the palaestra, "crippled, bent, crushed, or altogether maimed,"[18] and those who suffered facial trauma: "[the trainers] even made the faces of some athletes completely shapeless and ugly, especially those practicing boxing and the pankration. When they finally smash or wrench some part of the limbs or strike out the eyes, then, I suppose, then especially is the beauty of their completed training clearly seen."[19] But significantly he is similarly hostile toward athletic diets, running, and riding, much of which had to be innocuous—his objections to horseback riding, for example, rest on the frequent damage it purportedly causes to the kidneys and seminal ducts![20] Influencing Galen are long-standing philosophical and personal objections to sport in general. As early as the sixth century B.C.E., philosophers objected to the enormous rewards paid to athletes: they felt that the intellectual leaders of the cities deserved such honor and remuneration much more. Xenophanes (sixth century B.C.E.) had asked what good a boxer or a runner did for the city; Plato also maintained that contemporary athletes were overtrained and overspecialized and would be ineffective citizens in his ideal state (see below). It is this philosophical tradition which underlies Galen's polemical treatise about the professions: "It is crystal clear to everyone that the athletes have never had even a dream of intellectual virtues. . . . Always gaining bulk in flesh and blood they keep their intellect smothered as if in a mass of mire, unable to discern anything clearly, but instead devoid of understanding like that of the brainless beasts."[21] It also no doubt irked Galen that his society looked upon the physician as a wage earner, a specialized tradesman, while sanctifying the athlete's compensation as a reward or gift. Accordingly Galen's treatise defends his professional skill and decries the athletes along with those who have noble birth without a skill.[22] Plato was unique in showing concern about the potentially anarchic attitudes that combat sport might cause, and for the ideal state he depicts in the *Laws* he wants only a pure style of wrestling: "Those tactics which Antaios and Kerkyon introduced in their styles for the sake of idle brawling, or the boxing tactics of Epeios or Amykos, are worthless in wartime encounters and do not deserve discussion." He does not base his objection, however, on the injuries and fatalities that occur or on the brutalization of society, for elsewhere he argues that the state should regularly hold practice battles in which Plato foresees unavoidable casualties and makes legal provision for them.[23] In summary, we find little opposition to combat sport along the lines of modern disapproval, which sees pugilism as senselessly cruel and dangerous, brutalizing fans as well as participants. In fact combat sport seemed to offer benefits to ancient society, and these comprise the reasons for its steady popularity.

MILITARY CONSIDERATIONS

Warfare was an inescapable reality of the ancient world, and it exercised profound influence on civic and political life; it is impossible to understand antiquity in general, to say nothing of its predilection for violent games, without considering what war meant in day-to-day concerns. The stakes were often exceedingly high: war, as Thucydides wrote (3.83), was in all respects a harsh master. The stark Near Eastern reliefs of siege and battle show rows of impaled prisoners. The subtle and civilized Athenians killed every man in the city of Melos when it fell in 415 B.C.E., sparing the women and children for slavery; equally brutal, though less known, is their massacre of the inhabitants of Skione in 421 B.C.E. Rival Sparta had perpetrated a similar war crime on Plataea in 427 B.C.E., and if the counsel of Sparta's ally Corinth had been persuasive, Athens and her citizens would have suffered extinction in 404 B.C.E. at the conclusion of the Peloponnesian War. In her early years, Rome sent the legions on campaign every year, almost without exception, and contemporary historians reported that Roman tactics showed a degree of ferocity that stunned the Greek world. Ancient states had to face the question of how to meet the regular, if not constant, sequence of military exigencies that threatened their existence. Some states like Sparta and early Rome chose to keep their citizens in perpetual readiness for war; others, like Athens, relied to a large degree on the conscientiousness of the citizenry to be physically and emotionally ready for immediate muster.[24]

By the early sixth century B.C.E., after a long period of transition, the Greek states came to rely upon a battle formation called the hoplite phalanx, in which the heavily armed soldiers formed tight ranks with a wall of overlapping shields for protection. Generals made good use of light-armed troops as well, but the phalanx remained the mainstay of the armies into Roman times. Safety and success depended on holding the ranks, breaking the enemy's formation without disturbing one's own. Since a full set of armor weighed fifty pounds or more, the troops would have to be in excellent physical condition merely to advance in formation. Opposing phalanxes closed on each other briskly, moreover, using the momentum of the collision to disturb the enemy's line; it is hard to envision completely the strength of spirit required to march quickly onto the opposing line of stabbing spears that were the principal offensive weapons of the hoplites. Experienced soldiers knew, moreover, that most wounds fell on the neck or groin, the two places least protected by the shields and armor. It was not easy at first to get troops to fight effectively in the phalanx, as war poetry from its early years shows.[25]

To what extent did games, in particular combative games, figure in military thinking? Sport played a role in military preparation, but there was hardly unanimity on its value. Circumstantial evidence strongly suggests that at some periods Egyptian society believed in its efficacy, and some Greek authors explicitly acknowledge it, though militaristic Sparta placed substantial restrictions on the role of sport, and the greatest military power of the ancient world, the Roman state, despised the Greeks for their games. The range of opinion went from acceptance to complete rejection; in some instances only the exercises, not competition, were sanctioned.

A remarkable amount of sport rhetoric from the pharaohs of the Eighteenth Dynasty (1554–1306 B.C.E.) has survived. For them, the first rulers of the New Kingdom, memory of the domination of the foreign Hyksos was fresh, as was presumably the resolve to be prepared for military exigency. Their personal prowess almost always lay in archery, which is not surprising, since the Hyksos had taught their Egyptian subjects the superiority of the compound bow. The unapproachable skill of the pharaohs was part of their imperial dogma, and theatrically demonstrated as it was, it gave an evident sign of the importance that the rulers placed upon paramilitary sport. The pharaohs, aloof and above other mortals, would hardly involve themselves in a contact sport like wrestling (see below), but it appears to have been important for their soldiers. Even before the New Kingdom, the wrestling scenes from Beni Hasan were painted side by side with military activities, which may suggest that wrestling was part of the soldier's training from early on. Certainly the New Kingdom carvings (figs. 9, 10) show clearly that Egyptian soldiers of that era were active wrestlers.[26] The wrestlers carved on the wall of a tomb in Thebes, for example, compete in front of the deified Pharaoh Tuthmosis III, and the victor vaunts, "Alas for you, O miserable soldier, who boasted with his mouth! I'll make you say, 'O the folly [?] of taking the hand of a soldier of his majesty!' Amun is the god who decreed the protection against every land to the ruler, O great troop of Usermare, Ruler of the Two lands, O general." So also in the carvings at Medinet Habu, again in the presence of pharaoh, a wrestler is shown exclaiming, "Stand up to me! I'll make you see the hand of a [real] warrior!" In these carvings, the Egyptian athletes defeat foreigners, some identified as Syrians, some as Negroes, and the carvings attribute to the spectators explicit acknowledgment that the safety of the country is at stake: "You are like Montu, O Pharaoh, our good lord! Amun overthrows for you the foreigners who come to set themselves up [?] [against you]!"[27]

In the nostalgic eyes of Greeks under Roman dominion remembering their former glories, it was sport that had protected the freedom of Greece. When the barbarian visitor in Lucian's retrospective *Anacharsis* mocks the Greeks for suffering the discomforts and injuries of the palaestra for the sake of an olive crown at Olympia, the lawgiver Solon explains the higher purposes of sport, chief among them military:

> [We train the youth in sport] not only for the sake of the contests so that they may be able to take the prizes—since few indeed out of all of them achieve those ends—but to obtain something greater for the whole city and for the youths themselves. For a certain other contest lies before all the good citizens, and its crown is not of pine or olive or celery, but a crown which holds together in itself the felicity of mankind—that is to say, freedom for each person individually and for the state in general, and wealth and glory. . . .
>
> These are the things [sc. athletics], O Anacharis, in which we train our youths, thinking them to be good guardians for our city and that we will live in freedom through them, conquering our enemies if they should attack, and instilling fear into our neighbors, to the extent that most of them cower before us and pay us tribute.[28]

Lucian's near contemporary Philostratos maintained that the Spartans first developed boxing for military purposes: their warriors did not protect themselves with helmets, but only a shield, and boxing gave them practice in parrying blows to the head and training in withstanding the ones that did strike home. Reveling in the better days of free Hellas, he adds that the Greeks discovered the military usefulness of pankration and wrestling at the battle of Marathon, when hand-to-hand fighting became necessary, and at Thermopylae, when the beleaguered Spartans snapped their weapons in the fighting and had to continue the battle unarmed. Philostratos epigrammatically summarized his report on the lives of the great athletes of the past, saying, "They made war training for sport and sport training for war."[29] In a dialogue on the order of athletic events in Homer, Plutarch insisted that "all these activities [boxing, wrestling, footrace] are imitations and exercises of war" and explained that the custom of breaking a section of the city wall for the triumphal entry of an Olympic victor is a sign that "walls are of no great importance to a city that has men capable of fighting and winning." He drew the same connections between combat sport and hand-to-hand fighting that Lucian and Philostratos did, adding that the Spartans lost the battle of Leuktra to the Thebans because the Thebans were better practiced in the palaestra.[30] By the time of Philostratos, Lucian, and Plutarch, of course, Roman domination of Greece had rendered irrelevant the question of military preparedness: it was Rome's legions who enforced the peace, not city-state armies. Sometimes athletic rhetoric even betrays the fact that the era of Greek warfare was past. The eulogy for the great boxer Melankomas acknowledged that there was no opportunity for martial deeds, but proceeded to argue that athletic training was more rigorous than military, especially true of the boxer's regimen. Melankomas, said his eulogist, had virtue no less than that of the legendary heroes who fought at Troy or the historical soldiers who fought off the Persians; in fact, the boxer had the greater virtue. The statue of the personification of contest, Agon, stood right next to the statue of Ares, god of war, on the prize table at Olympia, and it is unlikely that this juxtaposition was a matter of chance. According to one late source, the great wrestler Milo led the people of his native Kroton to victory wearing the many wreaths he had won in the festivals: the story has the air of legend, but still it illustrates the popular assumption that great athletic achievement signals military prowess. A Greek author living much later, in the time of Augustus, drew the conclusion that Kroton practiced both war and athletics. Although most of these nostalgic and patriotic statements come from the later period of Greek history, the comedies of Aristophanes show that at least some Greeks in the fifth century B.C.E. also subscribed to them. One of his characters in *The Clouds* maintains that the old style of physical education produced the fighters of Marathon, who had saved Greece from the Persian invasion in 490 B.C.E., whereas in his degenerate times (later fifth century!), the youth neglect the palaestra for the baths and marketplace. So also in Aristophanes' *Frogs,* the good youths were athletes and loyal soldiers, but then deserted the palaestra and also became undisciplined in military life.[31]

How much historical reality underlies these traditions of sportsman soldiers? Eurybates of Argos, victor at Nemea in the pentathlon, was a general of his city and fought formidably in single combat long after such encounters became uncommon in Greek warfare. Promachos of Pellene, an Olympic victor in pankration, served valiantly in the war against Corinth; so also Timasitheos of Delphi took two crowns at Olympia and three at Delphi in pankration and served with great distinction in battle. In all of these cases, the sources explicitly note the athletic and military achievements side by side. The strange story of Dioxippos of Athens, moreover, deserves consideration here. During a drinking party in the camp of Alexander the Great, a Macedonian named Koragos challenged Dioxippos, victor at Olympia in pankration in 336 B.C.E., to a duel. Alexander appointed a day for the fight and thousands of his soldiers came to watch. The Macedonian appeared like Ares himself in full armor, Dioxippos came naked and oiled, carrying only a club. Koragos first hurled a javelin, which Dioxippos dodged, then attacked with a stabbing spear, only to have his opponent smash it with his club. Finally Koragos reached for his dagger; Dioxippos, in the best Olympic form, grabbed Koragos's right hand with his left, and with his other hand pushed him slightly off his feet, then kicked his legs out from under him. Dioxippos completed his triumph by putting his foot on his opponent's throat while raising his club and looking to the crowd.[32] Such events, of course, have more symbolic than practical implications, but other evidence suggests more regular military applications of the palaestra. The clubs of the ephebes in the Greco-Roman period record with pride that their members participated in high-level competitions in all athletic events, including the combat sports; since the purpose of the ephebes had once been military training and patrol, it is possible that this conservative institution was preserving the practices of its earlier, military era, and other signs also point to this conclusion. Aristotle makes the significant observation in the fourth century B.C.E. that there were two ways to prepare for war, the Spartan system of brutal training for youth and athletic training. He has nothing but contempt for Spartan education, which he finds both savage and counterproductive, but approves of athletics (though with misgivings about the overtraining and early burnout of athletes). The Spartan Agesilaus instituted contests in both athletic events and military drill for his troops in Ephesos in order to keep them in good fighting condition during the winter. Although our sources do not say which athletic events the troops contested, this stands as a strong piece of evidence for the military use of sport by a successful and famous general. Most important, there were postephebic clubs: free, private bands of young men devoted purely to physical culture, with both athletic and weaponry contests. The existence of such groups shows that the state could rely on this informal means of keeping citizens in serviceable condition for military purposes, and, judging from the fact that it was normal to see old men exercising in the gymnasia, the training persisted almost lifelong. Athletes' honorary inscriptions are worded in language quite similar to that of soldiers' inscriptions: the athlete finds much the same terms of approval that the warrior does, praise for his toughness and perseverance. Like the soldier, the athlete might receive a public funeral.[33]

The nostalgic and rhetorical flavor of much of this testimony, therefore, should not obscure the fact that clearly a substantial number of people believed rigorous athletic training, quickened by competition, would keep men ready for war. On the other hand, many Greeks (to say nothing of the Romans) held that sport had certain undesirable features for the training of soldiers, and it had critics in all Greek states.[34]

MILITARY CRITICS

In one of Euripides' plays, now lost but for a few lines, an unidentified character had some very harsh things to say about athletes: "What outstanding wrestler, what swift-footed man, or discus hurler, or expert at punching the jaw has done his ancestral homeland a service by winning a crown? Do they fight with enemies holding discuses in their hands or by kicking through shields with their feet expel the country's enemies? No one standing next to steel indulges in this stupidity."[35] It is impossible, without context, to determine Euripides' intent from this fragment, especially since the work was a burlesque satyr play, but Galen quoted the lines in earnest. Literature and history record other disapproving voices. It was reported that the general Philopoimen (fourth century B.C.E.) was a gifted wrestler but learned from friends that athletes did not make effective soldiers, so he ceased to participate in sport and later forbade soldiers to become involved in athletics. As we have seen, Plato had strong misgivings about the general effectiveness of the athletes of his day for civic responsibilities. He does warmly recommend wrestling for training the youth, but not athletic competition: he envisions instead of the combat sports, imitation warfare, which is, quite simply, an admisson that military ends are better served through games which require team participation and which closely resemble battle—a few generals in fact made this part of their routines for training their troops. Plato uses the telling phrase "athlete of war" in the *Republic* to describe the purpose of training, and Epaminondas, the formidable Theban general of the fourth century B.C.E., showed in his career the same sort of skepticism about athletics. He applied himself to the palaestra as a youth, emphasizing speed rather than strength, for this, he felt, was more useful in war. Hence he exercised more in running and wrestling, reaching the point where he could resist on his feet when caught in holds. His biographer notes, however, that above all he devoted himself to practice with weapons. As a leader, his opinions about the value of sport seem to have been even more mixed. On campaign he told his troops to winter in the camp, not the city, in order to make a strong impression on the enemy when seen exercising with weaponry and wrestling. Yet for all his use of wrestling as training (nowhere do we hear of competition), he admonished his city that in order to enjoy peace for a long time, the citizens had to practice in the war camps, not in the palaestra. Alexander the Great sponsored many musical and literary contests, but is said to have had little respect for athletes in general and for boxing and pankration in particular. He did admire fighting with staves, which suggests that, like Plato, he desired contests which came closer to the use of weapons.[36] Xenophon, general, statesman, and historian, writes frequently of the need for good conditioning and laments what he considered the unhealthy habits of his day, but nowhere does he prescribe the festivals, or even sport—it is Xenophon who reports that the boxer Boiskos was an unreliable soldier. In one instance he describes (perhaps with a large amount of editorializing) how Socrates scolded a boy named Epigenes for being out of shape. Socrates told him that he would be useless when Athens went to war and that it was his duty to be as concerned with physical training as an Olympic athlete. "Just because the city does not have public training for war doesn't give the private citizen the right to disregard exercise—on the contrary, he should train no less," the philosopher insists. Xenophon's Socrates does not tell the boy to get involved in the athletic festivals: very little in Xenophon or Plato suggests that Socrates found such practices useful to the state.[37]

A verdict demanding serious consideration is that of Sparta, for it was the most militaristic of all Greek states. The business of war was a daily affair for the Spartans—far more than in other city-states, her citizens steadily drilled battle tactics. They had good reason to fear, since by 700 B.C.E. they had enslaved so many of the surrounding peoples that they found themselves outnumbered almost fifty to one by bondsmen called Helots smouldering with hatred for their masters and ever threatening to revolt. At six, a Spartan boy left his mother to live with other boys under the tough, if not brutal, leadership of an older youth, enduring floggings, starvation, and endless drill—as one British historian wrote, "Everything was designed to produce toughness, endurance, and discipline, and all these of a kind which even the least sensitive champion of the English public school would hesitate to defend as likely to 'make a man of' the victim."[38] At twenty, he graduated to a more actively military group and joined one of two Spartan teams, whose purpose was to instill spirit and rivalry, achieved by regular scrapping and gang fighting between the teams. Thirty brought full citizenship, after which the Spartan could marry, but he continued to eat and train with his battle mates; the Spartan term for a citizen, *homoios* ("equal"), is a good indication of the priority which the state gave to corporate identity. Spartans boasted that they were the only Greek soldiers who could regroup and effectively fight alongside new comrades if their battle line collapsed, so precise was their training. Aristotle, however, concluded that this training made them more like beasts than men.[39]

Spartan disaffection with sport started early; the state reduced its role in civic life and developed new, "utilitarian" events atypical of the rest of the Greek world. Although Spartan kings, according to Plutarch, surrounded themselves with victors in the crown games when they went to war,[40] the seventh-century Spartan war poet Tyrtaios was singularly unimpressed with athletic achievement: "I would not give a thought to or praise a man for skill in running or wrestling, not even if he had the Cyclops' size and strength and outstripped in the race the Thracian North Wind . . . not even if he had every glory, except for bold courage. For a man is not good in warfare unless he dares look upon bloody slaughter."[41] Quite simply, according to the poet, the bold athlete is not necessarily a bold warrior. This is no condemnation of athetics, but it is certainly not an endorsement, and it helps explain why Spartan law guided the people's games toward military efficiency.

Unlike the citizens of other states, the Spartans cultivated combative group contests. Each year, the two youth teams would gather on an island, fighting each other wildly, gouging, biting, and punching, until one team drove the other into the water. Spartans also had team sports that involved quite a lot of fighting over the ball. It of course makes perfect sense that if play is to be at all useful for war it should include corporate activity like that of a battle squadron. The most shocking of all Spartan "utilitarian" contests was the yearly ritual at the festival of Artemis, in which Spartan boys would submit to flogging, vying to see who could stand the pain and loss of blood longest. Gone was any sense of individual expression or skill: this was the ultimate submission to Spartan authority. Image abroad also mattered. Although Sparta permitted a high level of violence in pankration, allowing the biting and gouging banned elsewhere in Greece, Sparta forbade her citizens to compete abroad in either pankration or boxing. The state could accept a Spartan losing abroad in a contest of skill, like running or even wrestling, but not in a fighting event—for these events, said Philostratos, the Spartans practice only for the sake of toughness, not sport.[42] Thus, Plutarch records, the Spartan who lost in wrestling at Olympia could respond to the heckling that his opponent was stronger by saying, "No, just better at the throw."

Plutarch, in fact, collected a number of Spartan sayings which display a peculiar attitude toward the festivals. In one, when a Spartan mother learned that her son died in battle, she exclaimed, "How much finer, o friends, it is that he died victorious in battle, than if he lived prevailing at Olympia!" A Spartan wrestler who was caught in a neck hold and began to bite his way out was not ashamed to be fouling his opponent, and when the wronged party scolded, "Spartan, you bite like a woman," he answered, "No, as lions do!" Sparta had no wrestling trainers, according to this collection of apothegms, for she wanted her youth to have valor, not skill; the athletic trainers she did employ were required to have a general knowledge of military tactics.[43]

The gap between athleticism and military training that characterizes the Spartan system is wider yet in Rome. The early Romans went to war almost every year, and a young aristocrat had to serve for a number of years in the army before he could qualify for office. Society laid down a rigid scheme of advancement, the *cursus honorum,* and military achievement was the indispensable foundation for it. So the Roman Vergil wrote, "Roman, remember to rule the nations by your power (these will be your arts) and impose proper behavior in peacetime" (*Aeneid* 6.851–52). A Greek observer in second-century B.C.E. Rome noted how the Roman youth were trained to endure even extreme suffering on behalf of the common good, in order to gain the traditional glory that Roman society bestowed on such valor. The indirect military training that the palaestra could provide seemed idle diversion to the Romans: even Cicero, who was by no means hostile to Greek civilization, considered the ephebic exercises absurd training for the army.[44] Roman poets mocked the Greek youths, "who are lazy from their devotion to the palaestra, who are hardly capable of carrying their weapons," youths who "have learned from their lazy pursuit of wrestling to endure [only] a soft, shaded contest, who delight in shining with oil."[45] Plutarch presents the clearest picture of the gulf between Greek and Roman attitudes:

> The Romans considered nothing to be the cause of the Greeks' enslavement and degeneracy as much as the gymnasia and palaestras, which gave rise to much time wasting and laziness in the cities, and also profligacy, paederasty, and the ruination of the youths' bodies through sleep, strolls, eurhythmic exercises, and precise diets, because of which they stopped practicing with weaponry and were happy to be called nimble and wrestlers and handsome instead of hoplites and good horsemen.[46]

There is, of course, a huge dose of Roman jingoism and national snobbery here, but the disdain for Greek athleticism was very real and often repeated. In Pliny's eyes (first/second century C.E.), the palaestra took the military spirit out of Roman bodies, and his contemporary Tacitus spoke of boxing as antithetical to Roman military ways.

The Romans did not eliminate exercise from military drill, however. Even highly conservative Romans like the Elder Cato believed in physical training: Cato, for example, personally taught his son to box and swim. But physical education and exercise are not the same as athletic competition, for which no Roman claimed wartime value. The Roman military handbook compiled by Vegetius recommended to commanders that the troops practice running, swimming, and jumping, but (unlike Cato) he does not mention the combat sports.[47]

Certainly war gives a partial explanation for the Greek society's toleration of violent athletics. It was at best an indirect means of training soldiers, but most Greek city-states were unwilling to submit to more practical (and regimented) exercises. Regardless of the value of combat sport in the training of soldiers, popular opinion saw in it the demonstration of courage, tenacity, and resourcefulness in a potentially hazardous situation, and many citizens viewed it as beneficial to the security of the city. Thus, for the states which did not wish to keep standing armies, sport provided a useful and enjoyable kind of indirect training for warfare. But the most serious military societies, Sparta and Rome, trained for war more directly and reduced the role of sport or condemned it. They recognized that it was an inefficient, haphazard training, and the seemingly undisciplined combat events were particularly suspect. Except in the most nostalgic Greek eyes, it also pulled its devotees into a regimen that did not meet the demands of a military campaign. The threat of foreign enemies therefore accounts in part, but only in part, for the palaestra.[48]

AN AGONISTIC SOCIETY

The will to compete is a basic human instinct, but different societies give varying amounts of encouragement (or discouragement) to the individual's attempts at measuring himself against others. For almost a century, it was popular to refer to the Greeks as an agonistic civilization, a people devoted beyond others to competition. In recent years this orthodoxy has been under scrutiny and attack, particularly from anthropologists and ethnographers—what, they ask, distinguishes the Greek contests from those of any other culture? Obviously many other societies enjoy and encourage competition, but I will argue here that nevertheless the Greeks distinguished themselves from other cultures in the number and nature of their competitions, and most significantly, in the way they institutionalized rewards and recognition for the victors. Their obsessiveness in this regard and the puzzling role of athletic violence among them become fully explicable only in the light of ancient Greece's orientation toward contest; this also explains more completely the differences between the athletics of Rome and Sparta and those of the other Greek city-states.[49]

Greek inscriptions speak well about the breadth and depth of devotion to the *agon* among the Greeks. Eight stones from Ephesos record a two-day contest under the direction of an *agonothetes* and gymnasiarch for doctors, in "events" such as surgery, instruments (use of), and presentation of a medical treatise; another inscription shows that Aphrodisias had a contest for sculptors.[50] Humbler trades too had their competitions. A vase from sixth-century B.C.E. Tarentum bears the inscription, "I am the victory prize of Melosa. She defeated the girls in carding wool."[51] The professional triumph of a fourth-century B.C.E. Athenian appears on his epitaph: "All Greece judged that Bacchios gained by his talent first place among rivals who skillfully gathered earth, water, and fire, into one. And in the contests [*agones*] that this city held, he won all the crowns."[52] He was, in other words, Athens's most successful potter. *Agon* runs the full range from the sublime contests of tragic and comic playwrights (all extant Greek drama was written for competitive performance against other works) to the ridiculous contests in eating and drinking, beauty, kissing. In the second edition of his comedy *The Clouds*, Aristophanes harangues the audience and judges for giving the prize to his rivals: such was the world of classical Greece.[53]

Against this backdrop of general competitiveness it is not surprising that athletic contests in particular multiplied in the Greek world, providing opportunities for the individual in a society which valued physical strength and prowess in competition at all levels, from the less demanding local festivals to the crown games. Within this agonistic society, sport emerges as the most widespread and highly rewarded expression of competition, and it was not by chance but out of social need that Greek cities had, even before the public gymnasia, a multitude of smaller, private establishments devoted in origin and design to wrestling. Enemies outside the walls were not the only threat to civic well-being: no Greek had to be reminded of the spectre of internal revolution (*stasis*), and a particularly fruitful way of viewing the *agon*, one which I will take here, is as an expression of the *polis*'s desire to give its citizens, particularly the traditionally ambitious nobility, safe and beneficial outlets for impulses toward self-assertion which could otherwise tear apart the fabric of civic harmony.

Among the unusual features of Greek sport, four aspects in particular make it different from the sports of most other societies. Viewed together, they are explicable only as manifestations of a deep and cultivated love for contest peculiar to the Greeks.

First, as must be obvious by now, athletics were serious activities for the Greeks, and athletic achievement brought honor and status. This attitude is clearly articulated in the earliest works of Greek literature. In book 8 of the *Odyssey*, Laodamas, the son of the Phaeacian king, Alkinoos, asks Odysseus to join in the contests:

> Friend, Excellency, come join our competition, if
> you are practiced, as you seem to be.
> While a man lives he wins no greater honor
> than footwork and the skill of hands can bring him.
> Enter our games, then; ease your heart of trouble.
>
> [8.145–49; trans. Fitzgerald]

Iliad 23.667–75 expresses the seriousness of sport even more starkly. There a boxer named Epeios makes athletic victory a surrogate for achievement on the battlefield. His substitution of combat sport for wartime heroism is prophetic of a major trend in later Greek history.

> Let the man who will carry off the two-handled goblet [loser's prize] step
>   forward.
> I say no other of the Achaians will find success at boxing
> and lead off the mule. I insist I am the champion.
> Is it not enough that I fall short in battle?—it seems somehow
> that a man cannot be a master in every endeavor.
> For I say straight out, and it will be a thing accomplished:
> I will smash his skin apart and break his bones on each other.
> Let those who care for him wait nearby in a huddle about him
> to carry him out, after my fists have beaten him under.

Second, winning was important, at times overwhelmingly important. In some of the smaller athletic festivals, second, third, and fourth places mattered, but at the four great Panhellenic Games one place only mattered, and that was the one at the top. Some late Greek inscriptions record with pride "participated at Olympia" but what predominated was an obsession with victory.[54] No voice is clearer than Pindar's in describing the stakes of contest:

Blessed with divine favor and true to his own
Bold virtue,
He has burdened the limbs
of his four rivals and not himself
with a return home most hateful,
with mocking tongues, by furtive,
shame covered paths.
But on his grandfather
Has this boy breathed a vigor to make age
of no account.

[*Olympian* 8.68–71]

Pindar's *Pythian* 8.81–87 shows the same sentiment: the defeated boys "do not find as they return to their mothers that sweet laughter arises, they cower watchful for their enemies in the back lanes, bitten by their disaster." The Greek so valued recognition as the best in a particular activity that no-contest (*akoniti*) victories are proudly recorded, a fact which seriously weakens romanticized views of ancient sporting ethics. One of Marcus Aurelius Asclepiades' (see chap. 7) many proud boasts is, *stesas tous antagonistas meta proton kleron* ("stopped his opponents after the first round")—he was so ferocious a pankratiast that after seeing his performance in the early rounds of a tournament, the rest of his potential competitors defaulted rather than encounter him. More striking yet is the victory inscription of Tiberius Claudius Marcianus, who won the wrestling at Antiocheia in Pisida—the stone reads, "When he undressed, his opponents begged to be dismissed from the contest!"[55] Even winning at Olympia was not enough of a goal for restless Greek ambition; there were special honors to seek beyond that. Athletes coveted the title *periodonikes* (see chap. 1) and other refinements of multiple victories. A man who won at Olympia in wrestling and pankration was a "successor of Herakles," and antiquity took note of this small sequence of distinguished Olympic victors. Inscriptions show that athletes used *paradoxos* ("amazing") when they won in two different sports. Details of the competition found their way onto stone: some athletes were "undefeated," "never caught in a waistlock," some "never took a fall." Unique combinations of victories gained recognition: Kleitomachos noted that he was the only man to win all three combat events at the Isthmus, and others claimed to be first of their respective homelands to achieve a particular distinction. Sometimes the agonistic impulse could grow to self-defeating proportions. According to a second-century B.C.E. historian, good wrestlers not uncommonly sought a draw, rather than a victory—that is to say, even the massive prizes could not overcome the deadly fear of losing.[56]

Third, Greek sport was with only a few exceptions completely individual competition. Only in militaristic Sparta do we hear about teams of ballplayers,[57] and some cities sponsored torch races for teams of runners or riders, but these did not give the victors the prestige that victory in the traditional athletic events bestowed.

The potter's inscription cited above is evidence of the fourth criterion: participation of all social classes in the agon. From a remarkably early date, well within the archaic age, nonaristocrats participated in the Greek athletic festivals. It was not easy for people of limited means to find the leisure and money to train for the contests, but no law obstructed them (see further chap. 7). The legends concerning certain early sport heroes are revealing: Glaukos of Karystos, the boxer who won at Olympia in 520, was said to be a ploughboy; Polymnestor of Miletos, who won the stade at Olympia in 596, a goatherd; Amesinas, the Olympic wrestling victor of 460, a cowherd. These accounts have a mythological air about them, but they do suggest that the Greeks did not find the idea of Olympic victors from humble origins unthinkable. Quite to the contrary, Greek society took remarkable steps toward making participation in the upper echelon of athletic competition accessible to all citizens. The rewards for local athletic victory could make the cost of training and travel to the national festivals affordable: a boy's victory at home could allow the young athlete of limited means to work his way up to competition at Olympia or Delphi; later, athletes were subsidized (see chap. 7). As early as 672 B.C.E. "corporate" chariots financed by groups of people were winning at Olympia: that is to say, the aristocrats' most prized prerogative, horsemanship, was being democratized, allowing groups of citizens to enter these expensive events.[58]

SPORT IN OTHER CULTURES:
THE CONTRAST WITH GREECE

A look at sport in other civilizations shows how distinctive these features of the Greek agon were. One will certainly find plenty of athletic contests, but nothing similar to the elaborate Greek system of singling out the winner, to name only the most obvious difference.

Egyptians engaged vigorously in sport, and there is evidence of a competitive spirit: "The Story of Truth and Falsehood," for example, tells of a schoolboy who "learned to write excellently and pursued all contests and surpassed all his older comrades who were with him at school."[59] But neither here nor elsewhere is there any hard evidence of organized contests whose purpose was the isolation and recognition of outstanding individuals; it seems that the element of hierarchy and control made a completely open agon impossible in ancient Egypt. Amenophis II, like other rulers of the Eighteenth Dynasty, was an avid, public sportsman. An inscription from Medamud tells how he challenged other nobles to match a superb bowshot of his, but the overwhelming majority of Egyptian accounts allow no contest with the pharaoh, even indirect. A stone from Giza records how the pharaoh shot through a copper target, concluding, "That was a deed that had never been done before and which man had never heard tell of . . . except in the case of the King who is rich in glory." In fact, Thutmose III, the father of Amenophis II, had explicitly used a feat of sport to reinforce the imperial dogma of his superiority: when he shot through a copper target (not, it seems, from a chariot, as his son later did), his panegyrist saw the deed as a confirmation that "he might fulfill the wish of his followers for success in might and victory."[60] (So also in Mesopotamia, the king demonstrated his prowess as a hunter in carefully arranged encounters to be witnessed by his nobles.)[61] More striking yet are the New Kingdom carvings from Medinet Habu, discussed in chapter 2 above. There Egyptians wrestle against foreign opponents, and in each case where a fall is scored, the Egyptian is the successful competitor. There is no way of proving (or disproving) the suspicion that the Egyptians had fixed the outcome of the contests to demonstrate the country's triumph over foreigners, but the focus is indisputably on pharaoh as the ultimate source of victory: one of the Egyptian wrestlers revealingly calls out, "Alas for you, O Syrian enemy, who boasted with his mouth. Pharaoh, my lord, is with me against you."[62] Sham fights with prearranged outcome were certainly not unknown elsewhere in the ancient Near East: the Hittites performed such a ritual every year.[63]

In contrast to the Greek emphasis on widespread popular participation, the role that sport played in Rome was for the most part entertainment—a show for spectators who had no thought themselves of ever joining the competition. The baths offered opportunity for acceptable exercise, and the army, as we have seen, in no way depended on sport for its success. Gladiatorial events help to explain the gap between crowd and participant. Instead of providing an institution for competition and self-expression, the arena most clearly displayed the power and control of its organizers—by the time of Augustus, of course, at Rome this meant the emperor or his representative. What the crowd learned was that the emperor (or earlier, the presiding official) was the arbiter of life and death; the crowd watched others die under state auspices and could feel (at best) both relief at their own continued existence in that cruel world and awe for authority. A modern analysis of the arena states, "At the psychological level, the gladiatorial shows provided a stage (as television news does for modern viewers) for shared violence and tragedy. They also gave spectators the reassurance that they themselves had yet again survived disaster. Whatever happened in the arena, the spectators were always on the winning side."[64] Perikles, Athens's greatest statesman, in the mid fifth century B.C.E. might boast about what we would call freedom of expression in ancient Athens: "We conduct our business as free men, both in regard to the community issues and concerning the suspicion towards one another that comes from everyday pursuits: we don't get annoyed at our neighbor if he does as he pleases; we don't even annoy him with hard looks, for harmless as they are, they are still irritating" (Thucydides 2.37). But Rome did not encourage such individualism. Romans who appeared on the stage forfeited citizen rights, and the wellborn Roman who participated in athletics bore thunderous denunciations for this affront to the dignity of his class. In the eyes of many Romans, sport was not only useless for war, it was a threat to societal values.

For the present-day Nuba tribes of the lower Sudan wrestling is perhaps the most important focal point of their culture, and youths live in close contact with older wrestlers and learn their techniques. A Sudanese song of praise shows, within its lively banter, how much prestige is at stake in wrestling:

> You are strong. You can throw ten men. But some time ago you weakened. You threw two men only, or you were sitting idle. Your cattle are strong and give plenty of milk. You have great strength. But now you dress up, you go to the village to be with the girls. Thus you can no longer throw ten men. You throw only three, or sit idle. Formerly, when the Kobane was here, he was stronger than you all.[65]

The annual competitions, a high point of the Nuba year, are thronged with spectators. Anthropologists report that young wrestlers who challenge the stronger athletes are encouraged and praised, even if defeated—contrast the institution of *akoniti* victories in Greece and the ominous boast *stesas tous antagonistas meta proton kleron* ("stopped his opponents after the first round").

In the annual wrestling festivals, the *lebolo*, the contrast with Greece most clearly appears. The anthropologist Siegfried Nadel, who lived among the Nuba, used the term *tournament* to describe their contests, but this is highly misleading for our purposes. In a Greek tournament, competition continued until one man emerged as winner, advancing through successive rounds without a defeat. For the Nuba, an athletic encounter is a meeting of two tribal teams. No attempt is made either to collect all the teams at once to ascertain the regional champion or to systematize the pairing of competitors. Nadel observed:

> When a wrestler has been successful in several fights or defeated a powerful opponent, [the older men] rush into the arena and form a solid ring about him, yelling and singing. He kneels down, a sheep skin with a slit in the middle is dropped over his head, the coveted wrestler's trophy, and he is lifted on the shoulders of one of the senior boys and carried in triumph around the arena. [They] are good losers, too: the defeated wrestler quietly retires and sits down among his friends and age mates, waiting for another chance.[66]

This calmness about defeat in an activity so prestigious in the community presents a remarkable contrast to what we have observed among the Greeks. What Nadel reports about attitudes toward competition is yet more striking:

> The competitive spirit is not allowed fullest scope; nor is the idea of individual

92. Nuba wrestlers, poised to begin the match. Their belts are adorned with gourds.

championship allowed to supersede the thought of team and community. There are no "finals" in which individual winners are matched against each other for a last, decisive fight. When the tournaments are over, one is content to sum up the position by stating, say, that "this year Kalkadda had two champions and Dordo only one."[67]

The Nuba also have more dangerous fights with shields and heavy sticks. Open wounds are common and fatalities not unknown. By Greek standards, however, the event is remarkably inconclusive. Nadel's report continues:

> There are essentially no victors and defeated in this contest. To have stood up well and braved its risks is sufficient proof of pluck and hardihood. . . . The idea of an all-out competition and individual championship is again alien to the spirit of these contests. Indeed, my question: who was the winner in this year's tournament was not understood. The answer was, "There were two grand fighters, one from Kalkadda and the other from Jokjob." And in the previous year, I was informed, there were no "champions" at all. Moreover, the memory of these tournaments does not last long; my informants had already forgotten the results of the contest of two years ago.[68]

Baron Pierre de Coubertin and all the other spokesmen for the Olympic ethic, with its stress on the sporting spirit of the athletes "not to win, but to take part," could more properly turn to the Nuba than to ancient Greece for a paradigm. The ideological differences between the individualistic, victory-obsessed Greek athletic agon and the genial, sporting ethic of the Nuba are immense. Nuba sport can engender an intensity and attain a level of danger that would put the Greeks to shame. The oldest, most advanced wrestlers compete with sharp bracelets on their arms, some of them two kilograms in weight, and suffer fearful cuts. But for all of that, in only the most rudimentary way are they interested in keeping score.[69]

The people of the Kirghis steppe offer another alternative to the Greek agon. In the 1860s a German linguist visited these Turkic tribes and witnessed the funeral games for a recently deceased chieftain. Five thousand gathered for the event; and extravagant prizes were awarded: the victor in the horse races won a fully equipped jurt (small house) complete with a woman and four hundred domestic animals. A singer circulated praising the important guests. Is this the Turkic version of Olympia? Only to a limited degree. There were ten winning places recorded and rewarded in the horse race, and in the wrestling there were fifty pairs of wrestlers and twenty-five prizes. Again, no structure existed for determining the ultimate victor. And class distinction prevailed: a herald proclaimed that the commoners should stay in their places because only the barons could wrestle.

Muey Thai, the style of boxing practiced in Thailand, is intense and deadly serious: all forms of kicks, punches, and chops are legal. One ring physician estimates that one boxer will die of subdural haemorrhage in every fifteen hundred bouts. Thai boxers, more than their counterparts in ancient Greece, earn the praises of a Pindar for their death-scorning boldness, but no Thai would ever ennoble a boxer: the Thai word for a man who boxes is the same word used to denote animals. Muey Thai plays a role more like the events of the Roman arena than of the Greek stadium: for the greater part of the society the experience is not agonistic but voyeuristic.

A number of Pacific cultures engage in sophisticated and highly individual sports, and these are occasionally characterized by a strong compulsion for victory. At the beginning of this century, a German anthropological expedition reported exhaustively on these games, but not a single instance of an elimination tournament occurs. Often at a wrestling festival the competition consists of one pair after another contending randomly. One Polynesian tribe allows the wrestling victor to choose his opponent for the next round. There are frequent instances of wrestling tournaments in which many pairs compete at once. Samoan boxing encounters allow a challenger to "cut in" on a match that has already been arranged. In a word, there is no parallel for the Greek style of progressive tournament.[70]

Admittedly small, this sampling of ethnographic data nevertheless reveals nothing even tantamount to the Greek athletic agon as it typically appeared in historical times, individualistic and organized to select one champion.

GREEK AGON AND SOCIAL NEED

What need did these contests fulfill for the Greeks in their long history, from the late archaic period virtually until late antiquity? The legacy of the heroic age weighed heavily on later Greeks. To call Homer the Bible of the Greeks is hardly to exaggerate; Homer's epics certainly became a standard work of education, an arbiter of correct behavior throughout the history of Greece. The tombstone of a Cyprian savant who lived at least a millennium after Homer boasted, "I was the one who once excelled in Homeric scholarship, pointing out the valor of the ancient heroes."[71] The expectation of a warrior was that he would distinguish himself as an individual champion, as the great warriors had sought out suitable opponents for themselves in the mêlées of the *Iliad*. Tyrtaios made fighting in the front of the phalanx a standard obligation in his admonitions to the Spartans, a joint act of courage, but it had formerly, in the Homeric world, been the prerogative and pride of the aristocrat; Hektor insisted that his heart did not know how to shrink back from battle, since the day "when I learned to be brave and always to fight among the front ranks of the Trojans, guarding my father's honor and my own also" (*Iliad* 6.444–46)," and his mother noted that he never remained back in a crowd of soldiers (*Iliad* 22.458–59). When the Trojan hero Glaukos encountered the fierce Greek Diomedes, he told how his father sent him to war with the admonition *aien aristeuein*, "always excel, and be preeminent above others, and not to bring shame on the line of my ancestors, who were the greatest in Ephyra and broad Lykia" (*Iliad* 6.207–11). The duel was not a phenomenon restricted to literature— Greek history offers a number of examples from its archaic past of such encounters (see the Appendix). Yet while the Greeks continued to admire the heroic deeds of their ancestors, enshrined in epic poetry, their own opportunity so to distinguish themselves vanished into the relentless facelessness of the phalanx.[72] As Pindar wrote, "Prowess without hazard has no honor among men or among the hollow ships": the violent Greek games had to fill the void that a lingering but inaccessible heroic ideal created.[73]

Homer's boxer, Epeios, seems a prophetic figure. He does not excel in war, and his compensation is his boxing prowess, so vital to his identity that a match with a fellow soldier elicits his most violent jealousy for honor and recognition. Not long after Homer's time, it became virtually impossible for anyone to excel in war the way Achilleus and Ajax had done, as the era of heroic single combat yielded to the superior power of the tightly organized and unified phalanx. Even the military leader had to put discretion over valor and stay behind the front; as early as Xenophon, military strategists begin to withdraw from the general his right to fight in the front lines. Thus the battlefield was no longer a proving ground for maverick skill and honor, and the city became the arbiter of glory and reward. Athens took over the responsibility for the funeral rites of its battle casualties and rigorously suppressed any attempts to garner individual repute from military success.[74] When Cimon and his colleagues asked Athens to reward their victory over the Persians in 476/5 B.C.E., the city allowed them to erect three statues, but without inscribing their names on them, noting that it was improper to glorify the general more than the city for a victory. Quite revealing for its emphasis on the community is one of the epigrams that the city inscribed for her generals:

Once from this city Menestheus went with the sons of Atreus
As a commander on the sacred plain of Troy,

A man that Homer said was from the throng of bronze armed Greeks
The man best at arranging battle.
So it is in no way unfit for Athenians to be called
Leaders in warfare as well as valor.[75]

The consciousness of Homeric heroism persists, but the focus turns from the individual (as in the *Iliad*) to the city of Athens. So also the great Miltiades, who masterminded the victory over the Persians at Marathon in 490, failed to persuade Athens to write his name on the painting of the battle in the Painted Stoa. Sparta was most emphatic in responding to the ambitious leader, and when Pausanias (the general) inscribed his name on the Delphic tripod celebrating the victory at Plataia, the Spartans had it erased and the inscription rewritten. It could be said with greater truth that the rise of the hoplite phalanx gave impetus to organized competitive athletics than that athletics supported the phalanx; the games represent displacement of certain military impulses, not training for them. The athlete, unlike the general, was most welcome to boast about himself on his monuments. Moreover in the political sphere, narrow kingship and clan rule had to broaden, accept new rules, and embrace a wider franchise; nothing could be more natural to the ambitious aristocrat, yet at the same time more perilous to the security of the city, than the assertion of individual superiority that led to revolution and tyranny.[76] Around the beginning of the fifth century B.C.E. Athens initiated ostracism—the exiling of citizens who were amassing too much power and influence—just for this exigency, and at least one century earlier than this, the city of Dreros in Crete passed stern laws against citizens who attempted to hold high office more often than once in ten years.[77] The language of the athletic inscriptions, "First from x to do y," is identical to that of political life: in place of competitive impulses that are destructive in military tactics or civic life Hellenic society cultivated the union of play and the serious, the agon. The word *agon* does not have its familiar meaning of "contest" in Homer: in the earliest epics it denotes an assembly or place of assembly for sport or other purposes. Nor do we find any Greek author using the verb *agonizesthai* ("to compete in a contest," "to compete for a prize") before the fifth century. Specialized vocabulary grew with the concept of contest as it steadily became a more important part of Greek life.[78]

Despite the obvious harshness and violence of the Greek combat sports, and the fierce, sometimes cruel competitiveness that surfaced, societal norms triumphed. Athletes might foul, but they received blows and sometimes lost their crowns for it. A row of bronze statues built with the fine-money paid by athletes convicted of corrupt practices lined the entrance to the stadium at Olympia, warning competitors to shun dishonesty. At times, the Greek feeling for honor was bafflingly acute. Theogenes made a special point of competing in both boxing and pankration at Olympia in 480, and after defeating Euthymos for the pugilist's crown had to default in pankration because of exhaustion. The judges made him pay a fine for withdrawing from the contest and an indemnity to Euthymos for spitefully taking away his chance at victory. While many vase scenes show a ruthless pursuit of victory, the Panathenaic vase in figure 93 shows at the same time the fruits of success and the reverence for authority expected of the athletes. The vase, as J. D. Beazley wrote, seems to say that the winner at the Panathenaia has a strong chance of winning an Olympic victory two years later, and so the deity Olympias looks with interest at the proceedings. But what she watches is not combative action; rather, it seems, she observes the referee admonishing the athletes before the contest begins. Winning mattered greatly, but so did honesty: the *agon* was not socially divisive or disruptive.[79]

It is nearly impossible to give a fully satisfactory analysis of a modern society's values—it is plainly impossible to do so for an ancient one which has left only partial records. But it appears that the athletic agon, for all its obsessiveness (and, in the particular case of combat sport, for all its violence) far more than it served practical ends, filled a crucial need as an outlet for the highly competitive and individualistic impulses Greece developed during the period from the seventh to the fifth centuries B.C.E. Not the least of combat sport's functions was to service the potentially volatile heirs of the warrior elite.

At the end of the nineteenth century, Thorstein Veblen's *Theory of the Leisure Class* mocked the "emulative efficiency" that sport instills, claiming that it is at best only indirectly serviceable to collective life in the community. Societies will, of course, have different attitudes toward the competitive individual (just as they will toward collective life). Veblen would have found few supporters in ancient Greece for his view of the agon.[80] The archaic farmer-poet Hesiod gives us the most fitting summary of Hellenic values:

> Clearly there has never been one type alone of Strife [*eris*], but there are two on earth. One you would praise on noticing it; the other is execrable, and they have opposite natures. One increases evil war and quarrels, miserable thing it is. No mortal man loves it, but under compulsion, by design of the gods, they honor grievous Strife. But the other, which dark Night first spawned . . . she spurs on to work even the delicate man, all the same. Potter envies potter and builder builder, beggar is jealous of beggar, and poet of poet. [*Works and Days* 11 ff.]

Sport encouraged, channeled, and refined these competitive impulses.

93. Referee instructing boxers before the fight. The personification of Olympia looks on with interest. Greek vase, 340/339 B.C.E.

THE PARTICIPANTS IN GREEK COMBAT SPORT

Who were the people who registered at the great festivals, drew their lots, and fought in the stadia? Who participated in the local festivals or merely relaxed in informal sport within the palaestra? We do not always know the social status of ancient athletes or the details of their lives, but at least a few have come through time with very complete histories, and we can also put together some general profiles of ancient participants; the task is easier, of course, for later antiquity, where we have more inscriptions to help us. Especially in the archaic period, before the Persian Wars, history and legend blend, but even these anecdotes are enlightening as an insight into the reputation and status of the famous athletes. The patterns, moreover, which ancient sources sometimes follow in narrating these legends reveal general societal expectations about the athlete: in such instances a fictionalized account may still be a witness to a common truth. This chapter will begin with a series of biographical portraits, chosen because of the fame of the particular athletes or for the value the stories have in illustrating the nature of the ancient competitors. The last part of the chapter will then sketch a general portrait of these men.

COMBAT ATHLETES OF THE ARCHAIC AND CLASSICAL PERIODS

Milo of Kroton

By far the most famous wrestler in Western history is Milo from the Greek colony of Kroton in southern Italy. He won at Olympia as a boy, probably in the 60th Olympiad (540 B.C.E.), then another five times as an adult; he also achieved seven Delphic crowns (one as a boy), ten at the Isthmus, and nine at Nemea—his career thus had to extend at least twenty-four years at the highest level of competition. Ancient accounts credit Milo with prodigious strength and tremendous size, which makes perfect sense, for only a huge and strong man could sufficiently compensate for waning endurance, and so continue to dominate the competitions for so many years. It is reported that he could hold a pomegranate in his hand without breaking a single seed, yet no one could move a finger from it; standing on an oiled discus, he defied challengers to push him from it, and when he held out his hand with his elbow bent perpendicular no one could move even his smallest finger. He could burst a band around his temples by inhaling air and causing the veins to swell. As I noted in chapter 1, legend also has it that he carried his own bronze statue at Olympia and put it in place, and once carried a four-year-old bull on his shoulders before killing and eating it in one day. But even this monumental strength did not suffice in antiquity to explain his success, and one author reported that he ate the gizzard stones of roosters, which made him invincible in contest. He finally failed to win on his seventh Olympic attempt (though it is unclear whether he lost or merely tied), probably because his opponent, a younger countryman of his, knew not to close with him: his strategy was to let time take its toll on Milo's endurance rather than risk grappling with the powerful man. The Greeks tended to attribute "significant deaths" to famous persons in keeping with their purported characters. So according to legend, overweening belief in his strength brought Milo to his death. Walking in the countryside, he came across a partially split tree with the wedges still stuck in the springy wood. He grasped the cleavage to pull the wood asunder but only succeeded in making the wedges fall out, and the tree snapped tightly on his hands, holding him captive until the wolves came and fell upon him in his defenseless state.[1]

Milo's social status poses interesting questions. Herodotos, who lived approximately one hundred years after Milo, recorded that the famous physician Demokedes married the great wrestler's daughter. The fact that he could accept a physician son-in-law suggests that Milo was not an aristocrat, for marriage to a wage earner, even an exceedingly wealthy and famous doctor, would have been a questionable liaison in an aristocratic family. That Demokedes paid Milo a large sum of money for the privilege of marrying his daughter puts him even farther beyond the pale of acceptable behavior among the nobility. This is not to say that Milo lacked status in his city, for at least according to an account that appears five hundred years after Milo's time, he valiantly led his countrymen in battle against vastly superior forces from Sybaris.

> One hundred thousand men of Kroton were stationed with three hundred thousand Sybarite troops ranged against them. Milo the athlete led them and through his tremendous physical strength first turned the troops lined up against him. For this man, six times victor at Olympia and having courage commensurate with his physical prowess, is said to have come to battle

crowned with his Olympic crowns and dressed up in the equipment of Herakles with his lion skin and club. [Diodorus Siculus 12.9.5–6]

If, moreover, he belonged to the Pythagorean circle of Kroton (see below), which was an integral part of the oligarchic government of Kroton, then he was clearly a man of political influence in a traditionally conservative city.[2]

Some ancient evaluations of Milo present him as a strong but mindless buffoon and glutton; indeed some sources give the story of his death as the ultimate example of his witlessness. For Galen he is a key example of the worthlessness of athletes, but this caricature does not square with the report of his military exploits, even less so with the testimony that he was a disciple of Pythagoras, the philosopher, and it probably serves better as an example of Galen's venom than as a biography. One tradition reports that Milo's wife was Muia, herself a Pythagorean or perhaps even a daughter of the great philosopher. It was said that Milo saved the lives of Pythagoras and his companions, for once, while dining at the communal meal of the philosophers, Milo jumped into the place of a crumbling pillar and held up the roof, escaping himself only when the others were free of danger. In another account, however, Pythagoras died in a fire in Milo's house. The stories linking him to the circle of Pythagoras vary widely and may even be ultimately unhistorical, but it is significant that he had a substantial reputation in antiquity for keeping company with philosophers and leaders.[3]

Diagoras of Rhodes

"Die, Diagoras, for you cannot go up into heaven!" So a spectator at Olympia said to the former Olympic boxing champion and *periodonikes* on the day when two of his sons won the Olympic crowns in boxing and pankration and lifted their proud father up onto their shoulders. Wellborn, praised by Pindar in a shimmering victory ode, father and grandfather of outstanding athletes, Diagoras showed all of the talents and assets that the fifth century prized.[4] His lineage, according to the tradition recorded by Pausanias, was as blue-blooded as can be found in the ancient world: his great-grandfather was a king, his great-grandmother, also descended from royalty, was the daughter of Aristomenes, the seventh-century leader of Messenia who for over a decade fended off Sparta's attempts to conquer his country. As was often the case in antiquity, a figure as great as Diagoras had to have divine parentage (even kings on both sides was not a satisfying explanation for such achievements), and Aristotle recorded the popular legend that his mother, tired by the heat, lay down in a sanctuary of Hermes where the god came and had congress with her. Other accounts attributed this son to Herakles.[5]

Diagoras was the first of a dynasty of combat athletes. Aside from his Olympic crown and a victory at Delphi, he won four times at the Isthmus, several times at Nemea (he was thus a *periodonikes*), also at Athens, Rhodes, Argos, Arkadia, Thebes (and elsewhere in Boeotia), Pellene, Megara, and Aegina. Pindar reports that he was a man of towering size. His older sons Akousilaos and Damogetos won their respective Olympic crowns in boxing and pankration, as we have seen, on the same day: their younger brother Dorieus, a boxer and pankratiast, alone collected almost as many victories as his father and brothers put together: three Olympic, four Delphic (one of which was *akoniti*),[6] eight Isthmian, and seven Nemean crowns. Diagoras's daughters Pherenike and Kallipatira each produced a son who took a boxing crown at Olympia, and Kallipatira herself achieved the unique distinction of seeing the Olympics as a married woman and living to tell of it. In one account she asked the Hellanodikai for admission and responded to their refusal by showing them the victory monuments of her father and brothers, an argument they found persuasive. Later accounts, however, vary in attributing the visit to Kallipatira or Pherenike and tell the more lurid story that the mother's desire to see her son in the boy's competition was so great that she dressed as a trainer and saw the contest. She was discovered, some say, when she ran to embrace her son. She stood in peril of execution for her sacrilegious invasion of Olympia and was saved only by the Greeks' regard for her father and brothers. The Olympic officials, however, passed an ordinance that henceforth trainers would have to appear naked, just like the athletes. These stories, of course, show signs of romantic embroidery; what is historical fact is that the six victory statues of Diagoras and two generations of his descendants stood together in a conspicuous group at Olympia, and portions of their inscriptions have survived to this day.

The family's importance contributed to the eventual death of Dorieus. During the Peloponnesian War, he led an anti-Athenian faction in Rhodes, and the revolt of the island against Athens' hegemony caused Athens to pass a death sentence against him. He fled to Thurii and fought on the Spartan side against Athens with ships he personally financed. Remarkably, when he later fell into Athenian hands they released him without ransom. Later, however, after the Peloponnesian War, when Rhodes broke its alliance with Sparta, the Spartans seized and executed him, in what may have been a total and rash misunderstanding of his role in the revolt.[7]

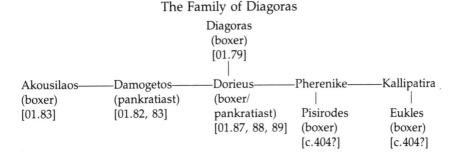

The Family of Diagoras

Diagoras
(boxer)
[01.79]

Akousilaos———Damogetos———Dorieus———Pherenike———Kallipatira
(boxer)   (pankratiast)   (boxer/ | |
[01.83]   [01.82, 83]   pankratiast)   Pisirodes   Eukles
                                [01.87, 88, 89] (boxer)   (boxer)
                                                 [c.404?]   [c.404?]

Theogenes of Thasos

Theogenes from the island of Thasos, pankratiast and boxer of the early fifth century, enjoyed a long, very successful, and exceedingly busy athletic life. There is an ancient discrepancy over the exact number of festivals he won—reports vary between twelve hundred and fourteen hundred.[8] Theogenes clearly gave up a lot to pursue athletics, for even if he had a long career, it still would have been necessary for him to spend a large part of his life on the road and fighting in order to visit so many contests. In major festivals, he won distinction with two Olympic crowns, one in boxing (480 B.C.E.) and one in pankration (476), three Delphic boxing crowns, one of them without competition (*akoniti*), nine victories in boxing at the Isthmus with a double victory there one year, for he gained a pankration crown on the same day, and nine Nemean boxing victories.

Theogenes' history is full of legend and folklore, but the anecdotal stories are in accord with the core of historical information in portraying a man full of pluck and charisma. At the games in Thessalian Phthia, homeland of Homer's Achilleus, he passed over the competitions in boxing and wrestling in order to win the long race "in the homeland of the swiftest of those known as heroes." At times he overreached himself and paid dearly for it, especially in the 75th Olympiad (480), when he attempted to win both the boxing and pankration crowns. Unfortunately, as noted above, his boxing opponent in the finals was the formidable Euthymos of Lokri (see below), champion in the previous Olympiad, who ultimately lost to Theogenes but not before he utterly exhausted him, leaving him incapable of meeting his pankration opponent. The Olympic judges fined him one talent (6,000 drachma) for defaulting, requiring him also to pay one talent to Euthymos in damages, since they felt he had entered the boxing competition merely to spite Euthymos. Success far outweighed setbacks, however, and he seems to have named his son Diolympos ("Two times at Olympia") in commemoration of his achievement. Centuries later, Plutarch considered him ambitious to the point of arrogance and tells how he once called all the guests at a banquet to fight in pankration against him in a fit of aggressive self-display. Plutarch concluded, "I don't praise his excessive love of honor and quarrelsomeness."[9]

Theogenes appears to have been active in civic life. His father was a priest of Herakles, which suggests that his family had already achieved some degree of importance, and certainly by 476, when he paid his one-talent fine to the Olympic officials, he was in possession of a large fortune, either the fruit of prize winning or inheritance. Centuries after his death, a Greek orator praised him for devoting himself no less strenuously to the common good than he had previously to athletics.[10]

Archaeology has confirmed ancient reports that the people of Thasos worshipped Theogenes as a divinity after his death and offered sacrifices to him. Excavations on Thasos uncovered among other objects a large inscribed stone with a hollow center, whose function was to receive the obligatory one obol donation from the faithful who came to sacrifice at his shrine. Legend concerning the foundation of the cult tells how one of his enemies vented his rage after Theogenes' death by whipping his statue and paid the price for this outrage when the statue fell and crushed him to death. As was typical of Greek procedure in cases involving bloodshed, the people of Thasos threw the statue into the sea, only to fall victim to the numinous rage of the divinity, which struck the fields with infertility. On the advice of the Delphic oracle, the statue, when finally found by a fisherman, was replaced, and Theogenes received appropriate cultic honors. Greeks from other cities as well as non-Greeks attributed to Theogenes magical powers of healing diseases.[11]

Euthymos of Lokri

Theogenes' boxing opponent Euthymos became a hero by virtue, it seems, of an encounter with a ghost. After his third Olympic victory (in 472), he erected a monument at Olympia with a simple, four-line inscription which survives to this day and was on his way home to his city Lokri in Italy, when he landed in Temesa and saw in preparation the strange rites of the local hero cult. Some sources speak vaguely about a ghost which "taxed" the inhabitants unduly. Pausanias, however, reports the local legend that one of Odysseus's sailors became drunk and raped a Temesan girl, for which outrage the townspeople stoned him to death. This did not trouble Odysseus, who sailed away with the rest of his men, but Temesa fell victim to the angry dead man: the ghost killed the townspeople without respite, until they were on the verge of abandoning the town. Finally, the Delphic oracle told them to honor the ghost by building him a temple and giving him each year the most beautiful maiden of Temesa. Euthymos arrived just after the townspeople had consigned the maiden to the temple; Pausanias tells that he first pitied her, then fell in love with her. The boxer, determined to rescue her, donned his armor and successfully fought the ghost, driving him away from the land. The ghost subsequently jumped into the sea, never to be seen again, and Euthymos married the girl he had saved. Pausanias describes a picture he saw, a copy of an ancient one, which depicted the fight—the ghost was black and frightening and wore a wolfskin. The boxer did not die as ordinary mortals do when his time came but departed "in some other way." Needless to say, Euthymos was credited with a divine father, the river god Karkinos.

Pliny the Elder records the story that lightning struck the statues of Euthymos at Lokri and at Olympia on the same day and maintains sarcastically that the only miraculous thing about Euthymos was that he ever received divine honors. The tradition of the greedy ghost, however, antedates Pliny: the Roman author is showing his ignorance of the legends here. Euthymos's confrontation with the Undead suggests that some very ancient and primitive traditions lurk beneath the tales we have: these, probably more than his great strength, explain why the Greeks numbered him among the heroes, but I am only guessing.[12]

Kleomedes of Astypalia and Diognetos of Crete

Also joining the ranks of heroized athletes is Kleomedes of Astypalia, whose name became a byword for savagery. At the 71st or 72d Olympiad (496 or 492 B.C.E.), he killed his boxing opponent, a man named Ikkos, using illegal tactics. According to the Church Fathers who retell the story as a condemnation of pagan culture, Kleomedes struck Ikkos in such a way that he tore open his rib cage: this seems unlikely, and the exact nature of the foul remains unclear, but whatever he did was serious mispractice, and one tradition holds that in addition to disqualifying his victory, the Olympic officials laid a fine of four talents on him. Kleomedes felt that he was unjustly treated and was so maddened with grief that when he returned to his city he overturned a column supporting the roof of a school, thereby killing many children. When the citizens naturally started to stone him, he fled to a temple, climbed inside a box and pulled the lid over him. But the townspeople found no one inside the chest when they forced it open, and the oracle demanded that they give offerings to Kleomedes, "the latest of the heroes, and no longer a mortal."

Diognetos of Crete killed his opponent in boxing, lost the crown for it, and was forced into exile. Despite all of this, however, like Kleomedes, he ultimately received a hero's honors. The two boxers quite naturally raise major questions about the definition of the Greek hero-athlete which I will try to answer at the end of this chapter.[13]

Glaukos of Karystos

Glaukos of Karystos was the son of a farmer and, like his father, worked the land. One day he astonished his father by using his fist to hammer a bent plowshare back into shape. The perceptive father took his son to compete in boy's boxing at Olympia (probably at the 65th Olympiad, 520 B.C.E.),[14] where his strength and determination took him into the finals, despite his being badly cut by his more experienced opponents. In his final contest, he wavered on the edge of signaling submission when his father or, in a different version, his trainer shouted, "My boy—the one from the plowshare!" At that reminder, Glaukos landed a powerful blow on his opponent and won. He went on to win two crowns at Delphi and eight at both Nemea and the Isthmus. After his plucky victory he seems to have much refined his technique, and Pausanias reports that he was an expert at light hand sparring, the sort of style that wears an opponent down rather than knocks him out.

Centuries later, Glaukos was still invoked as the consummate boxer: the orators Demosthenes and Aeschines referred to him in their suits, and his status remains intact even in late antiquity. The number of his victories, especially at the two top festivals, is somewhat small for an athlete of such legendary stature: one at Olympia, two or possibly three at Delphi, eight at the Isthmus, nine at Nemea. Presumably after his rough and ready debut at Olympia, he added a skill commensurate with his strength and through that became proverbial.

If there is any truth in the story of his farmboy origins then Glaukos provides a good example of how a person of moderate income in archaic Greece could rise rapidly to prominence through athletic skill. It seems most likely that his family was reasonably comfortable rather than poor peasantry: farming had far more status than other kinds of work in antiquity, to the extent that even a family with some social pretensions might still do some work on their own land,[15] and it is hard to imagine that Glaukos could have taken the year of training for Olympia if his presence on the farm was essential for the family's income.

The prominence Glaukos achieved ultimately seems to have been more bitter than sweet. The Sicilian tyrant Gelon appointed him governor of Kamerina, a high enough honor, but he perished in a revolt, some say by the designs of his patron Gelon himself.[16]

COMBAT ATHLETES OF LATER ANTIQUITY

Aelius Aurelius Menander of Aphrodisias

Aelius Aurelius Menander was from "eminent and well-reputed lineage."[17] During his pankration career in the mid second century of our era, he gained distinction for winning as a boy, youth, and man in three consecutive years and took crowns at Delphi, Nemea, the Isthmus, Naples, Rome, and a host of other festivals. In Rome he received his crown for victory in the Capitoline Games from the very hand of Caesar, a fact which his inscription proudly records. Menander was a serious athlete who traveled immense distances in his festival itinerary, competing among other places in Arabia, Palestine, Bithynia, and Italy. Later he served as xystarch, the head of an athletic synod, and received, as successful athletes often did, citizenship and the office of senator in several different cities. Menander himself was sufficiently wealthy (and philanthropic) on one occasion to facilitate the staging of some local games, and in particular, underwrote the cost of the athletes' prizes. For this beneficence, his synod[18] sent a letter of commendation to the emperor Antoninus Pius and resolved to erect statues and images of him prominently in his city. Not missing an opportunity for philanthropy, Menander's brother, Zenon, absorbed the cost of his brother's honors.

Another inscription from Aphrodisias tells of the more limited athletic success of a different Menander, quite possibly the grandson of Aelius Aurelius. Menander, the son of Menander the senate executive, as he is introduced on the inscription, competed "brilliantly" in the Philemonieion Games of Aphrodisias but failed to win. The senate (quite possibly in deference to his grandfather, if this identification is correct) decreed that it would erect a statue in his honor at its expense. Four years later, however, he won at this particular festival, and his inscription was duly augmented to take note of this achievement; the senate also granted him a second statue.[19]

Marcus Aurelius Demetrios and
Marcus Aurelius Asclepiades

The family of Diagoras could boast six Olympic victors and so reigns unrivaled in the history of Greek sport as a dynasty of distinguished athletes. Later antiquity, however, offers the history of Marcus Aurelius Demetrios and his son Marcus Aurelius Asclepiades as a weighty reminder that the highest achievements in combat sport continued to extend from one generation to the next.[20] The son was in no way reticent about his achievements, and the long inscription he erected in Rome reveals much about his character and the careers he and his father had.

The son's victory monument records that he was a *periodonikes* in pankration and won contests "among three nations: Italy, Greece, and Asia," noting specifically Olympia, Delphi, the Isthmus twice, Nemea twice, the Heraia in Argos, the Capitoline Games twice, the Sebasta of Naples twice, the Actian Games twice, and a host of other festivals. Asclepiades proudly recorded that at a number of these festivals he "stopped his opponents" after a certain number of rounds of the tournament, that is, they withdrew from the tournament rather than face him in contest. He gives, moreover, a long list of honorary epithets, some of which are unique in extant Greek literature:

> I was a pankratiast, a *periodonikes*, undefeated, never pushed out of the *skamma*, never challenged, I won all contests in which I registered and I never myself challenged an opponent, nor did anyone venture to challenge me, I was never tied, never assaulted an opponent, never avoided a contest, never left a contest, nor won one by royal favor, nor did I win in irregular contest, but was crowned in the *skamma* itself in all the festivals for which I registered, having passed all their preceding inspections.[21]

In this inscription, we also learn that the father, Marcus Aurelius Demetrios, was an outstanding wrestler and a *periodonikes* in pankration; he received the honors such an athlete could expect: lifetime presidency of the athletic guild with a high priesthood in it and superintendence of the imperial baths. His son went much further—whereas Demetrios was a citizen of Alexandria and Hermopolis, the son names six important cities on whose senates he served and notes that there were many others in which he held citizenship and civic office.

Interestingly, Asclepiades felt that he should record his athletic achievements, including such subtleties as "never pushed from the *skamma*," in official government correspondence, even when it had nothing to do with sport; a papyrus letter he wrote to the city council of Hermopolis still exists, showing this habit of his. Athletic achievement was a significant asset, and a public figure like Asclepiades was with good reason careful of his reputation. The upper echelons of sport formed a complex world, as we have already seen through the troubles Theogenes had at Olympia, and not only the athletes' achievements, but also his intentions (or what the officials perceived them to be) mattered greatly; it is not surprising that Asclepiades' inscription stresses his honorable life and behavior alongside his crowns and titles. At the end of his inscription he alludes to "dangers" and the "envy" of others which drove him into early retirement at age twenty-five after only six years of competition; he was apparently then at his prime, for he did make one comeback, some fourteen years later, to win at the Olympics of Alexandria. But what the tensions were between this eminent athlete and his contemporaries will forever remain a mystery.

Most remarkable of all perhaps, and a good reminder of how often stereotypes prove false, is the fact that Asclepiades was elected a member of the Museum, the prestigious literary coterie of Alexandria. By the third century, political leaders occasionally appear in its ranks, and probably it was Asclepiades' civic virtues which gained him the appointment: whatever the reasons, his membership argues that he was hardly the mindless hulk that Galen's polemic describes as the normal makeup of heavy athletes.[22]

Tiberius Claudius Rufus of Smyrna

High-level performance also characterized the aristocratic family of Tiberius Claudius Rufus from Smyrna. At some time in the first or second century, having already won in one or more of the sacred festivals, he pursued an Olympic crown in pankration, made his way to the finals, and there fought his opponent until darkness forced the judges to consider it a draw. According to the inscription honoring him, his perseverance so moved the officials that they considered him worthy of a victor's rewards and privileges. The inscription notes that he fought without a break (*anephedros*) against an opponent in the finals who had drawn a bye; what might have persuaded the judges in his behalf as much as merit was the fact that he was also influential enough to be an acquaintance of the emperors.[23]

By the third century, members of what seems to be the same Claudius Rufus family boast that they were descendants of consuls—the family had moved from local prominence to the highest Roman magistracy. Combat sport, interestingly enough, continued to play an important role in their lives, for Claudius Apollonius of Smyrna was twice *periodonikes* and his son, Claudius Rufus, was "a successor to his father" and likewise a *periodonikes*. An inscription erected by an athletic guild honors their memory and notes that they came from a family that had produced consuls.[24]

A writer and intellectual named Rufus of Perinthus (a city with close ties to Smyrna), who lived in the latter half of the second century and achieved great distinction for his erudition, may represent a branch of this family. Like the two *periodonikai* of the Claudius Rufus family, the learned Rufus had ancestors of consular rank, and one contemporary author noted that "he achieved mastery over his body with physical training, subjecting it to rigid diet and hard exercise, almost like athletes in competition." The evidence for a family connection is only circum-stantial, but, if true, it is vivid evidence for the survival of classical beliefs in the harmony of the intellect and the life of the athlete.[25]

GENERAL OBSERVATIONS ON ATHLETE-HEROES

Reviewing the stories of Kleomedes and Theogenes, a Church Father cynically remarked that he learned from them that boxing is a truly divine pursuit and that it had escaped the notice of purportedly wise people that they should give up being righteous, be-come boxers, and win divine favor. The polemic raises an important question, however: what was it about combat athletes that predisposed them in Greek eyes to immortality? As we have seen, Kleomedes was honored as a hero, Theogenes received the offerings due to a god; he also was credited with the ability after his mortal lifespan to cure illness, a capacity shared by the wrestler Poulydamas. Euthymos the boxer did not die a mortal death, and Diognetos the boxer, who like Kleomedes killed his opponent, received a hero's honors.[26]

There were many paths to becoming a hero in Greece; sometimes local political or family forces were at work in forming a cult, and it is mis-placed ingenuity to try to isolate one particular essence of the athletes that accounted for all their separate translations from the human to the divine. On the other hand, by looking at the general nature of Greek heroes, it is possible to see certain patterns in their lives and deeds to which these athletes conform quite closely. It is necessary, of course, at the outset to come to a working definition of the hero, since *hero* in Greek religion is a very broad term. The hero's existence begins like that of an ordinary mortal, but he does not die as normal people do; rather his powers persist after his human life ends. He is thus a super-natural entity, and even the Greeks sometimes blurred the distinction between heroes and gods. A proper hero cult involved special nighttime sacrifices of blood and holocaust (complete burning of the victim) at a grave site, things not done in normal divine service, but the same hero could also receive the offerings appropriate to the worship of a god. For the purposes of this section, we can use the term *hero* to refer to any mortal elevated to a divine or semidivine status; the nature of the cult is less interesting sociologically speaking than the fact that the athlete was viewed as superhuman.

State gratitude was a strong force in turning athletes into heroes: among many examples, the soldiers who fell fighting the Persians in 490 B.C.E. were named heroes (and were feared as powerful and poten-tially dangerous spirits), and so also the soldiers who fell in the battles at Plataia and Thermopylai received heroes' honors. Athletic victors, who brought delight and honor to their cities, easily fell into the category of public benefactors: the predominance of combat athletes over other sportsmen who received these honors may reflect the high popularity and esteem of those events. None of the great athletes of later antiquity received such honors—as we have seen, they were usually citizens of many different cities simultaneously, and thus the bond of athlete and city-state was no longer so close.[27]

Combat athletes possessed other features typical of heroes, like gigantic size and strength. The bones of Theseus, for example, were readily identifiable as those of the hero because of their size, and Greek art also reflects this difference in stature of mortal and hero. Of all sportsmen, the heavy athletes filled this expectation best. So also violence and a jealous sense of personal honor were typical of heroes: an ancient lexicon, for example, offered the following definition: "'The stronger ones': So they call the heroes. And some seem to be malicious. For this reason, even those who pass by the hero cult sites keep silent lest the hero do them harm in some way. And the gods are also this way."[28] Heroized combat athletes were prime examples during their mortal lives of pride and rage. Beyond even the harsh reality of their sports, two killed their opponents, and one of these, Kleomedes, then killed a number of children, adding crime upon crime. Theogenes, whose ego was proverbial, outraged guests at a religious fest by fighting the pankration against them. The legends of the athlete-heroes are full of accounts of the desecration of the hero's statue, exile, and dishonor, leading to the hero's revenge: heroes were beings on the margins of their societies who could do both good and evil. Once again we see the Greek admiration for the uninhibited and unbridled assertion of self to which the agon gave expression and release. Society may well have found the hero difficult to accommodate, but he was an embodiment of passions whose existence the Greeks were too honest to deny.[29]

SOCIAL BACKGROUND OF THE ATHLETES: EGALITARIANISM AND TRADITION

Although the custom of heroizing the great athletes does not extend beyond classical times, the status of the athletes remained high in later antiquity. Though clearly all social classes were free to enter the contests,[30] it is also clear that throughout its history, sport in the Greek world claimed the attention and participation of the nobility and was molded by its ideology.

In the latter half of the fifth century B.C.E. an anonymous author now popularly called the Old Oligarch wrote a pamphlet attacking the Athenian democracy. In it he made the grossly exaggerated charge that the masses have disbanded those training in sport and knowledgeable in music, thinking that these are unworthy pursuits and knowing that they themselves are not able to learn these activities. Of course, only a little later the same author noted that the masses built gymnasia for themselves, and nowhere does he set the contradiction right. What is interesting to note, however, in this fifth-century context, is the prejudice that sport, like music, is the preserve of the upper classes.[31] Some evocative lines of Aristophanes also display this sentiment when they speak of "solid citizens, people we know to be wellborn and decent men, people of justice, fine gentlemen, and nurtured in the palaestras, in the choruses, and in music" (*Frogs* 727–29). Showing similar thoughts, the prosecution in a fourth-century B.C.E. trial articulated his fear that a witness for the defense might make a very favorable impression because he was once a general and knew how to conduct himself "like one who has been in the palaestras and in learned discourse" (Aeschines, *Against Timarchos* 132). A fourth-century B.C.E. caricature displays this stereotype in a more amusing way: the boor, who only late in life is able to acquire an education, frequents the palaestra, struts around the baths pretending to throw imaginary opponents over his hip, and even wrestles with the bull when assisting at a sacrifice.[32] The modern equivalent of this would be the efforts of some nouveaux riches to enter the "horsey set" and master the accoutrements, techniques, and jargon of that exclusive subculture. We have already encountered a number of blueblooded, wealthy aristocrats in all eras who were willing to bear the blows and danger of the combat sports, often with tremendous success, as in the case of, for example, Diagoras and family. I might note others too: Timasitheos of Delphi, who won twice at Olympia and three times at Delphi in pankration, then later played a major part in a right-wing oligarchic (aristocratic) plot to seize the government of Athens, for which he suffered the death penalty; Kallias of Athens, *periodonikes* in pankration, who was exiled (ostracized) in the middle of the fifth century B.C.E., was almost certainly the victim of the struggle of the democratic leader Perikles to consolidate his power against the old guard. Harder to evaluate is Chairon of Pellene, twice victor at the Isthmus and four times victor at Olympia in wrestling. He was a pupil of Plato, whose students tended to come from the upper class, but later he instituted a tyranny in his own city and enfranchised slaves while exiling the nobles. Much later came Atyanas of Adramyttium, Olympic victor in boxing— and of the tough, sharp-thonged variety as well—whom Cicero called "a nobleman, whose name almost all of us have heard." The young

Marcus Aurelius enjoyed wrestling, and also from the Roman period comes Flavillianus of Oenoanda, among whose forebears were consuls and senators, and who himself "practiced pankration and won crowns at sacred competitions."[33]

On the other side of the coin were competitors from the middle and lower classes. It is unlikely that many made it to or even near the top in the earlier years of Greek sport. In Athens, at least, the lowest class of citizenry, the *thetes*, did not receive ephebic training, and thus their entry to the world of sport was difficult. Even a youth of hoplite status who had the advantage of some gymnasium experience would not necessarily find the time and money for higher level training. As an inscription c. 300 B.C.E. from Ephesos requesting a subsidy shows, even a Nemean victor from a poor family could not on his own afford the training and travel expenses necessary for a bid at an Olympic title despite the handsome reward he collected for his earlier success.[34] Moreover, not all festivals were lucrative. At the Delian Apollonia, for example, the top prize listed in the inscriptions is 10 drachmas, hardly enough to cover transportation. The festivals could have a massive number of entries; we have already seen examples of six, eight, even nine rounds of competition in the Roman period (see chap. 1), and formidable athletes, like Theogenes, might show up at seemingly obscure games. Thus the aspiring athlete without the wealth to train properly could well find himself badly beaten, with only the proverbial "pocketful of mumbles, such are promises" to show for his potential and courage. Aristotle, for example, takes note of a fishmonger who went on to win the Olympics but adds that such success is rare, beyond the person's powers, beyond expectations. The possibility, however, was always present that raw talent could succeed against those athletes with the money and leisure to train: unlike the nineteenth-century elitists who coined the notion of amateurism with the express purpose of excluding the working classes from sport, the man who entered the Greek agon could not hide behind title or birth. After the fourth century B.C.E. it becomes easier to see how people without familial wealth could succeed in athletics, namely, through subsidies provided by their cities for their training. In the Greco-Roman period the presence of less affluent people is quite noticeable. A late second-century C.E. treatise on the interpretation of dreams noted that the middle-class woman who dreamed of giving birth to an eagle was fated to raise an outstanding athlete, while an upper-class woman or a poor woman could expect different progeny: what is implicit here is that professional sport was acquiring the reputation of being largely (but not exclusively) a middle-class phenomenon, for this group would be able, given the huge rewards to be had for success, to scrape together the capital necessary to get a promising child started in athletics. From a papyrus letter dated 257 B.C.E., we learn how the wealthy Zenon paid a trainer in Alexandria named Ptolemaios to give instruction to a boy named Pyrrhos for whom Zenon acted as patron. Zenon's agent, reporting enthusiastically that the boy showed great promise under Ptolemaios's tutelage, wrote, "I expect you will be crowned," which seems to indicate that the prizes and honors that Pyrrhus might win in the athletic festivals would accrue to Zenon. Another correspondence shows that the relationship between the trainer and the master could be quite close: Zenon was apparently sufficiently interested in cultivating a friendship with Ptolemaios even before he had contact with him that he did some considerable service for the coach: athletic patronage was serious business. Slaves, too, could participate in some of the festivals of later antiquity, though it is unclear whether they could keep much of their earnings if successful.[35]

The great pankratiast M. Aurelius Asclepiades, whom we encountered earlier in this chapter, retired to the Museum of Alexandria, antiquity's greatest coterie of the arts, after six years of terrifying his opponents. In the same era, however, were men like the boxer Herminos and those who signed his guild membership certificate (second century C.E.), in some cases semiliterate but catapulted by their victories into high office in the athletic guild. The editor of the papyrus recording Herminos's entry to the guild noted, "The grammar of the two first subscriptions [signatures and titles of the officials] is so bad as to leave the construction rather doubtful." And the formidable Herminos, who could not sign his own name, served as priest at the important festival at Sardis: one senses social mobility in this athlete's life.[36]

Looking over the athletic scene in later antiquity, one encounters many signs of a full-blown professional world of sport: subsidies for athletes, slaves competing, massive numbers of festivals. We hear on one occasion of a cash advance offered to a famous athlete to lure him to lend his prestige to a festival by competing in it.[37] But for all this, the world of sport—at least in its ideology and vocabulary—remains ennobled. Athletes assuredly competed for money, but consistently they received *dora* ("rewards"), like those the heroes of old received for their labors. Their guilds, notwithstanding the fact that they supervised a big business, fostered in them a sense of respect for one another and for their pursuit. One Kallikrates, according to the monument erected by his fellow athletes, "has obtained with sweat and toil a glorious reputation" and was renowned "among all men throughout the world because of the perfect wisdom that was the object of his dedicated effort." The inscription continues, "He took care of his soul." A group of athletes mourned the death of a man named Alfidius, "since it struck down the most potent example of both moderation and achievement . . . for he was most amazing in regard to his inimitable moderation and gentleness, which he showed throughout his whole athletic career." An inscription from Aphrodisias records Ephesos's praise for Aurelius Achilles, "who took up the training of his body and was most noble in contest and most pious in his manner of living and conduct, to such a point that he blended as much virtue of soul as of body." Professionals of later antiquity they were, but they lacked neither mind nor soul.[38]

VIII

METAPHOR, MYTH, AND REALITY

The evening before his dreaded encounter with Esau, Jacob, son of Isaac, sent away his household and wrestled with a man until dawn. Despite an injury, he held his adversary fast and exacted the stranger's blessing as his victory reward. The book of Genesis narrates:

> Jacob was left alone. And a man wrestled with him until the break of dawn. When he saw that he had not prevailed against him, he wrenched Jacob's hip at its socket, so that the socket of his hip was strained as he wrestled with him. Then he said, "Let me go, for the dawn is breaking." But he answered, "I will not let you go, unless you bless me." Said the other, "What is your name?" He replied, "Jacob." Said he, "Your name shall no longer be called Jacob, but Israel, for you have striven with God and man and have prevailed."[1]

In the story of Jacob and the mysterious stranger, wrestling functions as a rite of passage; only after the contest can the potential patriarch begin to fulfill his destiny. He is thus an early and famous example of the many heroes in history and myth for whom a wrestling victory served as a symbol of power and, more important, leadership: this tradition extends in place and time from the ancient Near East through the Greek world into Christian thought and European politics.[2] The ideological significance of combat sport and its possible moral lessons go far beyond the contests; indeed even the critics and enemies of the palaestra returned over and over again to vivid metaphors and imagery of the combat sports, showing how deeply they had influenced, at least at one time, ancient life and thought.

Certain details in the biblical story point to a folk tradition in which the wandering hero has some kind of athletic trial. One might well ask why a divine emissary needs to leave at dawn: this characteristic of Jacob's adversary is more typical of a ghost or vampire than a celestial being. It seems that beneath the account in Genesis as we now have it lies a folk story of the hero defeating a local spirit or demon. This simple motif is not discarded from the biblical narrative but is transformed into a higher spiritual test involving an encounter with God's power.[3] In the epic of Gilgamesh, which antedates Genesis, a wrestling match is even more crucial in determining the direction of the hero's career. Gilgamesh, the mighty, divine hero, ruler of Uruk, has oppressed his people, forcing great numbers of women and perhaps young men as well into sexual union with him. The gods send against him Enkidu, a rival in size and strength, who blocks Gilgamesh from entering the meeting building of Uruk, where he intended to exact the *ius primae noctis*, that is, deflower maidens engaged to be married:

> Enkidu barred the
>   gate with his foot,
> They seized each other,
>   they bent down like
>   expert [wrestlers],
> they destroyed the
>   doorpost, the wall
>   shook.
> Gilgamesh and Enkidu
>   were holding each
>   other,
> like expert [wrestlers]
>   they bent down,
> they destroyed the
>   doorpost, the wall
>   shook.
> Gilgamesh bent [his
>   one knee],
> With the [other] foot on the
>   ground.[4]

[Gilgamesh, Tablet II (trans. Sjöberg)]

Unfortunately the text in the damaged form in which it has come down to us does not make it clear that Gilgamesh won the encounter, though this is the likeliest interpretation.[5] Enkidu was created to be Gilgamesh's equal and to keep the sovereign so busy fighting with him that the city would have peace (I.col 2); only later do the two heroes become loyal companions, in accordance with the dream Gilgamesh's mother revealed to him. Whether Gilgamesh bending over with his foot on the ground signifies victory or not, his life is different after the encounter.[6] Enkidu duly acknowledges Gilgamesh's sovereignty:

> Thy head is exalted above [all other] men;
>   The kingship over the people
>   Enlil has decreed for thee.

More important than the proof of sovereignty for Gilgamesh, however, is the sea change in his character. Immediately after the wrestling, the hitherto dissolute and promiscuous man takes his companion Enkidu off on a series of heroic adventures; he emerges from the contest a more serious and determined leader.

Wrestling continued to have an important role in demonstrating power and authority in early Islamic times. In the following story from *The Life of Muhammad*, the prophet persuades the skeptic, mighty man though he was, of his truths by defeating him in wrestling:

> My father Ishaq b. Yasar told me saying: "Rukana b. 'Abdu Yazid b. Hashim b. 'Abdu'l-Muttalib b. 'Abdu Manaf was the strongest man among Quraysh, and one day he met the apostle in one of the passes of Mecca alone: 'Rukana,' said he, 'why won't you fear God and accept my preaching?' 'If I knew that what you say is true I would follow you,' he said. The apostle then asked if he would recognize that he spoke the truth if he threw him, and when he said Yes they began to wrestle, and when the apostle got a firm grip of him he threw him to the ground, he being unable to offer any effective resistance. 'Do it again, Muhammad,' he said, and he did it again. 'This is extraordinary,' he said, 'can you really throw me?' 'I can show you something more wonderful than that if you wish. I will call this tree that you see and it will come to me.' 'Call it,' he said. He called it and it advanced until it stood before the apostle."[7]

The legendary wrestling matches of Jacob, Gilgamesh, and Muhammad reflect, of course, ancient expectations about the leader. These expectations also had political implications, and one historical personage, Shulgi the Sumerian king, whose court hymns claimed that Gilgamesh was his "bosom friend," boasted of his prowess in wrestling as well as in warfare, hunting, racing, and other contests of strength and skill.[8]

An institution as central to Greek life as combat sport could not fail to appear as part of the gods' lives as well. One legend records that Zeus wrestled his father Kronos at Olympia for control of the universe. The poet Aeschylus went further and made two rounds of divine succession the outcome of encounters in combat sport: first Ouranos (father of Kronos, grandfather of Zeus) controlled the cosmos, "bristling with a pankratiast's strength," but he retired into obscurity when defeated by Kronos, who then fell to Zeus, the *triakter* ("winner of the three falls"). Another legend held that Zeus instituted the Olympic Games in honor of his victory over Kronos, and in this primeval Olympiad, Apollo, whom the Greeks often invoked as a patron of boxing (see chap. 4), defeated Ares the war god in that sport.[9]

So, too, the Greek heroes were frequently involved in contests of combat sport. Theseus, the most important hero in Athenian legends, was considered the patron and inventor of wrestling (and in one tradition, pankration). His wrestling victory over Kerkyon appears often in literature and art (see figs. 23, 35, 40), most notably in the sculptures of the Athenian Treasure House at Delphi. Kerkyon had his own palaestra and, like Antaios (below), forced travelers to wrestle him, killing his victims. He had a wrestling style of his own—Greek tradition claims he developed the tactics of attacking the legs, but Theseus, relying on greater skill, ended his gruesome career: in one tradition he lifted Kerkyon high in the air and smashed him to the ground.[10] Skiron, who hurled guests to their deaths from his home atop a cliff, perished at Theseus's hands when he attempted this outrage on the hero. The legends concur that Theseus punished the outlaw by hurling him to his death from his own cliff, and though no literary source mentions that the two wrestled, figure 95 shows that the tactics of the sport were on the vase painter's mind: Theseus tips his foe over with an elegant leg-lift (cf. fig. 57). The adventures of Herakles offer yet more legends of wrestling and pankration. The hide of the Nemean lion was unpierceable, and Herakles had to strangle the beast, a detail which naturally suggested to the vase painter a great array of wrestling tactics. In one instance, Herakles executes the shoulder throw on the lion (fig. 96), in others a standing headlock; often he interlocks his fingers in the familiar wrestler's grip. Many were the brigands who fell to him in wrestling or boxing. One of his most famous encounters was with Antaios, the son of Earth. This ogre, according to Pindar, was decorating the temple of Poseidon with the heads of those who had the misfortune to visit him; later accounts report that he forced guests to wrestle with him, then killed them, burying their bodies in his palaestra. Pindar stresses how small Herakles was in comparison with the giant; his triumph (presented in literature as wrestling, though often shown as pankration in Greek art) marks the success of Hellenic skill over barbarian savagery.[11] Later traditions held that Antaios, as the son of Earth, could constantly draw sustenance from his mother, and Herakles was able to defeat and kill him only by lifting him completely off the ground.[12] Here also, the encounter is clearly one between a Greek tutored in wrestling and a barbarian relying on magic for his strength. In another set of legends, Eryx challenged Herakles to a wrestling match (or, in a few accounts, a boxing match) for possession of his cattle and died in the bout. According to one version of the story, Eryx and Herakles agreed that if Eryx lost the match he would forfeit his land and Herakles if unsuccessful would hand over his cattle; but since Eryx felt that the wager was uneven, Herakles offered his immortality as the stakes of the contest. This was not the only encounter in which Herakles' wrestling adventures involved death or the underworld. His victory over Hades himself forced the otherwise relentless god to restore Queen Alkestis to life, and Menoites, herdsman of the Under-

94. Old Babylonian tablet of the Gilgamesh epic, c. 2000–1600 B.C.E. The text shown here tells of the wrestling match between Enkidu and Gilgamesh.

95. Theseus throws Skiron, lifting the leg as if in a wrestling or pankration match (compare figs. 27, 41, 57). Greek vase, c. 490–480 B.C.E.

96. Herakles throws the Nemean lion over his shoulder (compare fig. 37). Greek vase, c. 530–15 B.C.E.

world, also challenged him over a cow and narrowly escaped destruction with broken ribs when Persephone, Queen of the Dead, interceded on Menoites' behalf. This notion of a wrestling match with the powers of death or with immortality at issue seems to be another example of the sport's role as a rite of passage, this time over the threshold between this world and the next.[13] Consideration of these legends as the expression of cultural ideals vividly shows the status and significance of combat sport. The labors of Herakles and Theseus naturally included clearing the world of monsters and highwaymen: what is remarkable is that weaponry plays a much less prominent role in their encounters than one would expect. Instead there was athletic verisimilitude, and even the mighty could succumb to impossible odds. A proverb current already in the seventh century B.C.E., "Not even Herakles can take on two," referred to the time when he attempted to wrestle at Olympia against two men at once and lost. We are looking at heroes created after the image of the Greeks' own experience and ambitions.

The Ptolemies, rulers of Hellenistic Egypt, knew well the potential force of wrestling imagery in imperial propaganda among Greeks and the native Egyptians, whose ancient traditions saw the pharaoh as an unrivaled sportsman. A contemporary poem about the young Herakles which clearly alludes to the young monarch Ptolemy II Philadelphos spoke of the wrestling, boxing, and pankration tricks which Herakles learned from his tutor. The facial features of Ptolemy III Euergetes and later those of Ptolemy V Epiphanes can be discerned in the depiction of the victor in a series of small bronzes showing a wrestler effortlessly stepping over his opponent (who has the distinctive features of a "barbarian" [non-Greek]), applying a clever and commanding hold (see fig. 43). At the same time, certain details of the victor's hairstyle are formal attributes of the Egyptian god Horos, who in Egyptian mythology defeats the embodiment of evil, Seth. Thus nakedness and wrestling tactics mark a Greek hero, hairstyle points to Egyptian mythology: the Ptolemies knew the nature of the mixed Greek and Egyptian populace they ruled. The origin of this imperial propaganda very likely goes back at least a generation earlier, for the barbarian about to fall to the Greek points to the famous victory Ptolemy II Philadelphos won against the Gauls. Philadelphos prided himself on this campaign (if it can be called that)—the renowned court poet Kallimachos celebrated it in a hymn to Apollo of Delos. His actual victory was in reality a tawdry act of cruelty; a group of his Gallic mercenaries started to mutiny, so Ptolemy led them to an island in the Nile where he burned them alive. Even noble traditions can be exploited for base purposes: we seem to have here an example of wrestling imagery employed to dress a gruesome deed in fair clothing.[14]

In ninth-century Byzantium once again a ruler was celebrated for his wrestling success (unlike Ptolemy, it seems, in an actual match). Basil I of Macedon rose from humble origins to steadily increasing influence at court, and among his noteworthy deeds was the defeat of a Bulgarian strong man who challenged all present at court to meet him in a wrestling match. What follows is from a court historian's account:

> Since at that time the Bulgarians—always being somehow conceited and arrogant—happened to have with them a Bulgarian who bragged about the might of his body and was outstanding at wrestling, whom hardly any wrestling opponent to that time had thrown, they seemed to have insufferable thoughts about him and bragged immoderately. When the drinking was progressing and the good cheer during the meal was running wild, that little man, Theophilos, said to the Caesar, "I have, lord, a man who, if you bid, will wrestle against this scandalous Bulgarian. For this will be the greatest disgrace to the Romans, and no one will ever take away the Bulgarians' arrogance, if this man should go back to Bulgaria undefeated." When the Caesar gave orders for the match to take place, Constantine the patrician, whom I

mentioned earlier, being very well disposed towards Basil feared that Basil might somehow slip, and asked as a favor from the Caesar for sawdust to be sprinkled on the floor. When this was done, Basil locked up with the Bulgarian and quickly pressed and squeezed him; like some light and lifeless bundle of hay, or a tuft of wool, dry and light, so he easily lifted him over the table and threw him. When this happened, there was no one present who did not honor and admire Basil.[15]

Another, more imaginative chronicler places this event later in Basil's life, when he was already king. In this version, Basil doffs his kingly garments and enters the palaestra incognito to defeat the upstart. Here is history in the process of becoming legend; but it is noteworthy that this court writer found nothing unreasonable or déclassé in this fantasy of the wrestling king of Byzantium.

One did not have to be a leader or hero to reap the spiritual benefits of sport. Pythagoras, it is reported, told his disciples that participating in sport, not winning, is the most important thing.[16] This was, as we saw in chap. 6, a highly atypical position in Greek thought, except for the philosophical schools, who found the training and self-sacrifice of the athletes to be of extreme interest, in fact, often of far greater value than sport itself. The athlete's ability to abstain from sex impressed Plato: "Don't we all know of Ikkos of Tarentum because of the reputation gained at Olympia and other contests, which he won through his competitiveness, skill, and the manly self-control of his soul—that is to say, he never touched a woman or a boy in all the period of his peak training. We hear the same about Krison, Astylos, Diopompos, and many others" (*Laws* 839e–840c). Plato concluded that if athletes could make such sacrifices of physical gratification for the sake of victory, youth could develop more self-control and strength of character. Like Plato, Aristotle lent only a little explicit approval to athletics, but he found the boxer's ability to withstand great pain for the sake of victory extremely enlightening: this, Aristotle noted, could teach a man even to sacrifice the life he enjoys for an important cause. The succeeding Stoic and Cynic schools made the athlete's training and contest, with particular attention to the grueling combat events, into an extensive metaphor for the good man's struggle to live properly. The most notable example of this is Dio Chrysostom's Melankomas (*Orations* 28 and 29). His flawless record of victory was only a small part of his glory: what distinguished him from all other boxers was his ability to win without giving or taking a blow. Dio informs us that he had trained to the point where he could hold up his guard for two days without letting his arms fall, and at least one opponent lasted a full day before giving into Melankomas's stalling. This makes no sense, of course, in light of what we know about the rules of

Greek boxing (see chap. 5), yet it is easy to see why Dio described Melankomas in the exaggerated way that he did: the boxer's style was in Dio's vision a display of pure continence and fortitude. Melankomas was "capable of exertion" in contest, but his character showed even greater accomplishment: "Yet indeed the most amazing thing for a man was to be undefeated not only by his opponents, but also by toil, heat, appetite, and sexuality." Dio thus used Melankomas as a starting point to explain in yet another light the Cynic doctrines of the good man's struggle against material and sensual temptation. Summarizing his discussion of Melankomas's practice of not giving or taking punches in his matches, Dio concluded: "I assuredly think that in the same thing [that is, boxing style] everything is said about manliness, courage, self-control, and moderation."[17]

As I noted in the previous chapter, the athletes themselves articulated their feelings about the character building aspects of their sports, at times with the help of philosophy. In the inscription honoring the pankratiast Kallikrates, his guild represents his life in terms of the famous story of Herakles at the crossroads, a story known to every Greek schoolboy. There the young Herakles has to choose between the soft road of pleasure and the hard road of virtue: Kallikrates, like Herakles, chose the latter.[18]

The detractors of sport might cut the notion of training free from its source in athletics: for all intents and purposes pagan antiquity had already developed a "denatured" metaphor of contest long before it found new life in Hellenistic Judaism and early Christianity. Isokrates (fourth century B.C.E.) complained, "I have often been astonished at those who hold festivals and set up athletic contests that they consider physical success worthy of such great rewards, but have not given any honor to those who personally labor for the common good and so prepare their souls that they are able to benefit others."[19] Diogenes the Cynic (fourth century B.C.E.), according to a follower centuries later, made a point of attending the Isthmian games, and when asked whether he came to watch the agon replied that on the contrary he came to compete. His opponents, he said, were "the toughest, most unapproachable contestants, whom no Greek can face up to, not by any means opponents like the runners, wrestlers, jumpers, boxers, javelin or discus hurlers— but those opponents who teach humility."[20] These teachers of humility or moderation he identified with labors and hardships that the wise man challenges and battles. Although Diogenes characterizes these opponents as athletes, never does he suggest that sport prepares a man for the real contest of life. According to Diogenes, Herakles was not an athlete, huge and well-fed, but was lean and hungry, given to toil and hardship. The philosopher is said to have shocked the officials of the Isthmian festival by putting the pine wreath of the victors on his own head, claiming that he won the greater contest by defeating hardship and pleasure. Epiktetos tells the story that once when Diogenes lay sick he called to people rushing to Olympia and told them that they were hastening to see the contest of worthless athletes and asked them if they wanted to see a real contest—one between a man and a fever! Epiktetos himself had strong words against athletics and favored only the abstract notion of training. He warned his disciples not to put their trust in the size of their bodies the way athletes did, for that would only make them undefeatable, "the way a jackass is": in his eyes the invincible athlete was the person who could withstand temptation.[21]

Both sides of Greek attitudes toward athletics are discernible in the writings of Philo Judaeus of first century C.E. Alexandria. Philo is the single richest source of athletic terminology in all of Greek literature; in keeping with his many-sided character (he was both a student of Greek philosophy and a ritually observant Jew) he makes particularly fruitful and original use of Greek traditions.[22] Although, as we shall see later, he had firsthand knowledge of the Greek games and endorsed athletics in the education of children, his interest in sport has overriding ethical and philosophical purposes, and in his enthusiasm for the spiritual, he can condemn the Greek festivals, just as Diogenes the Cynic, Epiktetos, and others had done before him:

> Do not regard as sacred the Games which the cities put on every other year, having built theaters to receive many thousands of people. For in these festivals, the man who outwrestles an opponent and stretches him on his back or prone on the ground, or the one powerful in boxing or pankration who doesn't stop short of violence and wrongdoing wins the first prize. . . . Now the Olympic contest which alone can rightly be called sacred the inhabitants of Elis do not hold, but it is the contest for the gaining of divine, truly Olympian virtues. [Philo, *de agricultura* 113, 119]

Still his vision of Jacob's spiritual struggles proceeds quite naturally from the biblical story, and he concentrates on the physical details of the encounter, using them for a spiritual homily. Since Jacob, coming from his mother's womb, had grasped Esau's heel, Philo could readily assign appropriate palaestra tactics to this metaphorical wrestler: "Although Pleasure expects to heel-trip and deceive the discerning mind, she will herself be heel-tripped by Jacob, trained in wrestling not of the body, but the sort which the soul wrestles with its enemies, the habits, fighting against passions and evil" (*Allegorical Laws* 3.190). Philo is hardly an advocate of sport, but his athletic imagery is often rooted quite concretely in the reality of Greek athletics.[23]

In early Christian writings, the metaphor moves steadily farther from its base in actual athletic activities. In I Corinthians 9 : 24–27, Paul gives an image of personal struggle that develops quite readily from the training and competition of ancient athletes: "I box not like a shadow-boxer," that is to say, he is a real fighter, he joins in the real combats in his pursuit of his faith. "I bruise my body and bring it into subjugation": he is an athlete of the Holy Spirit observing his regimen. Quite different is the metaphorical language of the fourth-century bishop of Constantinople, John Chrysostom, who praised a woman for the victory she won by patiently bearing illness. By this, he said, she has taught others to enter the wrestling ground. Her victory, said the bishop, was all the more amazing because she did not win it in the center of the city, as athletes do, but from her sick bed. The ultimate step in this process of abstraction of the spiritual lessons from sport is the creation of the metaphorical wrestler from a figure who originally had nothing to do with sport. The appearance of Job as a wrestler in Christian writings stands as the most intriguing example of this process.[24] I will quote only one of the many texts that describe Job as a wrestler, this one from a Byzantine lexicon:

> Job was that truly great and also noble striver for the truth, who first opened that athletic stadium shared by the whole world, who threw his opponent in every wrestling bout, who received blows and bruises to his very bones yet remained undefeated, who was full of worms yet also crowned. Death was not able to lay him out or to put dust on his shoulders, but he stood unturned like a statue or an anvil unstruck, wrestling throughout his whole life and smashing his opponent. He raised a monument of victory over the Evil One, not by contesting at Nemea, Olympia, the Isthmus, and Delphi, even the contests of which Greek histories boast, but by seeing with brave heart instead of children, substance, flocks, slaves, and a course of life free from calamities, the households of his own children turned into their tombs, a common grave. The Opponent's madness and envy were not sated up until the point when he challenged this athlete naked to the dung heap, making him completely spotted with sores and full of worms . . . and until finally the Cursed One brought the defeat upon himself and drew the lot of final shame. You have now the prize of this philosopher. You have also the Bible, which sings much sweeter than Homer or mellifluous Plato. . . . Job gained the ultimate and finest from his contests, to be raised with Christ. [Suda, s.v. "Job"]

The philosophers' hostility to sport in Greek civilization is surely directed at a culture that still admired athletics. But to what extent do these Jewish and Christian palaestra metaphors represent a branch

nolhoxes muemat q̃ ipfa fua cvebvefi
igar. quamus ẽ quifq̃ congi
uruum qualitate ũ ualet pfonarũ faln
uperur. Sic fic inhoc angelox hommi

97. Job wrestles against Satan; in keeping with athletic traditions, both are naked. Manuscript illumination, thirteenth century.

lopped completely free from the Greek athletic traditions from which they grew? There are a few signs that despite the thunderous denunciations of Greco-Roman sport which often surface in Christian texts, all athletics, including combat sport, continued to have a role, albeit a small one, in daily life: the athletic metaphors which Church Fathers used did not fall on the ears of a public completely devoid of knowledge of sport. The so-called Apostolic Constitution (in fact a work of the fourth century, not of the apostles) barred from baptism those who participated in or even watched athletics, but Clement of Alexandria spoke with approval of parents who send children to the gymnasium for instruction.[25] Even official strictures against sport occasionally give hints that some pulpits dissented. Novatian was clearly angered by this liberal approach:

Among the faithful and those who lay claim to the dignity of a Christian calling, some find no shame, no shame, I say—in vindicating from the heavenly Scriptures, the vain superstitions of the pagans that are intermingled in the spectacles. . . . "Where," they ask, "are such things mentioned in Scripture? Where are they prohibited? . . . A struggling apostle paints for us the picture of a boxing match and of our own wrestling against the spiritual forces of wickedness. . . . Why then should a faithful Christian not be at liberty to be a spectator of things that the divine Writings are at liberty to mention." I can with reason state here that it would have been far better for such people to lack knowledge of the Scriptures than to read them in such a manner! [*On the Public Shows* 2 PL 4.811, trans. de Simone]

So also Tertullian found that some coreligionists read Scripture differently: "Now if you insist that the stadium is mentioned in Scripture, you will win that point. But you will not deny that what is done in the stadium is unworthy of your sight, blows of the fists, kicks, poundings, every assault of the hand and attack upon man's face, which is the image of God. . . . Wrestling is also the Devil's work."[26] The Rabbis forbade the nudity and idolatry normally associated with Greek sport: "They should cover their shame, and should not uncover themselves as the Gentiles uncover themselves" (Jubilees 3:31); sometimes they condemned the institution as a whole. Thus the Rabbis explain Psalm 1 : 1, "Happy is the man . . . who sat not in the seat of scorners," as referring to those who refrained from attending stadia, camps, and mimes. But official doctrine never tried to ban participation in the palaestra, and one passage in the Mishna, an early codification of the Oral Law of Judaism, shows relatively broad tolerance for athletics. The Mishna tractate *Shabbat*, which prescribes appropriate behavior on the holy day of rest, specifies: "They may oil and massage the stomach, but not exercise and not scrape. They may not go down to the wrestling area and may not use artificial emetics" (*Shabbat* 22:6). Since this tractate deals with what is forbidden on Sabbath, by implication the activities are permissible on other days of the week. Certain peculiarities of the Hebrew diction make it clear that we have here a version of the law current in Palestine as well as in the Diaspora: in other words, this text represents mainstream Jewish practice in the second and third centuries c.e. The Mishna is not dealing with dilettante athletes: the inducing of vomiting (see chap. 1) was a sign of high-level training methods, and as one scholar noted, "Like their Gentile neighbors, the Jews used to perform all kinds of exercises of the body, and the Rabbis tolerated it."[27] In the Diaspora, there is evidence that Jews energetically engaged in sport. Some inscriptions show Jewish members of ephebic clubs, and huge dissension broke out in Alexandria when Jews tried to enter athletic festivals sponsored by the gymnasium.[28] Philo's athletic imagery shows a unique immediateness and directness: he unashamedly admits his firsthand experience as a spectator at the games. In a treatise arguing that only a virtuous man is truly free, Philo writes in the first person that he saw a competitor in the pankration fight aggressively only to succumb to exhaustion because of his opponent's attack (see chap. 1). Elsewhere he recounts, again in the first person, how he saw foolish spectators at the horse races lose their lives because they left their seats and stood too close to the chariots as they raced past. Most significantly, in a work on Jewish Law, he speaks with approval of parents who send their children to athletic trainers so they may gain good condition and gracefulness, just as they send children to learn the liberal arts.[29]

We have, of course, come a long way from the boxer in *Iliad* 23, who boasts he will crush his opponent's skull, and from the shamed losers described in two of Pindar's *Odes*. The role that combat sport played in the lives of Greco-Roman Jewry and early Christians was modest. Although Greek sport certainly did not end with the closing of the Olympic Games, as is often alleged, it lost the exalted status it once had and no doubt much of its popularity. The realization that life presents a series of contests and that success depends on steady training to meet these challenges continued with renewed conviction, but few would learn this lesson through the intensive experiences of the palaestra that had once characterized normal Hellenic existence.

APPENDIX:
COMBAT SPORT, FUNERAL CULT, AND HUMAN SACRIFICE

"For the life of the flesh is in the blood; and I have given it to you upon the altar to make atonement for your souls; for it is the blood that makes atonement by reason of the life" (Lev. 17 : 11). That blood is sacred and redemptive is one of the most widespread beliefs, and many cultures go a step further, maintaining that the dead thirst for blood, human or animal. Normal Hellenic sacrificial practice at a hero's tomb involved cutting an animal's throat over the grave or into a trench so that the blood would find its way to the hero. In *Odyssey* 11, when the hero sacrifices black sheep at the entrance to Hades, the squeaking ghosts flock to lap at the fresh blood; the fact that Patroklos's companions pour the blood of slaughtered animals around his body suggests that the deceased had an active interest in the blood.[1] Some ancient authors held that the origin of gladiatorial combat was human sacrifice to the dead, and one modern theory argues that this armed contest was initially part of a ritual to "find" and "punish" the person who was "responsible" for the death of the man who was being buried. This leads to another, more difficult question, the principal subject of this section, whether the combat sports which frequently appeared in association with Greek funeral rites are a later and milder development of contests which were originally offerings of human blood, or whether they represent an activity coincidental and ultimately irrelevant to the burial. Although the evidence for *blood offerings* at Greek funerals is quite ample, it does not warrant connecting these sacrifices with sport, and one can better explain Greek combat sport without recourse to the cult of the dead.

Reports of human sacrifice to the dead appear occasionally in Greek literature and history, leaving little doubt that such events occurred, though sometimes the motive for the sacrifice is obscure. When Achilleus attends to the burial of his friend Patroklos, he tells his dead companion (*Iliad* 23.20–23): "All that I previously promised you I am already fulfilling, having dragged Hektor here to give to the dogs to eat raw, and the throats of twelve of Troy's best youths will I cut before your pyre, angry at your death," and the hero honors his word, also burning four horses and two dogs on the pyre. Other evidence shows that the element of personal anger that Achilleus claims as motive for slaughtering the princes is a thin rationalization more suited to the world the poet creates in the *Iliad* than to the primitive sacrificial ritual which underlies it.[2] In another legend, when Achilleus himself fell before Troy, his son sacrificed Polyxena, the daughter of King Priam, over his tomb: although in some traditions Achilleus loved this enemy princess and desired her even in death, Euripides' version of the sacrifice stresses the vampiric aspects of the dead Achilleus, when his son invokes him, "O come that you may drink the black, undiluted blood of the maiden" (Eur. *Hecuba* 536–37). These legends of human sacrifice probably reveal popular belief and perhaps archaic practice as well:[3] there are also a few instances in later Greek history of Greeks ostensibly appeasing a dead man with human victims. Alexander the Great had the conspirators in his father's assassination killed over the grave (336 B.C.E.), and in 183 B.C.E. Greek soldiers stoned Messenian prisoners at the tomb of the general Philopoimen. Alexander's explosion of grief after the death of Hephaistion included the crucifixion of his friend's doctor and a hunting expedition into the Kossaian territory in which humans were the indiscriminately slaughtered quarry: this was called an offering (*enagismos*) to Hephaistion.[4] It is especially hard to separate the motive of anger and revenge from ritual intentions here, and it must be noted, moreover, that myths and at least purportedly historical accounts also report human sacrifice in Greece and Rome for purposes other than funeral offerings, for example, to ensure the success of an army or to propitiate a hostile deity.[5] Thus the question might arise, Is human sacrifice in any way *integral* to any form of the Greek cult of the dead or are our few literary descriptions evidence only of aberrant practice more indicative of the rage of the living than the demands of the dead? This seems to be undue skepticism; since ancient sources and archaeological evidence clearly show a belief in unquiet bloodthirstiness among the dead, it is a reasonable hypothesis that at least some of the human sacrifices at funerals represented offerings to appease the dead.[6]

The late Karl Meuli, relying on Freud's *Totem and Tabu* and a multitude of ethnographic data, developed further this theory of sacrificial origin and argued that what underlies the Greek agon is a ritual contest to determine the person responsible for the death of the man being buried and to make him atone by his own defeat and death for his act of killing. This is distinct from human sacrifice, the planned slaughter of victims, since the element of contest is central to discovering the purported malefactor. Primitive cultures, Meuli noted, citing the work of Lucien Lévy-

Bruhl, perceive every death as the result of murder, and even when age or sickness is the apparent cause, the tribe postulates poison or magic and seeks a culprit to punish. With the "guilty" man's death, "the deceased is avenged, and the living are protected from his wrath." One example will have to suffice here. A Melbourne aborigine died of natural causes. As was traditional, his friends dug a small hole under his body and waited until the first insect appeared; from the direction in which it walked they determined the direction in which they had to go to find their friend's "murderer." They proceeded toward Joyce's Creek, where they met a group of hunters, attacked them, and killed a youth. The friends of this victim, although they witnessed his death, dug a hole under his body and determined (as the other group had) the direction in which to seek his killer. The insect pointed toward the Goulboura tribe, and one week later the body of a murdered Goulboura was found. Such practice according to Meuli is a cultural common denominator, as it were: "these customs are rooted in the deepest levels of the human soul, there where ethnic differences now truly for once no longer play a role. All over the world, man feels and acts towards the deceased in the same way, and will for all time." This is a controversial theory—but if for the sake of argument we accept that avenging death with a direct human sacrifice or by the death of the losing competitor in an ordeal of combat is a universal phenomenon and explains the little Greek evidence we have about such practices, we can move on to the main question, whether funeral games (in which death was accidental, not the goal of the contest) could derive from this institution.[7]

The custom of holding games at funerals is very common and appears in the earliest works of Greek literature and art. A Mycenaen *larnax* (sarcophagus) recently found in a grave in Tanagra (central Greece) has depictions of a funeral accompanied by armed combat and bull leaping: it is strong evidence that the custom of holding funeral games was current in the thirteenth century B.C.E. After the sacrifice of the Trojan youths and the burning of the pyre, Homer describes the funeral games for Patroklos in full, giving us an exceedingly important document, and elsewhere he mentions in passing funeral games for Oedipus of Thebes, Achilleus, and others.[8] Many references to funeral games may be found outside of Homer for different Greek heroes and sometimes even more or less unrenowned figures. In some accounts these games are "command performances," with the angry dead making the demands. For example, in the mid sixth century, the Etruscan inhabitants of Agylla in southern Italy stoned to death a group of Greeks from Phokaia. Afterward whenever any man or beast from Agylla passed the place where the bodies lay, he suffered dislocations of his own bones. The Delphic oracle prescribed a solution: the Agyllaeans had to give funeral sacrifices and celebrate games in honor of the murdered Phokaians.[9] But why do the dead want games? Is the motive for sport in such a context, service to the dead (and if so, in what sense are the dead gratified?) or a spectacle in their honor for the living? On this point, unfortunately, our fullest and earliest account casts a confusing light and leaves room for many hypotheses. The Homeric epics as we have them sometimes incorporate extremely archaic epic traditions, which even in Homer's day were obscure and foreign, and those exist side by side with later elements;[10] therefore, no compelling a priori reason exists to think that the legends concerning the human sacrifice and the games even have the same origin or reflect similar values. I shall invoke some non-Greek material for comparison of funeral customs, as Meuli does, but it is also necessary to let the Greek texts speak for themselves; at least as Homer presents the games of *Iliad* 23 they take place the day *after* Achilleus sacrifices the twelve princes and the animals and burns Patroklos on the pyre, the ritual which frees the spirit from the body and allows it to enter the realm of the dead, there to remain forever (*Iliad* 23.70–76, cf. 23.179). Thus, according to Homeric views of the soul, the games should have no direct influence on Patroklos, and it is impossible to determine whether the legend(s) which inspired Homer's games had a different religious outlook.

The nature of the athletic events argues in part (but only in part) for a ritual of bloodletting that would be suitable in a sacrificial context. The games for Patroklos consist of eight different contests: chariot racing, boxing, wrestling, a foot race, single combat with weapons, hurling a weight, archery, and throwing a spear. One notices at once in this, our earliest literary description of funeral games, that the contests include violent events, but also a preponderance of nonlethal and even noncontact events. The funeral games for Amarynkeus which Nestor describes (*Iliad* 23.630–44) similarly mix contact and noncontact sports: boxing, wrestling, foot racing, spear throw, and chariot racing. If a fatality or bloodletting is needed to appease the dead, then these epic games must already represent a late and sophisticated development in which competition and spectacle have to a large extent usurped the place of sacrifice. This is quite possible, but the burden of proof still rests on those who wish to show that death, not athletics, is the wellspring of Greek games.[11] The hypothesis that the core of the funeral games was originally boxing and, more important, dueling, signs of the agon's more primitive, bloodthirsty past, is also problematic, since only the thinnest evidence suggests that murderous games preceded noncombative ones. The Olympic records start in 776 B.C.E., and though the authenticity of the early years of the register lies open to serious doubts, for many years tradition records only a footrace at Olympia, and at the Pahatheneia the footrace continued to enjoy the prestige of a greater victor's prize than the combat events, even in postclassical times.[12] Plutarch is unique in reporting that once lethal armed combats were held at Olympia, but he himself claimed that, dulled with wine, he could not recall the source of this report: his account hardly inspires confidence.[13]

Thus the priority of murderous games is questionable, but still, the peculiarity of the fight in armor, if not the boxing match as well, calls for some explanation. These stand out as the most likely events to fit the theory of games as funeral offerings.

In the boxing match, Epeios at first threatens that his opponent will receive frightful injuries: "This I tell you and it will be a thing completed: immediately I will break apart his flesh and smash his bones against each other. Let those who care for him remain thronged here to carry him away when he has been beaten down under my fists." Viciousness in competition, as we have already seen, is a permanent feature of all Greek contests, and Epeios's blustering may portend no more than what Marcus Aurelius Asclepiades must have done in pankration to convince his opponents to default to him early in the tournament. Some scholars, however, have suggested that the incongruity of Epeios's sudden kindness in picking up his fallen opponent and setting him on his feet indicates that an original story with a gorier ending in which Epeios acts upon his threat has yielded to the more moderate one we have. Such a story (whose existence is purely hypothetical) would argue for ritual bloodletting, but there are perfectly good thematic reasons for showing an athlete controlling his temper and displaying cooperative virtue: the wrath of Achilleus and his lingering quarrel with Agamemnon have, after all, led to Patroklos's death, and in book 23 the characters to some degree rise above their earlier antisocial behavior. Ethnography, perhaps, suggests a more sinister agenda: according to Frazer's *Golden Bough,* boxers in Laos at the funerals of important persons are expected to batter each other's heads with utmost vigor while the funeral pyre is blazing. If anything of the sort happened in our accounts of Greek funeral games it would make quite a strong connection between sport and cult sacrifice, but as it is it seems highly tendentious to argue that this ethnographic observation of a nineteenth-century traveler reveals the rationale for boxing in a society far removed in time and space. In fact, the differences seem more significant than the similarities between the funeral of Patroklos and the Laotian custom; none of the characters in *Iliad* 23 at this point take note of Patroklos's wishes, and neither here nor in any other description of Greek funeral games is there a suggestion that the pain and injury of the boxers is a service to the deceased. Meuli argues that there are signs of lethal intentions in other Greek accounts of boxing and even wrestling, but of the many examples he cites, only a few have a fatal outcome: Amykos and Polydeukes (in one variant), Antaios and Herakles, Theseus and Kerkyon—and none of these (in their extant versions) have anything to do with funerals.[14]

Armed dueling is clearly more dangerous and bloody, and its appearance in ancient Italy (see below) seems to have had direct connections to funeral sacrifice. The custom certainly existed in Greece, though as the account in *Iliad* 23 shows, even by Homer's day there is considerable hesitation and embarrassment about this deadly contest. Achilleus set out as victor's prize the armor which Patroklos had stripped from Sarpedon and calls for the best two men to fight over it (23.798–804). Achilleus continues: "Whichever one first reaches the fair flesh and touches the entrails, through the armor and black blood—to him will I give this beautiful, silver-studded Thracian sword, which I stripped from Asteropaios. Let both men take away this armor as a common possession, and we will set a good banquet for them in our hut." Two great warriors, Ajax and Diomedes, then step forward. This is a very odd arrangement for a duel and strangely narrated as well. Lines 808–09 suddenly introduce the sword as the real victor's prize, while the armor (which Achilleus told the competitors to fight for in lines 798–804) is to be the common possession of the warriors. Achilleus's nonchalance about the injury—he is certain that both men will still be alive to come to dinner with him—is exposed as preposterous when the troops fear for Ajax's safety and call a halt to the fight (822–23), awarding equal prizes. Neither combatant received a wound, which Achilleus had set as the goal of the fight, but Diomedes gets the sword anyway (824–25).

This narrative, which one scholar called "as self-contradictory as it is obscure," possibly conceals a primitive ritual, no longer comprehensible to Homer, in which one fighter must satisfy the dead man with his blood. Evidence from ancient Italy may support such a conclusion. A sarcophagus from Caere shows on one side an armed combat in front of male and female spectators and on the other the funeral meal, also a part of Achilleus's arrangements. Several third-century B.C.E. Italian funerary urns shows duels, one between two Gauls, presumably prisoners; and numerous Oscan, Campanian, and Etruscan wall paintings from the fourth century B.C.E. show such scenes. These artifacts give a gruesome glimpse into ancient practice, but by themselves they tell us little about the cultic purpose of the contests: other activities like boxing and chariot racing often appear alongside scenes of dueling and leave open the possibility that the lethal combat was not integral to the funerals. The Romans, who adopted gladiatorial combat from their Italic neighbors, may tell more about its religious context. Gladiators appeared in Rome in 264 B.C.E. at the funeral of D. Junius Brutus Pera, and not until 105 B.C.E. did they appear in any context except funerals. Servius, citing the Roman antiquarian Varro, wrote, "Women are accustomed in grief during funerals so to lacerate their faces that they satisfy the dead with their blood. From this, it even became an established custom for victims also to be butchered at the graves. Among the ancients men also used to be killed, but when J. Brutus died, and many nations sent captives to his funeral, his grandson paired them and thus they fought (*ad Aen.* 3.67)." In a note on *Aeneid* 10.519, moreover, Servius observed, "It was the custom to kill captives during the funerals of brave men. Since this later seemed cruel, it was considered proper for gladiators to fight in front of the sepulchres." These accounts betray the guesswork of their authors: the Romans in 264 B.C.E. were not the first in Italy to use gladiators at funerals—we have already seen that the Oscans, Campanians, and Etruscans long preceded them—nor is it likely that human kindness moved the Romans to change from purported sacrifice to combat.[15] But together with the fact that gladiators appeared so regularly on funerary decoration these traditions suggest that possibly ancient opinion was at least partly correct in seeing them as funeral offerings.

The Greek world has left similar monuments showing single combat, but unlike the southern Italian and Roman evidence, no Greek author explicitly offers the unquiet dead as the reason for the contest. Some sarcophagi from Clazomenai probably do depict dueling, though this mute evidence cannot completely exclude the possibility that a battle encounter, symbolized by a pair of soldiers fighting, is what the sarcophagus shows.[16] There are also some historical references to armed combat at funerals, though these seem consistently to take place on the edge of the Greek world. In 317 B.C.E. the Macedonian Kassander had four of his soldiers fight an agon of single combat (*monomachia*) at the funeral of the king and queen of Boeotia. The Thracians, Herodotos reported, regularly held single combats at funerals, though Xenophon noted an instance in which they held wine drinking and horse racing in honor of the dead.[17]

It is hard to argue from the instances of duels in or near Greece that they had an integral role in the service to the dead, more than any other popular activity like the chariot race. Their role most frequently seems to be settling succession and property disputes. By means of such encounters the parties avoided large-scale loss of life between quarreling states; it is probably not the hazard of time that far more reports of duels with pragmatic objectives than funeral duels have come down to us.

According to tradition, a duel resolved the dispute over the borders between Attica and Boeotia; Argos and Sparta sought to resolve their long fight over Thyreia with a battle of champions, and in 612 B.C.E. Pittakos of Mitylene killed Phrynon of Athens in single combat, settling the ownership of Sigeion.[18] Herodotos gives a particularly vivid history of a pentathlete, a victor at Nemea, named Eurybates, who apparently excelled also in single combat. In a conflict between Aegina and Athens he served as general (*strategos*) and killed three of the enemy in single combat before falling to a fourth. Strabo, discussing a duel which decided ownership of the territory of Elis, said that single combat was an ancient Hellenic custom.

These examples suggest that there are better ways to explain the duel in *Iliad* 23 than as a blood offering to the dead. Aside from its practical purpose in settling quarrels, it gains a high status in Homer as a demonstration of courage and prowess. For example, the duel between the adulterer Paris and the aggrieved Menelaos in *Iliad* 3 is a pragmatic attempt to settle the Trojan War; conversely, in *Iliad* 7, Hektor and Ajax fight a duel while the other troops watch, purely out of a sense of daring and honor.[19] In a quarrel between states, the risk of losing one or both heroes was the price of avoiding the risk of losing large numbers of soldiers. But for obvious reasons, such an encounter in a noncrisis situation and between important warriors in the same camp would not enjoy much sanction. The source of Homer's armed contest at Patroklos's funeral may have been a story of a savage duel between Ajax and Diomedes over the division of Achilles' possessions or as a primitive display of bravado, while the poet, in working it into his narrative, may have been hesitant about it because he felt it was neither an appropriate part of camp life nor a regular part of funeral games, and therefore its conclusion is quite contrary to the expectations raised by its introduction.

The theories presupposing funerary origin for Greek sport depend on a number of hypothetical steps. We must first assume that either human sacrifice or ordeal by combat was an essential part of prehistoric Greek life. This is quite possible, but the paucity of clear instances of human sacrifice among the Mycenaeans makes one wonder how widespread the practice was. Ritual combat at funerals to "find" the "murderer," as Meuli describes it, is yet more difficult to accept, for it requires faith that all primitive societies have essentially the same attitude toward the dead, a postulate that does not enjoy universal support. For both explanations, we must also assume that the funeral games are a survival from more primitive times, a form which has lost its original form, and, with almost no evidence, also to assume that they originally consisted only of lethal sports which served as human sacrifice or trial by combat; then only later did they shift their focus from death to competition. The silence, however, is somewhat surprising, if the instinct either to sacrifice a human victim or to find and punish a malefactor was once so integral to the agon: there is no trace in myth or history of such an explanation, though, as we have seen, there are many ancient speculations on the fate of the soul and at least a few firmly attested duels at funerals.[20]

It seems better to let the evidence we have suggest an explanation. Homeric heroes valued above all else their immortal glory, their *kleos*— Achilleus makes the clear choice between long life and *kleos*. Sport, an important part of Greek life from its earliest days and an activity that appears in the *Iliad* and *Odyssey* in nonfuneral contexts, is a fitting offering to the memory of a dead warrior, just as Apollo delighted in the boxing along with other activities at his festival. The boldness displayed in a duel was also not unsuited for a soldier, though society recognized the potential for disaster in such an activity and undoubtedly discouraged it. Prehistory invites speculation, and my discussion of the origins of combat sport will undoubtedly remain a *non liquet*, but the cult of the dead as an explanation for combat sport is fraught with more difficulties than other theories.[21]

■■■■■ *ABBREVIATIONS*

Abbreviations will follow the system of Liddell, Scott, Jones (*LSJ*) for Greek authors, Lewis and Short (*LS*) for Latin authors, the Chicago Assyrian Dictionary (*CAD*) for Mesopotamian texts, and *L'année philologique* for classical periodicals, though the abbreviations of some authors and texts will deliberately be expanded for easier recognition. Certain standard abbreviations which may be found in *LSJ*, especially for collections of inscriptions, are nevertheless repeated in the table below for convenience. In some places, I have taken the liberty of translating the titles of ancient texts; in such cases the traditional Latin title will follow in parentheses. Other abbreviations in the notes will follow the system below:

ABV	J. D. Beazley. *Attic Black-Figure Vases*. Oxford, 1956.
ARV	J. D. Beazley. *Attic Red-Figure Vases*. Oxford, 1963.
BE	Jean and Louis Robert. *Bulletin épigraphique*. In *Revue des études grecques*. Entries are listed by year and entry number, not by page number.
Burckhardt, *GK*	Jacob Burckhardt. *Griechische Kulturgeschichte* 4. 1898–1902; new ed. Darmstadt, 1977.
CAD	*The Assyrian Dictionary of the Oriental Institute of the University of Chicago*. Chicago, 1964–84.
CIG	*Corpus Inscriptionum Graecarum*. Berlin, 1828–77.
DS	Ch. Daremberg and E. Saglio. *Dictionnaire des Antiquités grecques et romaines*. Paris, 1877.
Delorme	J. Delorme. *Gymnasion*. Bibliothèque des écoles françaises d'Athènes et de Rome 187. Paris, 1960.
Ebert	Joachim Ebert, *Griechische Epigramme auf Sieger an gymnischen und hippischen Agonen*. Abhandlungen der Sächsischen Akademie der Wissenschaften zu Leipzig 63.2. Berlin, 1972.
Gardiner, *AAW*	E. N. Gardiner. *Athletics of the Ancient World*. Oxford, 1930.
Gardiner, *GASF*	E. N. Gardiner. *Greek Athletic Sports and Festivals*. London, 1910.

Harris, *GAA*	H. A. Harris. *Greek Athletes and Athletics*. London, 1964.
Harris, *SGR*	H. A. Harris. *Sport in Greece and Rome*. London, 1972.
IG	*Inscriptiones Graecae*. Berlin, 1877–.
IGUR	Luigi Moretti. *Inscriptiones Graecae Urbis Romanae*. Rome, 1968–.
IK	*Inschriften griechischer Städte aus Kleinasien*. Bonn, 1972–.
IvOl	Wilhelm Dittenberger and K. Purgold. *Die Inschriften von Olympia*. Die Ergebnisse der von dem Deutschen Reich-veranstalteten Ausgrabung 5. Berlin, 1896.
Jüthner, *AT*	Julius Jüthner. *Antike Turngeräthe*. Abhandlungen des ar-chaeologisch-epigraphischen Seminars der Universität Wien. Vienna, 1896.
Jüthner, *Philostr.*	Julius Jüthner. *Philostratos über Gymnastik*. Leipzig, 1909.
Jüthner-Brein	Julius Jüthner and Friedrich Brein. *Die athletischen Leibes-übungen der Griechen*. Österreichische Akademie der Wis-senschaften, philosophisch-historische Klasse, Sitzungs-berichte 249, I. Vienna, 1965.
Jüthner-Mehl	Julius Jüthner and Erwin Mehl. Art. "Pygme" in Pauly-Wissowa. *Real-Encyclopaedie für classische Altertumswissen-schaft* Suppl. 9 (Stuttgart, 1962), 1306–51.
Kaibel	G. Kaibel. *Epigrammata Graeca*. Berlin, 1878.
KBSW	*Kölner Beiträge zur Sportwissenschaft*. Schorndorf 1972–76; St. Augustin, 1977–.
Krause, *GAH*	J. H. Krause. *Gymnastik und Agonistik der Hellenen*. Halle, 1841.
Liermann	Otto Liermann. *Analecta epigraphica et agonistica*. Disser-tationes Philologicae Halensia. Halle, 1889.
LIMC	*Lexicon Iconographicum Mythologiae Classicae*. Zurich–Mu-nich, 1981–.
MAMA	*Monumenta Asiae Minoris Antiqua*. London, 1928–62.
Meuli, *Agon*	Karl Meuli. *Der griechische Agon*. Cologne, 1968.
Meuli, "Ursprung"	Karl Meuli. "Der Ursprung der Olympischen Spiele." *Die Antike* 17 (1941): 189–208.
Moretti, *IAG*	Luigi Moretti. *Iscrizioni agonistiche greche*. Rome, 1953.
Moretti, *Olympionikai*	Luigi Moretti. *Olympionikai, i vincitori negli antichi agoni olimpici*. Atti della Accademia Nazionale dei Lincei 8. Rome, 1959.
Para.	J. D. Beazley. *Paralipomena*. Oxford, 1971.

Peek, *VersInschr.*	Werner Peek. *Griechische Vers-Inschriften* I. Berlin, 1955.
Pleket, "Soziologie"	H. W. Pleket. "Zur Soziologie des antiken Sports." *Medelingen van het Nederlands Instituut te Rome* 36 (1974): 57–87.
Pleket, "Ideology"	H. W. Pleket. "Games, Prizes, Athletes, and Ideology." *Stadion* 1 (1976): 49–89.
Poliakoff, *Studies*	M. B. Poliakoff. *Studies in the Terminology of the Greek Combat Sports.* Second ed. Beiträge zur Klassischen Philologie 146. Meisenheim, 1986.
Robert, "Épigrammes"	Louis Robert. "Les épigrammes satiriques de Lucillius sur les athlètes, parodie et réalités." *L'épigramme grecque.* Entretiens sur l'antiquité classique 14. Geneva, 1968.
RE	Pauly-Wissowa. *Real-Encyclopaedie für classische Altertumswissenschaft.* Stuttgart, 1884–.
Syll.[3]	Wilhelm Dittenberger. *Sylloge inscriptionum Graecarum*[3]. Leipzig, 1915–24.
TAM	*Tituli Asiae Minoris.* Vienna, 1901–.
Weiler, *Agon*	Ingomar Weiler. *Der Agon im Mythos.* Darmstadt, 1974.
Weiler, *Sport*	Ingomar Weiler. *Der Sport bei den Völkern der Alten Welt.* Darmstadt, 1981.
Young, *Olympic Myth*	David C. Young. *The Olympic Myth of Greek Amateur Athletics.* Chicago, 1984.

▬▬▬ NOTES

Introduction

1. For example, the city senate pays for the monument of Menander, son of Menander (see chap. 7); the athletic guild for that of Kallikrates (chap. 7).
2. Paus. 6.13.8 notes that Corinth and Nemea, in contrast to Olympia and Delphi, did not have their own records in earlier times. There may have been some retrospective supplements to the early years of the register, but there certainly was a set of records at these latter two sites. See further, J. H. Krause, *Olympia* (Vienna, 1838; repr. Hildesheim and New York, 1972), vi.
3. On this problem, see Poliakoff, *Studies*, 48–49.
4. Galen, *Thrasyb.* 37 (=5.877 K., 84 H.); for discussion and further references, cf. Jüthner-Brein, I.33–34, and Jüthner, *Philostr.*, 22–26, 51–59.
5. On the common problems of retrospective visions of the past in these authors of the Second Sophistic (as this group is called), see E. L. Bowie, "Greeks and Their Past in the Second Sophistic," in *Studies in Ancient Society*, ed. M. I. Finley (London, 1974), 166–209 (=*Past and Present* 46 [1970]). On Plutarch, see chap. 1, n. 13. Concerning problems of athletic details in Philostratos, see Poliakoff, *Studies*, 143–48.
6. On the reliability of Philo as a witness to ancient sport, see Louis Robert, *Hellenica* 11 (Paris, 1960): 337 n. 1, 442 n. 4; *Rev. Phil.* 41 (1967): 30–31 n. 6; *BE* (1965): 182; H. A. Harris, *Greek Athletics and the Jews* (Cardiff, 1976) provides a thorough overview of Philo. Concerning the importance of the Church Fathers as a source, see in general, Alois Koch, "Leibesübungen im Frühchristentum und in der beginnenden Völkswanderungszeit," in *Geschichte der Leibesübungen* 2, ed. H. Überhorst (Berlin-Frankfurt-Munich, 1978): 312–40; M. B. Poliakoff, "Jacob, Job, and Other Wrestlers: Reception of Greek Athletics by Jews and Christians in Antiquity," *Journal of Sport History* 11.2 (1984): 48–65; Louis Robert, *BE* (1968): 147; M. B. Poliakoff, *ZPE* 44 (1981): 78–80; W. Weismann, *Kirche und Schauspiele* (Würzburg, 1972), with the review of Joachim Ebert, *Stadion* 1 (1975): 185 ff.
7. On vases as evidence, cf. Julius Jüthner, "Verzeichnete Athletendarstellungen auf Vasen," *Jahrs. österr. archaeolog. Inst.* 31 (1938): 1–18. Note the red-figure kylix, Bologna 362, which shows a wrestler with three shoulders. A particularly vivid example of modern tampering involving a wrestling scene is the Panathenaic vase 1911.272 in the Ashmolean Museum, Oxford (*ABV* 412.1). D. M. Robinson, *AJA* 15 (1911): 504–06, noted the extensive problems with this vase: once the modern restorations were removed from the ostensibly perfect scene, barely half of the figures remained; not nearly enough to reconstruct the upper body holds the restorer had invented. A marble statue in the Louvre (Clarac de poche pl. 327, no. 2042 in Salomon Reinach, *Repertoire de la*

statuaire grecque et romaine I [Paris, 1897], sometimes attributed to the sculptor Pythagoras of Rhegium (cf. S. Lagona, *Pitagora di Reggio* [Catania, 1967], 52–53) shows the sharp thongs (see chap. 4) over a century before their first certain appearance on Greek monuments. It turns out, however, that the arms are completely modern restorations—only the torso survived antiquity; cf. Henri Lechat, *Pythagoras de Rhegion,* Annales de l'Université de Lyon, n.s. 14 (Lyon, 1905): 104–08, on its state of preservation. Jüthner, *AT,* 84 n. 76 discusses another example of misleading restoration of a boxing statue, this one extant in two damaged Roman copies, one in the Louvre (Clarac de poche pl. 279, no. 2187), one in the Villa Albani collection (Clarac, pl. 858 D, no. 2187 A); cf. further, Charles Waldstein, *JHS* 2 (1881): 341–43, and Adolph Furtwängler, *Meisterwerke der griechischen Plastik* (Leipzig, Berlin, 1893), 491, on the nature and date of these statues. The famous Vatican relief popularly known as "Dares and Entellus" has fallen under suspicion of being a Renaissance forgery; see Jüthner, *AT,* 85–86 n. 77; Jüthner-Mehl, 1321.

Chapter I

1. On ancient fencing, see Krause, *GAH,* 612–14; Poliakoff, *Studies,* 88–100. Pl. *Laws* 833e–834a envisions dueling competitions to replace the idle games of his day; significantly, he mentions that the founders will have to call in experts to set up a system for determining victory. Concerning the nature of gladiatorial combats, G. Ville, *La Gladiature en Occident des origines à la mort de Domitien* (Paris, 1982), 15 ff., argues for agonistic *origins* of gladiatorial combat which then yielded to "un simple spectacle, pour l'amusement du public" (p. 16). According to Ville, comparing *Iliad* 23.802 ff. and Livy 41.20 (*vulneribus tenus*), such contests in Greece and Southern Italy "s'arrêter avant mort d'homme" (p. 17). But it is hard to know what realities underlie Homer's episode (see App. 1), and Livy 41.20 refers to the attempt of Antiochus Epiphanes to introduce Roman gladiatorial practices to the Greek world in the second century B.C.E.; Epiphanes was a despot who had no scruples about dispatching gladiators, as Livy, in fact, makes clear: "modo vulneribus tenus, *modo sine missione.*" Ville finds (perhaps) better evidence of an agonistic element in the fact that Campanian gladiators always bear equal arms, unlike the later Roman gladiators (p. 31), but the extensive wounds seen on the gladiators in southern Italian art suggest a fight to the death. Gladiators' circumstances are well described in Keith Hopkins, *Death and Renewal* (Cambridge, 1983), 1–30, and Louis Robert, *Les gladiateurs dans l'orient grec* (Limoges, 1940), 120–21.
2. On interrelations between the combat sports, see Poliakoff, *Studies* 7, 14 nn. 15, 16. Theogenes' victories appear in Paus. 6.11.5 and Plut. *praec. rei publ. ger* 15 (*Mor.* 811d–e) as well as on an inscription *Syll.*³ 36a (= Moretti *IAG* 21, = Ebert 37).
3. *AP* 9.588 (= Ebert 67). (We find more concerning the deeds of Kleitomachos in Ps. Kallisthenes 133–34 R., discussed in Joseph Fontenrose, *CSCA* 1 [1968]: 95–97.)
4. Concerning victories in more than one combat event, see R. Knab, *Die Periodoniken* (Giessen, 1934), 6–7, which also notes that heavy athletes account for more *periodonikai* than other athletes. For examples of victors in more than one combat event, cf. *IG* 4.428 (= Moretti *IAG* 40); *I Delos* 1957 (= Moretti *IAG* 51); *IG* 12.3, 390 (= Moretti *IAG* 55); *I Magnesia* 149 (= Moretti *IAG* 62); *IG* 14.747 (= *IGR* I.446, = Moretti *IAG* 68). Note also Kaibel, 942, 944; *IK,* Ephesos 4.1123; Leon in Chr. Habicht, *VII Bericht über die Ausgrabungen in Olympia* (1961) 218, Marcus Aurelius Damas (Moretti *IAG* 84), and

Nikostratos, Olympic victor in 37 C.E. on the same day in wrestling and pankration (Moretti, *Olympionikai*, 762–63). Incompatibility of track and field, see Diod. Sic. 4.14; Theogenes' *dolichos* victory discussed in Paus. 6.11.5; another example is Aurelius Septimius Irenaios, *IGR* 3.1012 (= *IAG* 85).

5. On heavy events, see also Krause, *GAH*, 257–58, 546–47; Jüthner, *Philostr.*, 192; and Poliakoff, *Studies*, 14 n. 14. Plutarch's observations about building the body for combat sport, *Kleomenes* 27. On the size of athletes, see Pi. *Olymp.* 7.15 (Diagoras the boxer); *AP* 6.256 (Nikophon the boxer); Afric. *Ol.* 33 (Lygdamis the pankratiast, cf. also Paus. 5.8.8 and Philostr. *Gymn.* 12); Paus. 6.5.4–7 (Poulydamas); Ebert (Add.), pp. 251–55 (Kleomrotos); vast size and appetites described in Athenaeus 10.412d–413c. Athletic tall tales collected and discussed in Krause, *GAH*, 435–37, 549 n. 2; Harris, *GAA*, 110–22.

6. Concerning *kartereia*, see Pleket, "Ideology," 76–78. Boxer's silence, Cicero, *Tusc.* 2.17.40; Aeschylus's observation, Plut. *de aud. poet.* 10 (*Mor.* 29f), *prof. virt.* 8 (*Mor.* 79e). Eurydamas of Kyrene in Aelian, *Var. Hist.* 10.19. On the date of the Olympic festival, see S. G. Miller, *Mitt. Deutsch. Arch. Inst. Ath.* 90 (1975): 215–31. Slaves threatened with Olympia, Ael. *VH* 14.18; there was no adequate water supply until Herodes Atticus (Lucian, *Peregr.* 19). Cicero, *Brutus*, 69; concerning the heat, cf. also Philostr. *Gymn.* 11, Paus. 6.24.1; and J. Chrys. *nom. mut.* 2.1 (*PG* 51.125). Boxer drinking from his glove, Philostr. *Heroikos* 15 (147 K.). Mockery of indoor athletes, Dio Chrys. 32.20. Note also Pausanias's account of Kapros's victory in wrestling and pankration at Olympia (6.16.1): he won "not without great toil and discomfort." Louis Robert discusses the frequent appearance of *ponos* and *mochthos* ("toil," "trouble") in descriptions of ancient athletes, *Hellenica* 11–12 (Paris, 1960): 345–49; "Épigrammes," 196 n. 2. Reinhold Merkelbach, *ZPE* 15 (1974): 99–104, on the pankratiast who perseveres until night. Boxer's inscription, "endurance of hands," is unpublished, noted in Robert, "Épigrammes," 288 n. 4. Melankomas in Dio Chrys. *Or.* 28, 29.

7. Philo, *Every Good Man is Free (Quod Prob.)*, 26. Cf. Seneca, *de ira* 2.14.2; *de const. sap.* 9.5.

8. Wrestlers' skill: *Il.* 23.725, scholiast to *Il.* 23.720. Page, *Epigr. Gr.* Simonides LII 283 ff. (= Ebert 34); *I. Priene* 268 (= Moretti 48, = Ebert 73); Plut. *Quaest. Conv.* 2.4 (*Mor.* 638d); *AP* 16.2 (= Ebert 12); Paus. 1.39.3; Nonn. 37.576. Emphasis on strength in *IvOl* 161 (= Ebert 36); *AP* 16.1 also perhaps *IvOl* 183, cf. Joachim Ebert, *Archiv für Papyrusforschung* 19 (1969): 140–42. Akkadian tablet cited and translated in J. M. Sasson, *Orientalia* 43 (1974): 407. Pankratiast's strength, see *IG* II.1301 (= Kaibel 941, = Moretti 22, = Ebert 40), Ebert, p. 134, offers many further examples. On pankratiasts' skill, see Pi. *Isthm.* 4.47–48, SM; Philostr. *Im.* 2.6. Skill in boxing, see chap. 5, noting esp. Demosth. 4.40; Dio Chrys. 8.18; strength, cf. *AP* 6.256; Robert, "Épigrammes" cited in n. 6, above; Ebert, p. 169, gives several examples with discussion. Ambidexterity, see Pl. *Laws* 795b, Philostr. *Gymn.* 41.

9. It is significant that the title *atraumatistos* ("unwounded") appears very rarely in regard to boxers, cf. Rudolph Knab, "Die Periodoniken" (diss., Giessen, 1934), 12. In addition to the passages given below, see also Pi. *Isthm.* 7.22: the pankratiast Strepsiades of Thebes is both "awesomely strong and beautiful to look at." See also Pi. *Ol.* 8.19–20; *Ol.* 9.65–66, 94.

10. *AP* 16.2 (= Ebert 12).

11. *IvOl* 225 (= Moretti *IAG* 64 = Ebert 76).

12. Loincloth in Homer *Iliad* 23.683–85; 710. Certain late sixth-century B.C.E. Attic pots—the "perizoma" series—show athletes wearing a loincloth. They also, however, show men at symposia wearing the same loincloth, and it is rash to infer that we have evidence for a change in Greek athletic habits rather than a passing artistic fancy. Thucydides I.6, which claims that the Greeks gave up the loincloth in athletics "shortly

before my time," i.e., the fifth century B.C.E. is more cogent evidence that there was a revival of partial clothing (cf. Pl. *Rep.* 452c), but the greatest amount of literary and visual evidence argues that the custom of nude competition experienced no interruption from its inception at the fourteenth or fifteenth Olympiad onward. Roman denunciations of Greek nudity, Ennius, fr. *scaen.* 395 V., quoted above; cf. also Tacitus, *Ann.* 14.20. Roman athletes wearing the loincloth, Dionysius of Halicarnassus 7.72. For ancient depictions, in addition to fig. 2, see e.g. Römisch-Germanisches Museum W. 162; 29 and H. B. Walters, *Catalogue of the Greek and Roman Lamps in the British Museum* (London, 1914), 808.

13. Wrestlers boxing during training: Paus. 6.23.4. There is slight confusion in the ancient sources concerning the presence of boxing in the palaestra. Plut. *Quaest. Conv.* 2.4 (= *Mor.* 638c-d) claims that athletes practiced only wrestling and pankration in the palaestra, but in *Praec. ger. reip.* 32 (*Mor.* 825e) he states that boxers practiced there as well. The first passage is demonstrably eccentric, see Poliakoff, *Studies,* 12–13 n. 7: all three combat sports appeared in the palaestra. Jüthner-Mehl, 1337, has many more references concerning boxing in the palaestra. On the etymology of palaestra, see P. Chantraine, *Dictionnaire étymologique de la langue grecque* (Paris, 1968–80), s.v. *palaio,* and Plutarch's ancient speculations *Quaest. Conv.* 2.4 (= *Mor.* 638b-c). On the rise of the gymnasium, see Delorme, 19 ff.; S. C. Humphreys, *JHS* 94 (1974): 90–91; Pleket, "Ideology," 54–55. Delorme, 253–71, points out that the features which most consistently distinguish gymnasia from palaestrae are architectural, in particular the gymnasium's track and open spaces. But even these features appear in Vitruvius's plan for a Roman palaestra. Reference to private gymnasia in Greco-Roman times, see *BGU* IV 1188, 1189 (first century B.C.E.); *BGU* IV 1201 (second century C.E.), discussed briefly in Aryeh Kasher, *The Jews in Hellenistic and Roman Egypt,* Texte und Studien zum Antiken Judentum 7 (Tübingen, 1985), 204–05. Evidence of public palaestrae in J. Oehler, *RE* 7.2009–11. E. Kalinka, *Die pseudoxenophontische Athenaion Politeia* (Leipzig, Berlin, 1913), 208–11, observes that in the controversial passage ps. Xen. *Ath. Pol.* 2.10 the author's reference to private gymnasia is a heavily exaggerated flattery ("Schmeichelei") of the rich. On ancient bathing establishments, see René Ginouvès, *Balaneutike,* Bibliothèque des écoles françaises d'Athène et de Rome 200 (Paris, 1962), 149.

14. Ps. Hippocrates, *Epid.* 5.212 L. on death from a hard fall. Cf. Philogelos 153, a joke in which an unsuccessful wrestler rolls over and over in the mud in order to look like a real athlete; Luc. *Anach.* 28 tells of the importance of training in the mud. Pankratiasts also need the *skamma,* see *IG* 14.1102.15 and M. B. Poliakoff, *ZPE* 44 (1981): 78–80. On the use of the pickaxe, see Theokr. *Id.* 4.10 with the scholiast's note and A. S. F. Gow, *Theocritus* (Cambridge, 1950), ad loc.; also Athen. 12.518 D. Importing sand described in Suet. *Nero* 45; Athen. 12.539 c; Ael. *VH* 9.3. Concerning the location of different wrestling rooms, see Jüthner, *Philostr.,* 297. On the mud/oil surface (*keroma*), see Louis Robert, *Hellenica* 13 (Paris, 1965): 167–70; Julius Jüthner, *RE* 11.326–28; *Jahres. Öster. Arch. Inst.* 18 (1915): 323–30; Poliakoff, *Studies,* 20–27. Note the hyperrefinement implicit in Plut. *Quaest. Conv.* 2.4 (= *Mor.* 638c-d): wrestlers have three facilities, sand, mud, and *keroma,* and eventually Greek developed a word for the pit filled with plain mud for the wrestlers, *peloma,* matching the pit filled with mud-oil, *keroma.* Cf. the important discussion in Saul Lieberman, *Greek in Jewish Palestine* (New York, 1942), 93–97, though Lieberman took *peloma* and *keroma* as purely synonymous.

15. On palaestra deities, see Krause, *GAH,* 169 ff.; Jüthner, *Philostr.,* 227. The relationship between the labors of Herakles and those of the athlete appears vividly in an inscription, *Altertümer von Hierapolis* 1898, no. 46, discussed by Jean and Louis Robert, *BE* (1971): 640. Cf. further, Reinhold Merkelbach, "Herakles und der Pankratiast," *ZPE* 6 (1970): 47–49.

16. On the *apoduterion* and the meetings there, Pl. *Lys.* 206e–207a; *Euthyd.* 272; cited and discussed in Delorme, 54–55, 296–301. René Ginouvès (n. 13, above), 138, discusses the development of the *aleipterion*; Cl. Foss, "Aleipterion," *Greek, Roman, and Byzantine Studies* 16 (1975): 217–26, agrees with this general description of the *aleipterion* but notes that in Roman times the term also acquires a general meaning synonymous with the

bathing complex as a whole. Concerning the use of the oil, see Luc. *Anach.* 24; Thuc. 1.6; and further Krause, *GAH,* 501. Christopher Ulf, *Stadion* 5.2 (1979): 220–38, argues that the original reason for the use of the oil was magical and cultic: it gave the athlete strength. Although explicit ancient testimony to this effect is lacking, there is much that is appealing in Ulf's wider look at the religious applications of oil. On the different oiling rooms, see Delorme, 301. Gymnasiarch's expense for oil discussed in G. Glotz, *DS* II.2, 1682–1684. Note also *SEG* 32 (1982): 555 (Elateia), for discussion and further references concerning an instance of a forty-way division of the cost of gymnasium oil. Benefactors who paid all by themselves noted this fact with pride, see, e.g., Jean des Gagniers, Pierre Devambez, et al., *Laodicée du Lycos* (Quebec and Paris, 1969), 261–75; Jean and Louis Robert, *BE* (1968): 462. See further Liermann, 80–83, 102.

17. Concerning cauliflower ears, see Pl. *Gorgias* 515e; Pl. *Protag.* 342b; Martial 14.50; Philostr. *Her.* 26 (167 K.), 37 (189 K.); Theokr. 22.45; Plut. *de audiendo* 2 (*Mor.* 38b), citing Xenocrates, discusses headgear for athletes and children. Headgear and exposed cauliflower ears appear on Metropolitan Museum (New York) statue 17.230.3 (third century ̄B.C.E.) and Stockholm NM SK 59, a mid-fifth-century statue, attributed to Myron (cf. O. Antonsson, *Antike Kunst* [Stockholm, 1958], 43–45). An excellent discussion of the Metropolitan statue with references to a number of other depictions of headgear appears in Gisela Richter, *Catalogue of Greek Sculptures in the Metropolitan Museum* (Cambridge, 1954), no. 184. Galen, *Thrasyb.* 37 (5.877 K., 84 H.). On hair length, see further Philostr. *Im.* 2.32, and Krause, *GAH,* 541 n. 6. On the *cirrus,* see Barbara Gassowska, "Cirrus in vertice," in *Mélanges offertes à Kazimierz Michalowki* (Warsaw, 1966), 421–27.

18. Sand coating, see Luc. *Anach.* 2; oiliness to avoid grips, Aristoph. *Eq.* 490–91. Medical properties of dust, see, e.g., Hippocratic Corpus, *Vict.* 2.65 (6.582 Littré); *Vict.* 3.68 (6.602 Littré); Galen 6.162 K.

19. For texts concerning cooperative partners, see Clem. Alex. *Strom.* 6.17 (*Die griechischen christlichen Schriftsteller der ersten Jahrhunderte* 2.514); *P Oxy.* 3.466; further references and discussion in Poliakoff, *Studies,* 161–72. Workouts described in Philostr. *Gymn.* 11. *Akrocheirismos* noted in Philostr. *Gymn.* 36; Suda s.v., "Showy shadow boxing," see Dio Chrys. *Or.* 28.2. Flute accompaniment, Paus. 5.17.10; Athen. 4.154a and 12.518b, which notes that this was Etruscan practice; ps. Plut. *de mus.* 26 (*Mor.* 1140c)—see further Jüthner, *Philostr.,* 301; W. J. Raschke, *Arete* 2.2 (1985): 177–200. In addition to pl. 91 a bell krater in Lecce (Jüthner-Brein pl. 13a) shows a boxer training to flute music.

20. For Milo stories, see Ael. *VH* 12.22; Harris, *GAA,* 111. Using weights to determine pairing, Jer. *in Zacch.* 3.12 (*PL* 25.1509-10). Use of light weights, see Galen, *de sanitate tuenda* 2.9 (6.141 K.); Lucian, *Lex.* 5. There is a full discussion of weight training in N. G. Crowther, *GR* 24 (1977): 111–20. On punching bags, see Philostr. *Gymn.* 57 with Jüthner ad loc.; Oribasius 6.33; Delorme, 280–81. Galen's exercises, *de sanitate tuenda* 2.9 (6.140–43 K.).

21. Washing facilities, see Delorme, 301–11; René Ginouvès, (n. 13, above). The obvious soothing qualities of hot water on overtaxed muscles were, of course, well known; M. R. Lefkowitz has kindly pointed out Pi. *Nem.* 4.4–5 as a particularly good example. This makes the absence of hot baths in early gymnasia all the more austere.

22. Aristotle, *EN* 3.3, 1112b. Public trainers, see Jüthner-Brein, 107–09, 165–66; private trainer, see Athen. 13.584c; Themistius, *Or.* 23 (290a) with Jüthner-Brein, 163. Subsidy of promising athletes, *P. Cair. Zen.* 1.59060; *P Lond.* 1941; see further, Louis Robert, *Rev. Phil.* 41 (1967): 14–32; Pleket, "Ideology," 72; E. N. Gardiner, *CR* 44 (1930): 211–13. Youths in local competitions, see Young, *Olympic Myth,* 158–60. Concerning training routines and diet, see Eur. fr. 282 N.; Pl. *Rep.* 3.404a; Sen. *Ep.* 15.2–3, 88.18–19; Gardiner, *GASF,* 126; and esp. Saul Lieberman, *Greek in Jewish Palestine* (New York, 1942), 96–97. "To eat like a wrestler" was an expression for gluttony in Aristoph. *Pax* 33–4 ff.; see further Jüthner, *RE* 7.2049–50. Four-day training cycle, see Philostr. *Gymn.* 47, 54; also Galen, *Thrasyb.* 47 (5.898 K., 99 H.) and *de san. tuend* 3.8 (6.208 K.), discussed in Jüthner, *Philostr.,* 19.

23. Galen, *Protr.* 11 (1.28–29 K., 122 M.).

24. Trainer striking pupil for showmanship, Ael. *VH* 2.6. Olympic training rules, Paus. 5.21.12–14; Philostr. *Gymn.* 54; *IvOl* 56 (on the isolympic games of Naples).

25. Wolfgang Decker, "Das sogennante Agonale und der altägyptische Sport," in *Festschrift Elmar Edel*, ed. M. Görg and E. Pusch (Bamberg, 1979), 98–99, tentatively suggests that certain native Egyptian elements underlie this festival noted in Hdt. 2.91. A. B. Lloyd, however, in *Herodotus, Book II, Commentary* 1–98 (Leiden, 1976), 367–70, argues that there is no connection between the Greek agon which Herodotus reports and the particularly Egyptian games honoring Min. On Mesopotamian athletic festivals, see J. H. Tigay, *The Evolution of the Gilgamesh Epic* (Philadelphia, 1982), 186–87, who cites and discusses KAV 218; A,ii,5–7, 13–15, and *The Death of Gilgamesh* (BASOR 94:7, 28–31); see also Åke Sjöberg, *Expedition, The University of Pennsylvania Magazine* 27.2 (1985), 9.

26. On size of rewards for victors at the period games, see discussion later in this chapter. Apples at Delphi, see Louis Robert, *Hellenica* 7 (Paris, 1949): 93 ff. Games which restricted participation to citizens: *CIG* 1586 (music contest); 5805, noted by Liermann 113; also *CIG* 2758 (= Liermann XXXVII I.A. col. ii 3–5), but it is unclear when such restricted festivals appeared. It is remarkable how honorific titles adjust to the expanding festival program in later antiquity. Under the Roman Empire, the *periodos* grows to seven contests, including the Actian Games inaugurated by Augustus to celebrate his victory over Antony, the Capitoline Games of Domitian, and the games of Hera at Argos; Robert also suggests that perhaps the Sebesta of Naples belong to this category. *Periodonikes* in this period comes to mean victory in any four of the seven festivals, on which see Louis Robert, *BE* 67 (1954): 57. On prizes given at festivals, and "iso-" contests, see Pleket, "Ideology," 56–71. On the proliferation of festivals, see H. I. Marrou, *Histoire de l'éducation dans l'antiquité*[6] (Paris, 1965), 181. Athlete known to three nations, *IG* 14.1102.17 (= Moretti *IAG* 79). Note also that Aurelius Achilles, a heavy athlete, boasts of his success in "all the stadia of the nations" (published in C. P. Jones, *HSCP* 85 [1981]: 107–29).

27. On M. Aurelius Aelius Menander, pankratiast from Aphrodisias, see Liermann, 94.

28. Harris, *SGR*, 40. In fairness to Harris, he does not omit the evidence for early prizes in Greek sport, but rather he ignores its full implications. Considering Solon, see Plut. *Solon* 23; Diog. Laert. 1.55 adds that Solon's rewards of five hundred drachmas to Olympic victors and one hundred to Isthmian victors represented an austere *limitation* of the usual grants to the successful athletes! Xenophanes on athletes' benefits, fr. 2 W. Note also *IG* I² 77, which promises free meals for life to victors at Olympia, Delphi, Nemea, or the Isthmus: it was this custom which Socrates ridiculed in Plato, *Apol.* 36d. Tithe dedication, cf. Ebert (Add.), pp. 251–55. Worth noting also is *IvOl* 56, an inscription concerning the [isolympic] festival at Naples, which speaks of *athla* ("prizes") to be given to the athletes. On rewards, see Pleket, "Soziologie," 67, 70, 84 n. 124. Two other excellent discussions of the inapplicability of modern terms are Pleket, "Ideology," and Young, *Olympic Myth*.

29. Requirement to stay after registration: Aristeides I.2 (To Zeus); deadlines and late entry, see *IvOl* 56 and Paus. 5.21.12–14. The five age categories are discussed in Th. Klee, *Zur Geschichte der gymnastischen Agone an griechischen Festen* (Leipzig, Berlin, 1918; repr. Chicago, 1980), 43–51. On registration and age categories, see J. and L. Robert, *BE* (1968): 147; Louis Robert, *Rev. Arch.* (1978): 283–84; *Hellenica* 11–12 (Paris, 1960): 334–35. Arguments over categories, see the history of the boxer Pythagoras, chap. 5. Winners in more than one division at the same festival, Marcus Lucius, in Louis Robert, *Hellenica* 7 (Paris, 1949): 105–13; Marcianus Rufus achieves the same, see Moretti, *IAG* 69.

30. On the guilds, see F. Poland, *Geschichte des griechischen Vereinswesens* (Leipzig, 1909), 107–52, 610 n. 26A; H. W. Pleket, *ZPE* 10 (1973): 197–227; Hans Gerstinger, "Zum 'Faustkämpferdiplom' des Boxers Herminos alias Moros aus Hermopolis Magna aus dem Jahre 194 n. Chr.," *Anzeiger der Österreichischen Akademie der Wissenschaften* (1954), 57–61; C. A. Forbes, *CP* 50 (1955): 238 ff. *P Oxy.* 2475–77 gives evidence for the great

privileges accorded to a guild of actors and musicians; *IK* Ephesos, 7.1 3005 tells of tax exemptions for athletic victors.

31. Philostr. *Vit. Ap.* 5.43; cf. further Paus. 5.24.9.

32. Birth requirements are evident in the account of Hdt. 5.22; Demosthenes 23.37 (*Against Aristokrates*), makes clear that in Athens those guilty of homicide were barred from festivals. J. H. Krause, *Olympia* (Vienna, 1838; repr. Hildesheim and New York, 1972), 132–33, is surely correct in assuming that this ban applied throughout the Greek world. Contrary to the claim of Baron Pierre de Coubertin that Greek athletes took "an oath of honor and disinterest" (*Revue Olympique,* July 1906), which he then applied to banning compensation for sport, the Olympic oath had nothing to do with reward or payment to the victors. Harris, *GAA,* 165, argues correctly against Gardiner that all competitions took place in the stadium, cf. also Philostr. *Gymn.* 54 for wrestling in the stadium. On stadia, see Paus. 2.27.5; 9.23.1 and Manfred Lämmer, *KBSW* 5 (1976): 45–46, 59–60 n. 54 for further references. Delphi inscription, *BCH* 23 (1899): 564–67.

33. Lucian, *Hermotimos* 40.

34. Ariston, *IvOl.* 225 (= Moretti *IAG* 64, = Ebert 76).

35. Winning without a bye, see e.g., *IvOl* 54 (= *Syll.*³ 1073), 227; Pindar, *Nem.* 6.62–63. For the tournament scheme, see Ebert 76, p. 229, whose pairing diagram I copy here. References to large tournaments in *TAM* 2.301; Louis Robert, *Hellenica* 7 (Paris, 1949): 108; J. G. C. Anderson, *JRS* 3 (1913): 283, 294–95. Galen, *de aliment. fac.* (6.487 K.) speaks of competitions lasting an entire day. As a caution to undue skepticism, cf. Matti Jukola, *Athletics in Finland* (Helsinki, 1932), who noted that single Greco-Roman wrestling bouts in the modern Olympics lasted up to twelve hours. On respites in boxing, see chap. 5. In the other combat sports, see Ambrose, *Comm. on Ps. 118.21* (*PL* 15.1567), Appian, *BC* 3.68; Philo, *Leg. Alleg.* 3.14, cf. further Harris, *GAJ.* Tie bouts, *IvOl,* pp. 115–16; Gell., *NA* 18.2.5, cf. Polyb. 1.58.5.

Chapter II

1. These are sentiments that Greek literature and inscriptions explicitly express about wrestling. See Plut. *Quaest. Conv.* 2.4 (*Mor.* 638d) on the craftiness of wrestling and Poliakoff, *Studies,* 14–15 n. 21, for further references; note in particular Page, *Epigr. Gr.* Sim. LII, 283–85. Quintilian 2.12.2 observes that a wrestler who rushes for his opponent often falls by his own momentum and is defeated by a weaker opponent. On perseverance, note the use of the word *kartereia* in discussions of wrestling (as well as other combat events), on which see chap. 1 above, and further, Lucian, *Anach.* 24; Plato, *Laws* 796a-b. There is one clearly attested wrestling fatality involving an athlete who fell onto a hard surface during the bout (Hippocratic Corpus, *Epid.* 5.14 [5.212 L.]), and a damaged inscription seems to record another accidental wrestling death (*Syll.*³ 274, = Ebert 44, = Moretti *IAG* 29). Outside of Galen's general polemic against athletes (see chap. 6)—and even he gives pride of place to the dangers of boxing and pankration—few surviving texts mention danger in wrestling, though there are frequent references to the hazards of the other two combat sports.

2. Seneca, *On Benefactions* 5.3; Plato, *Euthyd.* 277d. See also Aeschylus, *Choeph.* 338–39, with scholia, *Agamemnon* 167 ff., and Krause, *GAH,* 424, for further references to the third fall.

3. Galen, *de nat. fac.* 2 (2.79–80 K.); *an arteriis sang.* 5 (4.717 K.); for more references, see Poliakoff, *Studies,* 8, and note in particular Aristophanes, *Knights* 571–73, which presents the vivid image of men brushing the dust off their shoulders so they could deny the fall and continue to fight.

4. Philo, *On Agriculture* 113 writes that in the Greek games, the competitor who outwrestles his opponent and stretches him out on his back or prone wins. Ambrose, *Commentary on Psalm* 36.51 (*PL* 14.1038–39) likens temptation to a wrestling match and claims that a wrestler may touch his knee to the ground, but once stretched out prone or tied up in a controlling hold, he has lost the match. For strangling in wrestling, cf. Lucian, *Anach.* 1.8; Nonnos 37.602–9—these matches are explicitly called wrestling,

not pankration. T. F. Scanlon, *CW* 77.3 (1984): 194–95, asked whether the late date of these sources indicates a change in rules: given a relatively high degree of conservatism, especially at the major Greek festivals, it is difficult to believe that wrestling in the first-century C.E. Olympics was vastly different from its counterpart in the fifth century B.C.E. The evidence does not warrant the conclusion drawn by W. Weismann, *Kirche und Schauspiele* (Würzburg, 1972), 63 n. 203, 64–65 n. 210 that the Church Fathers show widespread confusion of wrestling and pankration.

5. Herodotos 6.27. Jüthner, *Philostr.*, 212–13 clearly explains this passage, cf. further Robert, "Épigrammes," 251–53, and Poliakoff, *Studies*, 17 nn. 36, 37. Ambrose (passage cited n. 4 above) observes that there were "many disputes" concerning the scoring of a fall. E. N. Gardiner, *JHS* 25 (1905): 18–23, argued that touching any part of the opponent's body constituted a fall. He later revised his view, agreeing with Jüthner (cf. *GASF*, 377–78 and *AAW*, 182–83), but his old theory has found wide acceptance nonetheless.

6. The small number of scenes does not allow a firm conclusion about the rules underlying these Middle Kingdom depictions. J. A. Wilson, *Journal of Egyptian Archaeology* 19 (1931): 218–19, suggests that throwing the adversary to the ground on any three points constituted a fall but notes that the Beni Hasan drawings pose problems for this theory.

7. This is the interpretation of J. A. Wilson (above, n. 6), 211. Helmut Wilsdorf, *Ringkampf im alten Ägypten* (Würzburg, 1939), 21, notes that the meaning of the text is ambiguous; he suggests that the wrestlers are to turn toward pharaoh during the contest, a philologically unexceptionable interpretation, but also a pointless action in a wrestling match in terms of both spectators and contestants.

8. Attempts at breaking the back, Quintus Smyrnaeus 4.224–26; Apollod. 2.5.12. Pausanias 6.4.3 on Leontiskos. Pollux 3.155 lists *anchein* ("to choke") as a wrestling term. Rule of the *skamma* in Nilus, *de voluntaria paupertate* 60 (*PG* 79.1049), on which see M. B. Poliakoff, *ZPE* 44 (1981): 78–80, with a response by Jean and Louis Robert, *BE* (1982): 115. Ambrose, *Comm. on Ps. 36.55* (*PL* 14.1040–41) clearly describes the rule against striking. Plato on the details of wrestling regulations, *Laws* 833e.

9. Weiler, *Sport*, 171, shows appropriate skepticism of modern attempts to draw sharp distinctions between wrestling and the other combat sports, "deutlicher als es die Quellen zulassen." For an important study of modern distortions of ancient athletic values, cf. Young, *Olympic Myth*. I learn of the unpublished Olympia inscription by the kind communication of Prof. Peter Siewert, who discussed the text in his lecture at the Epigraphical Congress of 1982 at Athens and expects to publish the text in collaboration with J. Ebert in 1987.

10. On limb holds in Mesopotamian texts, see BIN 2.22:172 f. Such tactics are also perhaps implicit in *umāšu*, if it indeed derives from a concept of an arm hook, but cf. the objections of Benno Landsberger, *WZKM* 56, 115–17. W. Von Soden, *Akkadisches Handwörterbuch* (Wiesbaden, 1965–81) cites s.v. *umāšu(m)* /*humā*/*ušum* ARM 10.4.13; TCL 1.230.25, which seem to be evidence for belt wrestling. Cyrus Gordon, *HUCA* 23/1, pp. 131–36, suggests that belt wrestling was an essential part of the warrior/hero's life, but he bases his article on an unsupportable translation of the Nuzi tablet JEN 331 (cf. *CAD* s.v. *sabatu* 2d, 3). On ARM 10.4.13, cf. J. M. Sasson, *Orientalia* 43 (1974): 405–10. Wolfgang Decker, *KBSW* 5 (1976): 11, makes the extremely interesting observation that the wrestlers on the Egyptian carving from Amarna wear a belt decorated with balls in principle similar to those worn by modern day Nuba wrestlers (see fig. 92) and gives evidence for contact between the ancient Egyptians and this isolated tribe.

11. Firdausi, *Shanamah* S.495–503, 633. Carsten Niebuhr, *Reisebeschreibung* I (Copenhagen, 1774), 169–70. Persian dislike of nudity, see esp. Herodotos I.10.

12. W. Armstrong, *Wrestling* (London, 1889): "Modern spectators do not much care about the recumbent style of wrestling, in which a man who is really down and underneath struggles with very small chances of success, but with laborious and tedious efforts to keep at least one shoulder off the ground."

13. Heliodoros, *Aethiopika* 10.31, gives an exact description of the stance.

14. Caricature of the parvenu in Theophrastos, *Characters*, 27.14; poem on the young Her-

akles, Theokritos 24.111–14; claim of injury in executing a leg trip, Lucian, *Ocypus* 60–61.

15. Scholiast to Homer, *Iliad* 23.711.

16. Waistlock as serious disadvantage, see *TAM* 2.741, 1206, 1207 (second century C.E.). For further examples and discussion of the waistlock, see Poliakoff, *Studies*, 40–53. Crushing ribs with the waistlock, Apollodoros 2.5.12. Countering the waistlock, Quintus Smyrnaeus 4.224–30.

17. Nonnos 48.152–58. Editors have almost without exception claimed that the text has not come down to us intact and that some number of lines are missing from this description. This is possible, but as a wrestling tactic, at least, what the text describes is plausible.

18. Myth of Kerkyon and Theseus, Scholiast to Plato, *Laws* 796.

19. Most scholarship on the series of Hellenistic bronzes of which figs. 43, 44 are examples considers the contest to be over at the moment the artist has chosen to show, arguing that since the bottom man's knees are on the ground, the top man has won and is standing in a victory posture, cf. E. N. Gardiner, *JHS* 25 (1905): 23, 289–93; Helmut Kyrieleis, *Antike Plastik* 12 (Berlin, 1973): 133–47. This chapter offers abundant evidence, however, that wrestling matches often continued on the ground; moreover, the pose of this series of bronzes is much too kinetic to be a victory posture—one should note in particular that the top man steps over his opponent's leg, *blocking* him from escaping the armlock.

20. Note that Pollux 3.155 lists *klimakizein* as a wrestling term.

21. For a line-by-line commentary on the papyrus *P Oxy.* 3.466, see Poliakoff, *Studies*, 161–72.

Chapter III

1. For discussion of the terms, see Krause, *GAH*, 535; Louis Robert, *Études épigraphiques et philologiques* (Paris, 1938), 89 ff.; Robert, "Épigrammes," 261. Poliakoff, *Studies*, 64–74.

2. Plato contrasted the wrestling tricks that Antaios and Kerkyon developed in their techniques for the purpose of worthless brawling with the type of wrestling he sanctioned in his ideal state (*Laws*, 796a).

3. Rule against biting and gouging, Philostr. *Im.* 2.6. Reference to illegal activities, Aristophanes, *Pax* 898–99 (erotic encounter); Epiktetos 3.15.1–4; and Galen, *Protrept.* 11 (1.31 K., 123–24 M.); nickname Lion, Lucian, *Demon.* 49: these noted and discussed in Harris, *GAA*, 107, 208 n. 65. (Two other texts which discuss eye injuries are not necessarily evidence of foul play: Libanius 64.119 speaks of pankratiasts with eyes knocked out, but this text does not point to illegal gouging as much as punching; so also Galen, *Protrept.* 12[1.32 K., 124 M.]). "Permissive" definition of pankration, Ambrose, *Ennar. in Ps. 36.55* (*PL* 14.1040–41).

4. An inscription from Pisidia orders the pankratiasts not to use wrestling holds but to employ upright striking (*Papers of the American School of Classical Studies at Athens* 3, no. 275, 167, = E. N. Gardiner, *CR* 43 [1929]: 210–12). More references and discussion in Krause, *GAH*, 537–38 n. 9.

5. *Gramm. Gr.* I, i/iii, 111, states that pankratiasts, unlike boxers, were not "armed." One assumes this refers to thongs, and scholars have generally argued that pankratiasts did not use the thongs. But the balance of the evidence supports the opposite view. Although one could suppose that one pankration vase showing thongs is a mistake, the new find at Eretria (fig. 59), which also shows thongs, makes this argument unconvincing. Moreover, the ancient commentary on Pi. *Nem.* 5.89 credits Theseus with the invention of "pankration without boxing thongs (*myrmekes*)": the implication of this phrase is that there was also pankration with boxing thongs, as the two vases show.

6. Kicking in pankration, Galen, *Protrept.* 13 (1.36 K., 127–28 M.); Theokr. 22.66. The pankratiast's broad foot, *AP* 7.692 (Philip or Antipater). Upright fighting, Lucian, *Anach.* 3 (quoted); Quintus Smyrnaeus 4.480. Cf. further Krause, *GAH*, 537–38 n. 9.

7. Readiness of pankratiasts: Aulus Gellius, *NA* 13.28 (quoted). Breaking fingers, Paus. 6.4.1–2 and Moretti, *IAG* 25 (= Ebert 39), an inscription honoring Sostratos. Hand position, Galen, *de motu musc.* I.6 (4.395 K.), as noted in Krause, *GAH*, 545–46 n. 8.
8. Winning by being trampled, Philostr. *Her.* 15 (146 K), with discussion in Gardiner, *AAW*, 215. Cf. also Theokr. 24.113–14. Pindar, *Isthm.* 4.48.
9. Death of Arrichion, Philostr. *Im.* 2.6. Fatality in pankration, *IK* Ephesos 7.1, 3446 (= Peek, *VersInschr.* I.680). Letter to the pankratiast's mother, Philostr. *Gymn.* 23. Cf. also Dio Chrys. 8.19. Changing order at Olympia, Paus. 6.15.5; dreams of sport, Artemidorus 1.62.

Chapter IV

1. For discussions of stick fighting, see J. A. Wilson, "Ceremonial Games of the New Kingdom," *Journal of Egyptian Archaeology* 19 (1931): 211–20; J. Vandier d'Abbadie, "Deux nouveaux ostraca figurés," *Annales du Service des Antiquités de l'Égypte, Cairo* 40 (1940): 467–88; A. D. Touny, S. Wenig, *Sport in Ancient Egypt* (Leipzig, Amsterdam, 1970).
2. On the connections between the practices of the Nuba and those of the Nubian athletes on the fourteenth-century B.C.E. carving, see the excellent discussion of Wolfgang Decker, *KBSW* 5 (1976): 10–13. Carsten Niebuhr, *Reisebeschreibung* I (Copenhagen, 1774), 169–70.
3. Pyramid Texts, Utterance 469, sec. 908 in Kurt Sethe, *Übersetzung und Kommentar zu den altägyptischen Pyramidentexten* IV (Glückstadt, 1935–62), 179–80, 184. Ramesseum Papyrus, scene 38, on which see H. Altenmüller, "Letopolis und der bericht des Herodot über Papremis," *Jaarbericht van het Vooraziatisch-Egyptisch Genootschap* "Ex Oriente Lux" 18 (1964): 271–79. Note that Altenmüller argues against the earlier interpretation of K. Sethe, *Untersuchungen zur Geschichte und Altertumskunde Aegyptens* 10 (Leipzig, 1928; repr. Hildesheim, 1964), 224, who considered the objects in question to be the forms of the uprights of a ladder for the deified king's ascent to heaven. Sethe, p. 166, also considers the ideogram in scene 18 which shows two men fighting with sticks to be a general character for struggle and not a specific hieroglyph for stick fighting.
4. Herodotos 2.63. Concerning cultic aspects, see in addition to Altenmüller, cited above, A. B. Lloyd, *Herodotus Book II, Commentary 1–98* (Leiden, 1976), 285; J. Vandier d'Abbadie (above, n. 1), 479–81. Vandier d'Abbadie makes the interesting observation in passing that stick fighting is particularly popular during the Islamic festival of Ramadan.

Chapter V

1. Kaibel, 942.
2. In addition to the well-known carving shown in fig. 68, two smaller fragments show the same types of gloves, Heraklion Museum inv. 255 (Peter Warren, *Minoan Stone Vessels* [Cambridge, 1969], 85) and another in the Boston Museum of Fine Arts (*Minoan Stone Vessels*, 86), the latter of which is of doubtful authenticity, see J. Coulomb, *BCH* 105 (1981): 29–32. Coulomb also argues in this article that the Minoan gloves, like the Greek light thongs, protect the hands and face of the boxer, giving special protection to the vulnerable thumb. The helmets, however, do not bespeak a gentle contest. The boxing boys on a fresco from Thera (now the Greek island of Santorini), also c. 1500 B.C.E., are less martial with their jewelry and long braids, and it is hard to imagine that they are engaged in a hazardous fight, but the fresco is too badly damaged to indicate more than the fact that they are wearing some kind of glove. Further discussion in A. J. Papalas, *Ancient World* 9.3–4 (1984): 67–68.
3. Note the very similar carving, Iraq Museum, Baghdad 10039; it is somewhat more eroded than the carving shown in fig. 69, but the wrist band is clear. The boxers in British Museum 91906, found at Senkereh, are also barefisted. Concerning Theban Tomb 192, see C. E. De Vries, "Attitudes of the Ancient Egyptians toward Physical-

Recreative Activities" (diss., University of Chicago, 1960), 222–38. De Vries also suggests that a caption in these scenes identifies some of the boxers as "defending" or "guarding," though this does not appear in the publication of Ch. F. Nims et al., *The Tomb of the Kheruef. Theban Tomb 192*, Oriental Institute Publications 102 (Chicago, 1982), 63–64.

4. On the application of the thongs, see Philostr. *Gymn.* 10 and Paus. 8.40.3, who says that the boxers wrapped them under the hollow of the hand and left the fingers free— a number of vase paintings show this very clearly, though others show boxers wrapping the fingers as well. Jüthner, *AT*, 72–73, argues that eccentric vase scenes represent the blunders of the painters; there are certainly some errors in vase painting, cf. intro. n. 7, but it seems unsound to explain away so many ancient monuments this way. On the purpose of the thongs, see W. Rudolph, *Olympischer Kampfsport in der Antike* (Berlin, 1965), 9–10.

5. Socrates' caricature of pro-Spartan Athenians, *Protag.* 342b. Akousilaos in Schol. Pi. *Ol.* 7.1.

6. Concerning the date of the appearance of sharp thongs, see A. S. F. Gow, *Theokritos* II (Cambridge, 1950), 394. Note that the Villa Albani boxer, late fifth century B.C.E. (Clarac, pl. 858 D, no. 2187 A, discussed intro., n. 7), has traces of the sheepskin lining characteristic of the fully developed sharp thongs on the authentic part of the arm. It is possible that the first half of the fourth century saw a gradual development of those gloves, cf. the discussion of Jüthner, *AT*, 83–84, with n. 76. Arguments for their gentleness in Harris, *SGR*, 22–23. References to the cutting qualities of these gloves appear in Apollonios of Rhodes 2.52–53, Quintus Smyrnaeus 4.338–39, 353–54; Nonnos 37.507. Philostratos, *Gymn.* 10, which claims they protected the face from injury, must be wrong; on this problem, cf. Poliakoff, *Studies*, 143–48. Protection of the boxers' arms, see Gardiner, *AAW*, 198.

7. On *sphairai*, see Pl. *Laws* 830a–831a; Plutarch *Praec. reip. ger. 32 (Mor. 825e)*; further references and discussion in Poliakoff, *Studies*, 88–100; T. F. Scanlon, *Stadion* 8/9 (1982–83): 31–33. Softer gloves, Trebellius Pollio (Script. Hist. Aug.) *Gallienus* 8.3, discussed in E. K. Borthwick, *CR* 78 (1964): 142. Note the discussion of T. F. Scanlon, *AJP* 107 (1986): 110–14.

8. On the *myrmex*, see Poliakoff, *Studies*, 54–63; T. F. Scanlon, *Stadion* 8/9 (1982–83): 31–45.

9. Philogelos 172.

10. Eustathius 1324.20 ff. *ad Il.* 23.683.

11. Lucillius, *AP* 11.78, cf. Robert, "Épigrammes," 209–12.

12. Concerning the use of the ladder, (*klimax*) as a barrier, see Hesychius and the Etymologicum Magnum, s.v. *ek klimakos*, and Eustathius 1324.48 (*ad Il.* 23.686, discussed in M. B. Poliakoff, "Melankomas, *ek klimakos*, and Greek Boxing," *AJP* (forthcoming). On the Sala Consilina scene (fig. 81), see Bernhard Neutsch, *Apollo, Bolletino dei musei provinciali del Salernitano* 1 (1961): 53–66, who first recognized the significance of the barrier in front of the boxers.

13. Onomastos, see Paus. 5.8.7; Afric. *Ol.* 23.

14. Boxers resting in epic accounts, Stat. *Theb.* 6.796–801; Ap. Rh. 2.86–87. Historical mention of boxers resting, Polyb. 27.9.7–13, see further Robert, "Épigrammes," 222; Jüthner-Mehl, 1338. See also chap. 1 for general aspects of the tournament progression. Ban on clinching, see Plut. *Quaest. Conv.* 2.4 (*Mor.* 638e–f).

15. Story of Pythagoras, Diog. Laert. 8.47; the epigram is Theaitetos VI 3368 (Gow-Page).

16. Prejudice about Ionia, see Hdt. 1.143.

17. Demosthenes 4.40.

18. Apollo as boxer, K. Ziegler, *RE* 23.2077; Weiler, *Agon*, 173–74; Plut. *Quaest. Conv.* 8.4 (= *Mor.* 724c), see also *Il.* 23.659–62.

19. Theokritos 22.83–86 (cf. also Nonnos 37.534–36).

20. Theokr. 22.95–98; further references to two-handed fighting, see Q.S. 4.360–69; Vergil, *Aen.* 5.457.

21. Ap. Rh. 2.90–92.

22. Note, however, the argument of K. Weiss in *Theologisches Wörterbuch zum neuen Testament* (Stuttgart-Berlin-Cologne-Mainz, 1969), 8.589, that when Paul speaks of bruising his body he leaves his previous image of the boxer for one of the sinner patiently receiving divine punishment. But Philo, *de agr.* 114, notes body blows in crown festivals, on which see Harris, *Greek Athletics and the Jews* (Cardiff, 1976), 58. R. and M. Brophy, *AJP* 106 (1985): 171–98, argue, but without reference to Paul and Philo, that body blows were illegal. Concerning stabbing with the thumb, note that one of the safety measures that contemporary professional boxing associations have begun to consider is requiring "thumbless" boxing gloves; such a measure would eliminate many eye injuries.

23. For descriptions of energetic boxing matches, see Theokr. 22.102–03; Stat. *Theb.* 6.766–805; Nonnos 37.523–26, 536–38. Q.S. 4.346–47 describes boxers on their toes. See also Dio Chrys. 8.18 and Manil. *Astron.* 5.162–64.

24. Philo, *Cher.* 80–81.

25. Herdsman at Olympia, Theokr. *Id.* 4.

26. Kleitomachos at Olympia in Paus. 6.15.5; Artemidoros, *Interpretation of Dreams* 1.61–62 on the relative dangers of boxing and pankration. On eye injuries, see Libanius 64.119 and Galen, *Protrept.* 12 (1.32 K., 124–25 M.); these texts refer to punching, which was a part of both pankration and boxing, not gouging (which would make the injury peculiar to pankration).

27. Lucillius, *AP* 11.81 (quoted), cf. also 77, 75; see further Robert, "Épigrammes."

28. Scorning death, Philostr. *Heroikos* 15 (147 K).

Chapter VI

1. Boxing in Sweden, Mats Hellspong, *Boxinngssporten i Sverige: En studie i idrottens Kulturmiljo* (Stockholm, 1982). AMA policy, *New York Times* (Dec. 6, 1984), discussed in M. B. Poliakoff, "Boxing Can be Good for Us," *Washington Post* (Jan. 12, 1985).

2. George Will, *Boston Globe* (Nov. 23, 1982).

3. John Hoberman, *Boston Globe* (Feb. 2, 1983). For a critique of boxing on societal grounds, see also Joe Brown, "And You Hear Your Name," "The Manly Art of Watching a Fight," (Princeton) *University Magazine*, Summer-Fall 1963.

4. Thucydides 2.39. See also Paus. 1.17.1 on the Athenian ethos.

5. It is difficult, of course, to make reasonable generalizations about the relative levels of cruelty in different societies, but the Greek world knew nothing like the Roman practice of decimation (killing every tenth man in an unruly or unsuccessful army)—on the contrary Greek military discipline was notoriously lax, see W. K. Pritchett, *The Greek State at War* II (Berkeley, 1974), 243–45. Nor did it tolerate the private execution of slaves, a custom banned only under the emperors in Rome. For further discussion of institutionalized cruelty at Rome, see Keith Hopkins, *Death and Renewal* (Cambridge, 1983), 1–2, 28. Initial Greek reaction to the arena was repugnance (Livy 41.20), although this yielded to enthusiasm in time. Worth noting also are the conclusions of A. Lintott, *Violence, Civil Strife, and Revolution in the Classical City* (Baltimore, 1981), 26–27, 173–76, on the lower level of tolerance for private acts of violence in Athens than in Rome, "Private violence was on the whole considered a danger to personal liberty in Athens, whereas in Rome it was for long held to be not only compatible with liberty but liberty's ally and guarantor." The opening chapter of F. E. Romer's book on the rise of Greek tyranny (in preparation) adds earlier and weightier considerations to Lintott's argument, noting that by the late seventh century Athenians were showing strong disapproval of private violence, as witnessed by Draco's homicide laws, which remove from the citizen the need and entitlement to revenge the murder of kin.

6. Leigh Montville, "A senseless 'game' on a Saturday afternoon," *Boston Globe* (Nov. 15, 1982).

7. G. J. M. G. Te Riele, *BCH* 88 (1964): 186–87, discussed by Jean and Louis Robert, *BE* (1965): 182.

8. Dio Chrys. 31.110.

9. *IvOl* 54/55 (= *Sylloge*³ 1073). See Reinhold Merkelbach, *ZPE* 15 (1974): 99–104.
10. Philostratos, *Im.* 2.6. Cf. *Gymn.* 21; Paus. 8.40.1–2.
11. Philo, *Every Good Man is Free (Quod Prob.)*, 110, 113.
12. There are, in fact, records of eight specific fatalities in the combat sports: in addition to Agathos Daimon, there were three others in boxing: Paus. 6.9.6; 8.40.3–5; Photius 190 B. (noted in A. Hönle, *Olympia in der Politik der griechischen Staatenwelt* [Bebenhausen, 1972], 100); another in pankration, in addition to Arrichion: *IK* Ephesos 7.1 (Metropolis Ioniae) 3446 (= Peek, *VersInschr.* 680); two in wrestling: Syll.³ 274 (Moretti *IAG* 29, = Ebert 44) and ps. Hippocr. *Epid.* 5.14 (5.212 L.). A Church Father, Athenagoras, maintained that Theogenes of Thasos killed an opponent at Olympia (*suppl. pro Christ.* 14.62) (Otto), but the silence of the other, ample sources argues convincingly that Athenagoras was mistaken. On the topic of fatalities, see Robert and Mary Brophie, *AJP* 106 (1985): 171–98, with additions and corrections in M. B. Poliakoff, *AJP* 107 (1986) 400–02. Three of the boxing casualties involved illegal tactics, but this should not be taken as evidence that the sport normally was much safer: Pl. *Laws* 865a–b, Demosthenes (Against Aristokrates) 23.53, and Aristotle, *Ath. Pol.* 57.3, all discuss the legal immunities of athletes who unintentionally kill their opponents in sport.
13. Demosthenes (Against Meidias) 21.45.
14. On *hybris*, see Michael Gagarin, "The Athenian Law Against Hybris," *Arktouros, Studies in Honor of B. M. W. Knox* (Berlin and New York, 1979), 229–36, who suggests that the institution of the *graphe hybreos* on top of existing civil sanctions against *hybris* represents an intense loathing of physical assault; note, however, that his discussion of Isokr. 20 (p. 231) does not take into account the orator's stress on the arrogant attitude and intent of Lochites in sections 9–11. D. M. MacDowell, "*Hybris* in Athens," *G&R* 23 (1976): 14–31, was correct in noting that the Greeks did not separate arrogance from its realization in assault. See also the evaluation in A. Lintott (n. 5, above), 173–76.
15. Isokrates (Against Lochites) 20.9–11.
16. Lucian, *Anacharsis* 11. Like other authors of the Second Sophistic, he enjoys looking back to Athens's early history. It is also relevant to note, as Prof. R. Merkelbach kindly pointed out to me, that Lucian, born in Syria, may have had a clearer ability to compare Greek and non-Greek ways than a native born Hellene.
17. Hippocrates on athletes' condition in *Aphorisms* 1.3, cited in Galen, *Thrasyb.* 9 (5.820 K., 43 H.), also *Protrept.* 11 (1.27 K., 121 M.).
18. Galen, *Small Ball* 5 (5.909–10 K., 101–02 M.)
19. *Protrept.* 12 (1.32 K., 124–25 M.)
20. On the dangers of horses, Galen, *Small Ball* 5 (5.909–10 K., 101–02 M.). Another noteworthy criticism based on safety considerations comes in the orator Libanius's exhortation on behalf of dancing, where he attacks wrestling for the broken bones it causes, other combat sports for eye damage, charioteers for killing opponents, and horse racing for its capacity to excite the crowds to violence (*Or.* 64.119), noted in J. P. V. D. Balsdon, *Life and Leisure in Ancient Rome* (London, 1969), 276.
21. *Protrept.* 11 (1.27 K., 121 M.)
22. Xenophanes of Colophon's polemic is fr. 2 W. Pleket, "Ideology," 84–89, discusses the sanctifying terminology of athletes' compensation: Greek *doron* ("gift"), not *misthos* ("wage") (which is what a laborer—or a physician—would receive). On the social status of physicians in the Greek world, cf. also L. Edelstein, *Ancient Medicine* (Baltimore, 1967), 323 ff., 336 ff. J. Scarborough, *Roman Medicine* (London, 1969), 108 ff., observes that the Roman attitude toward the physician was highly ambivalent; although aristocratic Romans sometimes valued the best physicians, they remained wage earners, and in general "the Romans viewed medicine as the province of slaves and freedmen." V. Nutton, *CQ* 65 (1971): 262, notes that no physician in Rome ever rose above equestrian rank. The explanation of M. I. Finley and H. W. Pleket, *The Olympic Games, The First 1000 Years* (New York, 1976), 122, for Galen's polemic as his disgust at the athletes' "failure to achieve an honorable livelihood" is perhaps too charitable an interpretation, given Galen's spitefulness about his own status (cf. esp. *Protrept.* 7 [1.11–15 K., 110–12 M.], which derides nobility without skills).

23. Pl. *Laws* 796a (quoted) on a pure style of wrestling; prescription of war games in *Laws* 830c–831a.

24. Melos discussed in Thuc. 5.115; Skione, Thuc. 5.32, and Isokrates 12.63; Plataea, Thucydides 3.68; proposed devastation of Athens, Xenophon *Hell.* 2.2.19, Isokr. 14.31–32. See further, Russell Meiggs, *The Athenian Empire* (Oxford, 1973), 337–38. On Rome, see W. V. Harris, *War and Imperialism in Republican Rome* (Oxford, 1979), 9–53, 263–64.

25. On the phalanx, see A. M. Snodgrass, *JHS* 85 (1965): 110–22; Y. Garlan, *War in the Ancient World* (London, 1975), 124–26; A. J. Holladay, *JHS* 102 (1982): 94–103; J. K. Anderson, *JHS* 104 (1984): 152. Weight of the armor, see Donald Engels, *Alexander the Great and the Logistics of the Macedonian Army* (Berkeley, 1978), 21 n. 31. The date and extent of the social change attendant on the introduction of hoplite armor and tactics are highly controversial; this, however, does not affect the thesis presented here. Even if the introduction of the phalanx affected only aristocrats for an extended period of time (and Garlan raises cogent objections to this view), these warriors would still make up the largest portion of the personnel of the Greek games in the preclassical era.

26. On military elements in Egyptian sport, Helmut Wilsdorf, *Ringkampf im alten Ägypten* (Würzburg, 1939), 31; Wolfgang Decker, *KBSW* 4 (1975): 47–48.

27. J. A. Wilson, "Ceremonial Games of the New Kingdom," *Journal of Egyptian Archaeology* 19 (1931): 211–20.

28. Lucian, *Anach.* 15, 30.

29. Philostr., *Gymn.* 9.11.43, for discussion, see E. L. Bowie, "Greeks and Their Past in the Second Sophistic," in *Studies in Ancient Society,* ed. M. I. Finley (London, 1974), 166–209 (= *Past and Present* 46 [1970]) and Poliakoff, *Studies*, 143–48.

30. Plutarch, *Quaest. Conv.* 2.5 (*Mor.* 639a–640a): the Theban general at Leuctra was Epaminondas (who, according to Nepos, was somewhat skeptical of the palaestra [see below]). Young, *Olympic Myth,* doubts the historicity of the reports of breaking the city walls, but concerning extravagant victory processions, see Diod. Sic. 13.82.

31. It is worth noting how persistent is the dream of unobtrusive military preparation, as the following quotation from Minute 2430 of the Interdepartmental Committee on Physical Deterioration (1904) shows: "Without recourse being had to any suggestion of compulsory military service, the male adolescent population might undergo a species of training that would befit them to bear arms with very little supplementary discipline" (from P. C. McIntosh, *Landmarks in the History of Physical Education*² (London, 1960), 201. Melankomas in Dio Chrysostom, *Or.* 28 and 29, esp. 29.9 and 29.14–15. Statue of Agon at Olympia, Paus. 5.20.3. On Milo as leader, see Diod. 12.9.5–6; concerning Kroton's prowess, Strabo 6.1.12 (262 C.). Aristophanes, *Clouds* 984–85, 1052–54; *Frogs* 1069–73.

32. Athletes and warriors: on Eurybates, see App. Pausanias 7.27.5–7 tells of Promachos and Paus. 6.8.6 of Timasitheos. Dioxippos's story appears in Diodorus Siculus 17.100.2; further references and discussion in Moretti, *Olympionikai*, 458; Harris, *GAA*, 122–23.

33. On ephebes and military considerations in general, see Pleket, "Ideology," 76–77; Finley and Pleket (above, n. 22), 113 ff.; C. A. Forbes, *Neoi* (Middletown, Conn., 1933); Julius Jüthner, *RE* 7.2051–54; A. Dumont, *Essai sur l'éphébie Attique* (Paris, 1875–76). Note with Dumont, I.1 ff., that the *ephebeia* is considerably more ancient than the first attestation of the word in the fourth century B.C.E.; so also P. Vidal-Naquet, *PCPS* 4 (1968): 49–64. H. Y. McCulloch and H. D. Cameron, *ICS* 5 (1980): 1–14, show evidence for the institution as early as Aeschylus. Ephebes in crown games, see Pleket, "Soziologie," 73. Aristotle, *Politics* 8.4, 1338b—the philosopher notes that few boy victors at Olympia return to win as men, and he recommends that youths only participate in light sports until their bodies are ready for tougher activities. Agesilaus's actions at Ephesos appear in Xenophon, *Agesilaus* 1.25–28 and *Hell.* 3.4.16–19. Old men exercising in gymnasia, cf. Plato, *Rep.* 452b. An important discussion of sport and military training appears in W. K. Pritchett, *The Greek State at War* 2 (Berkeley, 1974), 208–21. Language of athletic and military honor, cf. Anton Stecher, *Inschriftliche Grabgedichte auf Krieger und Athleten*, Commentationes Aenipontanae 27 (Innsbruck, 1981), 48 ff. It is

remarkable to note how close, e.g., *OGI* 553 (= *TAM* 2.265), a military inscription, and the praise of the *kartereia* and *ponos* of the athletes are to one another; on these similarities, see further n. 73, below.

34. On sport and war, cf. J. H. Krause, *Olympia* (Vienna, 1838; repr. Hildesheim and New York, 1972), 39–40 n. 15. Homer makes at least a circumstantial connection between athletics and war when he presents the great heroes as the outstanding sportsmen in the funeral games of bk. 23: on this see Matthew Dickie, "Phaeacian Games," *Papers of the Liverpool Latin Seminar* 4 (Liverpool, 1984), 241–43. The incident of Tydeus at Thebes, reported in *Il.* 4.370–400; 5.800–13 is better evidence for a connection of warrior and athlete, though it still falls short of proving that sport provided *training* for battle. Moreover, in *Odyssey* 3.111–12 Nestor describes his son as "fastest in running and a great warrior."

35. Euripides, *Autolykos* fr. 282 N., cf. Jüthner-Brein, I.95.

36. Philopoimen in Plutarch, *Philopoimen* 3. Plato's misgivings about the serviceability of athletes in war appears in *Republic* 403e–404b, his recommendation for a pure form of wrestling in *Laws* 796a-b, and his preference for team war games in *Laws* 829e–831b (on the nature of Plato's sphaeromachia, cf. Poliakoff, *Studies*, 91–95; the phrase "athlete of war" in *Rep.* 416d, 422b, 521d, 543b, as noted by Pritchett (n. 33, above). Epaminondas's opinions about athletics appear in Nepos 15.2 and 15.5; Plutarch, *reg. et imp. apopth.*; *Épamin.* 3 (*Mor.* 192c-d); *seni reip. ger.* 8 (*Mor.* 788a). On mock battles, see Pritchett, 221. Alexander the Great in Plutarch, *Alexander* 4

37. Xenophon's belief in physical education, *Memorabilia* I.2.4, III.5.15; the story of Boiskos *Anab.* 5.8.23, cf. Pritchett, p. 219 n. 45. Socrates and Epigenes, *Memorabilia* 3.12 (quoted), see also A. Delatte, *Le troisième livre des souvenirs Socratiques de Xenophon* (Paris, 1933), 162–66. Protagoras insisted that the good physical condition achieved under the *paidotribes* saved a person from having to show cowardice in war, but does not specify what sort of physical education he deemed appropriate (Plato, *Protag.* 326b-c).

38. W. G. Forrest, *A History of Sparta, 950–192 BC* (London, 1968), 51–55.

39. Superiority of Spartan tactical training, ps. Xen. *Const. Laced.* 11.5–10; for further examples and discussion, see Garlan (n. 25, above), 165–68, and Pritchett (n. 33, above), 208–13. Aristotle on Spartan training, *Pol.* 8.4, 1338b.

40. Spartan kings surrounded by athletic victors, see *Quaest. Conv.* 2.5.2 (*Mor.* 639e) and *Lykourgos* 22.

41. Tyrtaios fr. 12 W.

42. Group combat sports, Lucian, *Anach.* 38; Paus. 3.14.8–10. Flogging contests, *Anach.* 38, cf. also Cicero, *Tusc.* 5.77. Spartan prohibition against competition in pankration and boxing abroad, Philostr. *Gymn.* 9, 58; Jüthner, *Philostr.*, 203, notes in addition, Plut. *Lykourgos* 19; *reg. et imp. apopth.* 44, *Lyk.* 4 (*Mor.* 189e); Sen. *de benef.* 5.3.1.

43. Plutarch, *Spartan Sayings (Moralia)* 233e, 234e, 236e, 242a-b. See also *AP* 16.1, a victory epigram for a Spartan wrestler: "They [from other states] rely on technique, I, as befits boys from Sparta, conquer by my might." On Spartan trainers, see also Jüthner, *Philostr.*, 232. Note the astute assessment in Burckhardt, *GK*, 82: "Auch Sparta mit seinem kargen Dorismus, wo sich das Agonale auf seine besondere Weise fixiert, steht auf der Seite; denn hier findet sich nicht eine wahre Gesellschaft, sondern ein hart herrschendes Eroberervolk, dessen gymnastisches und sonstiges Tun wesentlich den praktischen Zweck hat, die Herrschaft zu behaupten." Ziehen, *RE* 18.43–45 connects Sparta's withdrawal from Olympia with her disdain for the technical developments of sport attendant on the rise of the career athlete. But the withdrawal starts early—it is more likely to be a result of the intensification of Sparta's militarism and its demand for pursuits closer to war; see also Hönle (n. 12, above), 126–39, esp. 136.

44. On the Roman ethos, see Polybius VI.52–54 and further D. C. Earl, *The Moral and Political Tradition of Rome* (London, 1967), 23–43, noting in particular his assessment, p. 23, "To a purely private cultivation of personal virtue the Roman tradition was always hostile." Cicero, *Rep.* 4.4.

45. Poets' scorn, Lucan 7.270–72; Sil. Ital. 14.136–37.

46. Plut. *Quaest. Rom.* 40 (*Moralia* 274d).
47. Pliny, *NH* 35.13; Tacitus, *Ann.* 14.20; see also Pliny the Younger, *Panegyr.* 13. Plutarch, *Cato Maior* 20. Vegetius I.9 ff. Further discussion in N. Petrochilos, *Roman Attitudes to the Greeks* (Athens, 1974), 177 ff.; Jüthner-Brein, 131–44; Weiler, *Sport,* 268–76.
48. Despite Perikles' boast in the Funeral Oration (Thuc. 2.37), Spartan hoplites were superior; see Pritchett (n. 33, above), 210–11, for references and discussion. Pritchett, 243–45, documents the traditionally lax discipline of Greek armies. Delorme, 24–30, argued that the city-states began to build gymnasia in the sixth century in response to the need for the development of hoplites. But S. C. Humphreys, *JHS* 94 (1974): 90–91, properly questions the suitability of the gymnasium for group hoplite exercises. It is, indeed, very hard to understand why the gymnasium assumed the form it did, if its origin lay primarily in marching exercises; further discussion in Pleket, "Ideology," 54–55. Mutatis mutandis, Thorstein Veblen's sarcastic appraisal of athletics in chap. 10, "Modern Survivals of Prowess," of *The Theory of the Leisure Class* would have found more than a few supporters in antiquity: Veblen concluded that the well-trained athlete would have little capacity for self-preservation in a hostile environment, and that "the relation of football to physical culture is much the same as that of the bull-fight to agriculture."
49. On the universality of play and games, see J. Huizinga, *Homo Ludens* (Engl. ed.) (Boston, 1950). The classic discussion of the agon in Greek life is that of Burckhardt, *GK,* 82–117, 201–06. Some, but hardly all, of his theories merit the criticism they have received in this century, and his work should still challenge us to get at the essence of the Greek contests. On the whole, Burckhardt's thesis that the Greek agon is unique and central to our understanding of ancient society seems sound, though not necessarily for the reasons which he gives. (*GK* is, incidentally, a posthumous edition of Burckhardt's lecture notes, and naturally its arguments have certain gaps.) Burckhardt restricts the true agonal spirit to "small free aristocracies" (p. 85), since the Homeric heroes did not need such an outlet, "Wer den Krieg hat, bedarf des Turniers nicht" (p. 88), and democracy was interested in gratification, not excellence (p. 203). This aristocratic bias runs counter to history—the democracies take an active interest in sport, both in building gymnasia, and, more to the point, in rewarding, hence encouraging, victors; the number of sport festivals grows rather than decreases (cf. chap. 1). V. Ehrenberg, *Ost und West* (Brünn and Leipzig, 1935), 63–96, made important modifications in Burckhardt's theories, particularly in noting the agon's influence on later Greeks and the void it filled when the phalanx took away the opportunity for individual heroism, "die Entheroisierung des Kriegertums sich ein Gegengewicht zu schaffen suchte, um diesen Kräften des Menschen Betätigungsmöglichkeit zu geben" p. 70): Ehrenberg's discussion has greatly influenced the argument in this chapter.
   The fiercest criticism of Burckhardt falls upon his restriction of the agonistic spirit to Greece. He does, in fact, acknowledge contest elsewhere (pp. 84–85) but maintains that the Greek impulse to excel in a contest with peers under objective judgment is unique. This verdict will not survive the criticism of modern or ancient ethnology (most of which was unavailable to Burckhardt). Huizinga (p. 71 ff.) sharply and properly attacked Burckhardt on these grounds, for the Greeks had no monopoly on serious athletics, but his own insistence that the "agonistic principle" continues into the spectator amusements of Roman civilization, like the arena, shows that his search is for a common denominator of play, not an understanding of the special and distinct features of a given civilization. Huizinga took the potlatch (contests in destroying property) as a sign that the non-Greek world had the same agonistic spirit as the Greeks; I, at least, fail to see the correspondence between a Greek tournament open to all citizens and designed to select one victor and a confrontation of two chieftains burning their goods to impress others.
   Most recently, Ingomar Weiler has devoted a series of publications to refuting the Burckhardtian concept of the agon. (See esp. *Agonales in Wettkämpfen der griechischen Mythologie,* Veröffentlichungen der Universität Innsbruck 19 [Innsbruck, 1969]; *Der Agon im Mythos* [Darmstadt, 1974], 300 ff.; "Aien Aristeuein," *Stadion* 1.2 [1975]: 199–

227; *Sport* [Darmstadt, 1981], 53–57.) A footnote, even a long one, is the wrong place to discuss his carefully documented studies, but it appears that Weiler's zeal to combat a large body of racist scholarship (e.g., E. Mehl, "Leibesübungen als Lebensform des nordischen Menschen," *Volk und Leibesubungen* 7 [1941], which denies not only competition but even sport to non-Aryan races), has prevented him from focusing on the distinctive features of sport in historical Greek times. On the problems of using myth (a principal source for Weiler) as a witness to ancient life, see the review of H. Eisenberger, *Grazer Beiträge* 8 (1979): 277–81. The key question is not the existence of sport, but its nature and ideological context, a point well taken by Erich Segal," To Win or to Die of Shame, A Taxonomy of Values," *Journal of Sport History* 11.2 (1984): 25–31.

50. Physicians' contests: *IK* Ephesos 4.1161–69. Sculptors' contest, *MAMA* 8.519, cf. further J. and L. Robert, *BE* (1972): 414. In this context, note also the Paionios inscription *IvOl* 259, recording his victory in a competition for the commission to make the temple *akroterion*.

51. The carding inscription appears in M. J. Milne, *AJA* 49 (1945): 528–33 (= L. H. Jeffrey, *Local Scripts of Archaic Greece* [Oxford, 1961], 280).

52. *IG* II-III² 6320 (= Peek, *VersInschr.* I. 897).

53. On contests in general, see Burckhardt, *GK*, 89, Ehrenberg (n. 49, above), 76, 78–79. Friedrich Nietzsche had some striking perceptions about the agon in *Homers Wettkampf*: "Every talent must unfold itself in fighting: that is the command of Hellenic popular pedagogy, whereas modern educators dread nothing more than the unleashing of so-called ambition. . . . And just as the youths were educated through contests, their educators were also engaged in contests with each other. The great musical masters, Pindar and Simonides, stood side by side, mistrustful and jealous; in the spirit of contest, the sophist, the advanced teacher of antiquity, meets another sophist" (trans. Kaufmann). Weiler, *Agon*, 300 ff., properly compares the Guinness Book of World Records to the Greek desire to set records. But one still needs to observe the elaborate *structure* of contests and rewards which the Greeks established. Modern society, for example, knows musical contests, but one could not argue that such competitions characterize the contemporary artistic scene as they did in the world of Greek drama and music. See further discussion at the end of this chapter.

54. Pride in having done well in a festival without victory, see, e.g., the inscription of Menander, son of Menander, discussed in chap. 7, and Robert "Épigrammes," 186–87, for several examples and discussion. The report in Porphyrius, *Vit. Pyth.* 15, that Pythagoras when advanced in wisdom advised people to compete in athletics but not to win, "since it is necessary to withstand toils, but to flee the envy that comes from victory," is virtually unique.

55. Marcus Aurelius Asclepiades appears in *IG* 14.1102 (= *IGUR* I.240, = Moretti, *IAG* 79), discussed by Louis Robert, *Hellenica* 7 (Paris, 1949): 106–10. On Tiberius Claudius Marcianus, see J. G. C. Anderson, *JRS* 3 (1913): 287 n. 12.

56. On special titles, see Krause, *GAH*, 549–52; Rudolph Knab, "Die Periodoniken" (diss., Giessen, 1934), 10–15; M. N. Tod, *CQ* 43 (1949): 105–12; Robert, "Épigrammes," 239 n. 2, 275 n. 2; Reinhold Merkelbach, *ZPE* 14 (1974): 94–96, on *paradoxos*. Concerning the recording of details of the contest, see Robert, "Épigrammes," 203–04, 242. Boasts of the pattern "first from x to accomplish y" discussed in Louis Robert, *Hellenica* 7 (Paris, 1949): 120–22; Ebert 31 (pp. 106–07). Tie to avoid loss, Polybius 29.8.9.

57. On ball games, see K. M. T. Chrimes, *Ancient Sparta* (Manchester, 1949, 1952), 131–36; A. M. Woodward, *BSA* 46 (1951): 191–99.

58. Young, *Olympic Myth*, 155–57, on the backgrounds of athletes; Young himself notes the legendary trappings of these stories. "Corporate" chariot races, Phlegon, *FGH* 257 fr. 6 (= Moretti, *Olympionikai*, 39); *P Oxy.* 222 (= Moretti, *Olympionikai*, 207,33).

59. Translated from Wolfgang Decker, "Sportlehrer im alten Ägypten," *KBSW* 1 (1973): 32–33. Decker observes in n. 21, p. 36, that the text implies practice in sport and the handling of weaponry.

60. On Amenophis II's records, see Steffen Wenig and A. D. Touny, *Sport in Ancient Egypt*

(Leipzig and Amsterdam, 1970), 34–38, 90–96; on Thutmose II, see C. E. De Vries, "Attitudes of the Ancient Egyptians toward Physical-Recreative Activities" (diss., University of Chicago, 1960) 201–03; and further, Wolfgang Decker, *Die Physische Leistung Pharaos* (Cologne, 1971), esp. 60 f. On the question of the level of competitiveness in ancient Egypt, see W. Decker, "Das sogenannte Agonale und der altägyptische Sport," in *Festschrift Elmar Edel*, ed. M. Görg and E. Pusch (Bamberg, 1979). Burckhardt, *GK*, 84–85, has exaggerated in maintaining that the hierarchical nature of Egyptian society "das Agonale völlig zurückdrängt": the Old Kingdom tombs of father and son Ptahotep and Akhethotep, which identify one of the wrestlers as Akhethotep and another as the son of the priest of the dead argue for some degree of competitive sport among the upper classes, even though the pharaoh's image as ultimate perfection was in general stifling to individual assertion. (Plato, *Laws* 819b offers an interesting, offhand example of an Egyptian math problem which involved arranging pairs and byes for wrestlers and boxers, but in the absence of corroborating evidence, I hesitate to conclude that this schoolbook exercise reflected native practice of holding tournaments.)

61. Mesopotamian royal hunts, discussed in Vera Olivová, *Sports and Games in the Ancient World* (London, 1984), 32–33.
62. Translation and discussion in J. A. Wilson, *Journal of Egyptian Archaeology* 19 (1931): 211–20; see also Helmut Wilsdorf, *Ringkampf im alten Ägypten* (Würzburg, 1939), and J. Vandier d'Abbadie, "Deux nouveaux ostraca figurés," *Annales du service des antiquités de l'Égypte*, Cairo 40 (1940): 477–78.
63. Sham fights with prearranged outcome among the Hittites, see H. Ehelolf, *SB Berlin* (1925), 267; A. Lesky, *Arch. Rel. Wiss* 24 (1926): 73 ff.
64. Analysis of arena, Keith Hopkins, *Death and Renewal* (Cambridge, 1983), 30.
65. Siegfried Nadel, *The Nuba* (Oxford, 1947), 136–37.
66. Ibid., 232.
67. Ibid.
68. Ibid., 233–34.
69. Concerning the Nuba, see also Leni Riefenstahl, *Die Nuba* (Munich, 1973); Leni Riefenstahl, *Die Nuba von Kau* (Munich, 1977); George Rodger, *Le village des Noubas* (Paris, 1955).
70. Meuli, "Ursprung," discusses the games of the Kirghis Steppe. On Muey Thai, see Hardy Stockman, *Thai Boxing* (Bangkok, 1979); on Pacific cultures, see H. Damm, *Die Zweikampfspiele, Die gymnastischen Spiele der Indonesier und Südseevölker*, pt. 1 (Leipzig, 1922). I thank Prof. A. Khazanov for his help on this section.
71. Cyprian tombstone, *SEG* 6.829.3–4 (= Richard Lattimore, *Themes in Greek and Latin Epitaphs* [Urbana, 1962], 286). On the educational impact of Homer, see Werner Jaeger, *Paideia* I (Oxford, 1939), 35–44; for a humorous but revealing glimpse of popular belief in Homeric authority, cf. Plato's *Ion*.
72. Tyrtaios, fr. 12.15–20 W., cf. also frr. 10,11. On Homeric and heroic tactics, see F. Vian, "La Fonction guerrière dans la mythologie grecque," in *Problèmes de la guerre en Grèce ancienne*, ed. J.-P. Vernant (Paris, 1968), 66–68, which stresses the extreme individualism of legendary heroes, "le guerrier est un individu en marge de la société et qu'il ne s' intègre à elle que d'une façon secondaire et parfois provisoire." G. S. Kirk, "War and the warrior in the homeric poems," in Vernant, 110–12, suggests that the single combats largely represent poetic license, but nevertheless (as Kirk acknowledges) the poem presents them as the center of the battle, and Homer leaves the reader with the impression that the great fighter must have his paroxysm of personal glory; (we should note, however, with P. A. L. Greenhalgh, *Historia* 21 [1972]: 528–37, that even within Homer certain community responsibilities can restrict the heroes' expression of self.) On phalanx tactics, see F. E. Adcock, *The Greek and Macedonian Art of War* (Berkeley, 1957), 4–13.
73. Pindar, *Ol.* 6.9–11: it is perhaps significant that Pindar notes the "hollow ships": this is a Homeric phrase (*e.g.*, *Il.* 1.89) and seems to link the world of battle and sport. For

similarities in the ideology of the citizen-soldier and the athlete see Robert, "Épigrammes," 288–89.

74. Obligation of the general to protect himself, see Garlan (n. 25, above), 146–48. Athens and public funerals, see F. Jacoby, *JHS* 64 (1944): 38, 61–62.

75. Aeschines, *Ktes.* 183–86, discussed in M. Detienne, "La Phalange," in ed. J.-P. Vernant (n. 72, above), 127–28.

76. Miltiades and the Stoa Poikile, see Aeschines, *Ktes.* 186. Thuc. 1.132 on Pausanias of Sparta. On the "will to power" looking for expression among the Greeks, cf. Friedrich Nietzsche, *Twilight of the Idols* ("What I owe to the Greeks," sec. 3).

77. Weiler, "Aien Aristeuein," *Stadion* 1.2 (1975): 226, argued that ostracism and the Ephesian custom of exiling the best citizen are witnesses for a democratic rather than an agonistic element in Greek culture. But Nietzsche seems to have had a better interpretation of this phenomenon in the fragment *Homer's Contest*: "Why should no one be the best? Because then the contest would come to an end and the eternal source of life for the Hellenic state would be endangered. . . . Originally this curious institution is not a safety valve but a means of stimulation: the individual who towers above the rest is eliminated so that the contest of forces may reawaken. . . . That is the core of the Hellenic notion of contest: it abominates the rule of one and fears its dangers: it desires, as a protection against the genius, another genius" (tr. Kaufmann). On Dreros, see Russell Meiggs and David Lewis, *A Selection of Greek Historical Inscriptions* (Oxford, 1969), no. 2: the inscription states that any one who holds the office of *kosmos* more than once every ten years is liable to a punitive fine and loss of status; V. Ehrenberg, *Polis und Imperium* (Stuttgart and Zurich, 1965), 98–104, notes that this was a measure against individuals trying to gain excessive power for their clans.

78. On "first formulae," in political life and athletics, see M. N. Tod, *CQ* 43 (1949): 110. Concerning agon, see the entry s.v. "agon" in B. Snell and H. F. Mette, *Lexicon des frühgriechischen Epos* (Göttingen, 1955–), also G. Glotz, *La solidarité de la famille dans le droit criminel en Grèce* (Paris, 1904), 277 n. 4. T. F. Scanlon, *Arete* I.1 (1983): 151, suggests that there are five uses of *agon* as "contest" in early Greek epic. Of these, two are from post-Homeric hymns, one an interpolation in Hesiod, and two are ambiguous Homeric uses (*Il.* 23.531, *Od.* 8.259) that could mean either "contest" or "place of contest." The most one can say is that Homer has begun to show the later semantic concept of *agon*, but this is not provable. In the absence of a convincing demonstration that *agon* necessarily has a relation to "contest" in early Greek epic, the existence of Indo-European cognates which can refer to "contest," though interesting, do not establish that the desired root meaning has to do with "contest." J. D. Ellsworth's arguments in "Agon: Studies in the Use of a Word" (diss., Berkeley, 1971), 196–216, that the assembly of ships (*agon neon*) in the *Iliad* refers to an "assembly of ships as the object of contest" are unprovable.

79. Victors losing crowns: Kleomedes, Kreugas, Diognetos (see chap. 7). On Zanes, see Paus. 5.21.2–18. Theogenes and Euthymos in Paus. 6.6.5–6. J. D. Beazley, *The Development of Attic Black-Figure*, Sather Classical Lectures 24 (Berkeley, 1951), 98–99. Cf. also M. W. Dickie, "Fair and Foul Play in the Funeral Games in the *Iliad*," *Journal of Sport History* 11.2 (1984): 5–17, and note the pride in victory achieved in a contest strictly judged in the recently published inscription from Miletus (inv. 1238 = Werner Peek, *ZPE* 7 [1971]: 213–16): "Those who conduct the festival strictly according to the rules crowned him. . . ." Cf. further Joachim Ebert, *ZPE* 35 (1979): 293–96, concerning an example of piety and solidarity among the athletes.

80. Comparing the observations of Clifford Geertz's classic study "Deep Play: Notes on the Balinese Cock-fight," in *The Interpretation of Cultures* (London, 1973), 412 ff., with this view of an agonistic Greece, we note that Geertz demonstrates how a culture can use games to instil its values at the very moment they give vent to forbidden passions. (Quite different is the pattern of private violence among the Tausug, who live on the island of Jolo, north of Borneo. "The level of formalized aggression is low. There are no wagers of combat, ordeals, hero combat, chivalry, ritual peaces, pre-arranged battles, formal challenges [T. M. Kiefer, *Man* n.s. 5 (1970): 591]"; instead one finds almost

apocalyptic intratribal violence, with feud-related casualty accounting for 1 percent of the deaths each year among males aged twenty to fifty.) A few Greek authors seem to have noted the cathartic value of sport or at least the good behavior of the athletes. Pindar's Diagoras of Rhodes, the boxer, is a man who "treads a path that hates *hybris*" (*Ol.* 7.90–91), Lucian claims in the *Anacharsis* 30 that in peacetime youth engaged in combat sport are much better than others, since they have no regard for shameful acts and do not turn to *hybris* out of idleness. Philo, *On the Contemplative Life* (*de vit. cont.*), 41–42, very favorably compares athletes to those who overindulge in symposia (but elsewhere he calls the activities of the stadium *hybris* and wickedness [*Agr.* 113]). One may gain other useful insights on Greek competitiveness from A. W. H. Adkins's studies of the tensions between what he calls "competitive excellences" and "cooperative excellences" in Greek society, see *Moral Values and Political Behaviour in Ancient Greece* (London, 1972). Cf. also K. J. Dover, *Greek Popular Morality in the Time of Plato and Aristotle* (Oxford, 1974), 229–34. Veblen, chap. 10, "Modern Survivals of Prowess," *The Theory of the Leisure Class.*

Chapter VII

1. Pausanias 6.14.5 claims that Milo won seven crowns at Delphi, which may well be correct, for as Ebert, 61, notes it is consistent with the report that Milo attempted a seventh Olympic victory; Africanus, however, says he won six Delphic crowns. General accounts of Milo in Modrze, *RE* 15.2,1672–76; Harris, *GAA*, 110–13; Ebert, 61; Augusta Hönle, *Olympia in der Politik der griechischen Staatenwelt* (Bebenhausen, 1972), 83–84; Moretti, *Olympionikai*, 122. Milo's feats of strength, see Paus. 6.14.5–8; Ael. *VH* 2.24. Most writers follow Ch. Scherer, *De Olympionicarum statuis* (Goettingen, 1885) in suggesting that these legends arose from an archaic statue of Milo depicting him holding an apple (part of the Delphic prize, see chap. 1), standing on a round base, with a victory fillet around his head, though the argument does not seem completely convincing. Philostratos, *Vit. Ap.* 4.28 describes such a statue of Milo, but in this case it is likely that the legend inspired the sculpture and, if Milo's victory statue at Olympia really looked like this, it is somewhat puzzling that Pausanias does not give any details of it, since elsewhere he tends to record unusual features of the victors' statues. W. W. Hyde, *Olympic Victor Monuments* (Washington, 1921), 105–07, has a balanced discussion of this question. How the legend got started, however, is relatively speaking inconsequential—it reflects Milo's reputation for tremendous strength, and this must be historical fact. Eating roosters' gizzard stones, Pliny, *NH* 37.144. Death described in Strabo 6.1.12 (263 C.); Paus. 6.14.8 ff. On "significant deaths" see M. R. Lefkowitz, *The Lives of the Greek Poets* (Baltimore, 1981), esp. 3 with n. 6, 23, 37, 85–86, 96–97. "Ironic death" also figures in ancient biography: according to *The Contest of Homer and Hesiod* and Tzetzes, *Life of Hesiod*, the moralistic Hesiod perished at the hands of two brothers whose sister he seduced; an unwitting woman's poison undid mighty Herakles.

2. Marriage of Milo's daughter described in Hdt. 3.137. H. W. Pleket (by correspondence) notes that Demokedes was an extremely accomplished and influential man, whose status would have been particularly high in the scientifically oriented city of Kroton. Milo's role in the battle with Sybaris is told by Diodorus Siculus 12.9.5–6, discussed in T. J. Dunbabin, *The Western Greeks* (Oxford, 1948), 363–66. Political activity of Pythagoreans, Kurt von Fritz, *RE* 24.213 ff. Milo's social status, Hönle (n. 1, above), 83 ff. Young, *Olympic Myth*, 153–54, asserts that there is no evidence that Milo was an aristocrat—he led the Krotonite forces, but nowhere is he called a *strategos*, which would be a clear sign of high office. Young perhaps goes too far in completely condemning the testimony of Diodorus—the chronological muddle Diodorus creates, which would make Milo 105 years old at the time of the battle, stems from putting the whole affair in the wrong Olympiad, a simple mistake which is easily corrected. There are, moreover, enough soldier-athletes in antiquity to make the story credible, see chap. 6.

3. For charges of Milo's stupidity, see Galen, *Protr.* 13 (= 1.34–5 K., 126 M.); Cicero, *de*

Senect. 9.27, 10.33. The gluttony and stupidity have a topical air about them: the prototypical strongman, Herakles, is similarly an ambiguous figure of physical strength and intellectual weakness in many Greek legends. For Pythagorean stories, see among others, Strabo 6.1.12 (263 C.), Diogenes Laertius 8.39, Iamblichos, *Vit. Pyth.* 35.249, 36.267. (On the highly uneven value of Iamblichos as a source, see Erwin Rohde, *RhM* 26 [1871]: 554–76; *RhM* 27 [1872]: 23–61 [= *Kl. Schrift.* (Tübingen and Leipzig, 1901), 102 ff.]). The ultimate source of some Pythagorean stories is probably Timaios, on whose questionable reliability, see Honigmann, *RE* 4A.1, 141. Antiquity had the tendency to bring famous contemporaries into association (concerning which see J. A. Fairweather, *Ancient Society* 5 [1974]: 261–62)—hence the greatest athlete and greatest philosopher of Kroton had to be intimate; the fact that there was an important trainer, Pythagoras of Samos, contemporary with the famous philosopher (who also lived in Samos before coming to Kroton) could easily explain how later Greeks came to see Milo as a student of philosophy, cf. K. Ziegler, *RE* 24.300–01. Walter Burkert, *Weisheit und Wissenschaft*, Erlanger Beiträge zur Sprach- und Kunstwissenschaft 10 (Nürnberg, 1962), 167–68, with n. 153, points out that the tradition of Milo as a Pythagorean must stem from the period before Pythagoreans acquired the reputation of being vegetarians (*i.e.*, before the fourth century B.C.E.). We must note, however, that already in the fifth century B.C.E., meetings of famous men who could hardly have met is a popular tradition, cf. Herodotos I.30 ff. on the encounter of Solon and Kroisos, discussed by W. W. How and J. Wells, *A Commentary on Herodotos*² I (Oxford, 1928), 66–67. For an interesting example of this tendency in our own century, cf. W. M. Calder III and E. Christian Kopff *CP* 72 (1977): 53–54.

4. According to Aristotle fr. 569 R. (= Schol. Pindar, *Ol.* 7), the boys won on the same day as their father. Other sources for the story are Plut. *Pelop.* 34; Cicero, *Tusc.* 1.46,111; Paus. 6.7.3. Pindar *Ol.* 7 praises Diagoras's victory of 464 B.C.E. General studies, Kirchner, *RE* 5.1, 309–10; Harris, *GAA*, 123–24.

5. Lineage, see Paus. 6.7.3 ff. and 4.24.1–3.

6. If *CIG* 1715 (= Moretti *IAG* 23) refers to Dorieus, he won four Delphic crowns. *IvOl* 153 speaks of three victories at Delphi, but it is, of course, possible that this inscription was cut before Dorieus's career was complete.

7. On Dorieus, see Paus. 6.7.4–6; Thuc. 3.8, 8.35, 8.84; Xen. *Hellenica* 1.5.19; *IvOl* 153; Moretti, *IAG* 23; Harris, *GAA*, 124. Further references and discussion in Swoboda, *RE* 5.2, 1560–61.

8. Orthography of Theogenes' name varies in antiquity. Epigraphical sources give Theugenes (so F. Bechtel, *Die historischen Personennamen des Griechischen bis zur Kaiserzeit* [Halle, 1917; repr. Olms]) and Theogenes (which I follow here, purely because it is more familiar to general readers); Pausanias has Theagenes. On the number of crowns, see Paus. 6.11.5; *Syll.*³ 36(= Moretti *IAG* 21, = Ebert 37); Plut. *praec. reip. ger* 15 (= *Mor.* 811e).

9. Theogenes' emulation of Achilleus, Paus. 6.11.5; note that the inscription at Delphi, *Syll.*³ 36, credits him with a victory in the long run at Argos. Paus. 6.6.5–6 tells of the problems with Euthymos. On Diolympos, see *IG* 12.8.278 C 31), discussed by R. Herzog, *Hermes* 50 (1915): 319–20. Theogenes' ambition, Plut. *praec. reip. ger.* 15 (*Mor.* 811d–e); cf. further Ebert, p. 122.

10. Theogenes civil service, Dio Chrys. 31.95. Father's priesthood mentioned in Paus. 6.11.2. Young, *Olympic Myth*, 150–53, has challenged the common assumption that Theogenes was an aristocrat. Young is certainly correct to view with extreme skepticism the fanciful biography which appears in Jean Pouilloux, *Recherches sur l'histoire et les cultes de Thasos* (Paris, 1954), 62–105. I am less inclined to discard the information that Pausanias records about the priesthood of Theogenes' father, however. The fact that Theogenes' father was a priest of the Herakles cult probably gave rise to the legend that Herakles was his father rather than representing, as Young argues, a late rationalization of the myth of divine parentage. Young suggests: "We cannot imagine a wealthy aristocrat spending every week, six months a year, for decades miles from his island home and ancestral estates—merely for the glory of hitting and being hit in an

athletic road show that toured more small towns than large ones," as part of his argument against the assumption that Theogenes was a wellborn aristocrat; this seems to be answered by Plutarch's account of Theogenes' restless, obsessive ambition.

11. Archaeological evidence, *IG* 12.8 Suppl. 425; R. Martin, *BCH* 64–65 (1940–41): 163–200. Healing diseases, Paus. 6.11.9; Luc. *Conc. deor.* 12.

12. Concerning Euthymos, see Paus. 6.6.4–11; Strabo 6.1.5; Ael. *VH* 8.18; Pliny, *NH* 7.47.152 (citing Kallimachos); *IvOl* 144 (= Moretti *IAG* 13), Eustathius, 1409 ad *Od.* 1.185. Cf. further Joseph Fontenrose, "The Hero as Athlete," *CSCA* 1 (1968): 79–82; Francois Böhringer, "Cultes d'athlètes en Grèce classique," *Revue des études anciennes* 81 (1979): 5–18. Euthymos has been the subject of much speculation in modern scholarship. Fontenrose suggested that Euthymos and the ghost are a "doublet," i.e., the identical character appearing in two slightly different forms in a later literary version of the myth (such as the one Pausanias relates). This theory is appealing (though it is only a theory), since the "Euthymos-ghost" figure conforms more readily to the pattern of other athletic heroes who are at some point in their lives pariahs of their societies (note esp. Theogenes, Diognetos, Kleomedes).

13. On Kleomedes, see Paus. 6.9.6–8; Plut. *Rom.* 28; Erwin Rohde, *Psyche* (Freiburg, 1898), 178–80. On the translation of the oracle's *hystatos* ("latest"), cf. Fontenrose (n. 12, above), 74. Diognetos in Photius, *Bibliothec.* 190 151a.

14. There is some discrepancy over the date of his victory, possibly a confusion of Glaukos of Korkyra with Glaukos of Karystos. Cf. Moretti, *Olympionikai*, 134, and the arguments against this traditional view in Fontenrose (n. 12, above), 99–103.

15. Note M. Balme, *Greece and Rome* 34 (1984): 145–46, citing Xen. *Oec.* 4–5 on the good reputation of farming in the Greek world.

16. On Glaukos, see Paus. 6.10.1–3; Philostr. *Gymn.* 20; Krause, *GAH*, 510–11, 645, 648. Concerning his death in Sicily, see Young, *Olympic Myth*, 162.

17. The inscription is slightly damaged at this point; the text reads *g[enous pro]tou kai endoxou*, but this formulaic acknowledgment of noble birth occurs elsewhere, cf. *e.g.*, *CIG* II.2766,2771 (also from Aphrodisias), and the fact that Menander's brother underwrote the cost of his victory statue suggests a family of established wealth.

18. That it was the synod and not the city of Aphrodisias who sponsored the inscriptions and monument is argued quite forcefully by Louis Robert, *Hellenica* 13 (Paris, 1965): 147.

19. The athletic career of Aelius Aurelius Menander is known only from two inscriptions, *CIG* II.2811b (= *MAMA* 8.421, = Liermann XV) and *CIG* 2810b (= Liermann XVI). Menander, son of Menander, is known from *CIG* 2811. The only discussion of these interesting athletes appears in O. Liermann. The names Menander and Zenon appear in several other inscriptions from Aphrodisias (*e.g.*, *CIG* II.2739,2749,2778,2837), but since the names are quite common in Greek it is impossible to tell if they refer to members of the same family.

20. Note also the family of the wrestler A. Aurelius Hermagoras. An inscription referring (it seems) to his father calls him "the offspring of victors in the crown festival," cf. Louis Robert, *Opera Minora Selecta* 2 (Amsterdam, 1969): 1142–44.

21. Asclepiades' inscriptions: *IG* 14.1102 (= *IGR* 1.153 = Moretti, *IAG* 79 = *IGUR* 1.240); *IG* 14.1104 (= *IGUR* 1.239). The terms Asclepiades uses have given rise to much controversy: Moretti, for example, changed his interpretation considerably between *IAG* 79 and *IGUR* 1.240. The translation I offer here can only be provisional, for Asclepiades uses some very rare words indeed in describing himself. G. E. Bean *AJA* 60 (1956): 198–99, suggested that *asynexostos*, which I have translated "never pushed out of the *skamma* [by his opponent]" means "never expelled along with an opponent for stalling." This is appealing on two grounds: first, there was a lot of deliberate stalling in ancient combat sport (see chap. 6), second, the prefix *syn-* most readily means "along with." But there are problems with this view. *Asynexostos* is an honorary title which Asclepiades also uses on an official letter to the senate of Hermopolis (*Corp. Pap. Hermop.* 7.2.3): it would seem very odd for him to refer to himself as "M. Aurelius Asclepiades, the undefeated pankratiast, periodonikes, who was never expelled for

stalling.": on this cf. M. B. Poliakoff, *ZPE* 44 (1981): 78–80. Bean (followed by H. A. Harris, *JHS* 82 [1962]: 19–20) further suggests that *anekkletos* ("unchallenged") and *ekkalesamenos* ("making a challenge") refer instead to appealing against a decision. I find it easier to accept this interpretation than that of *asynexostos* because *anekkletos* does not appear in the *Corp. Pap. Hermop.* letter. Bean is right to note that *prokaleisthai*, not *ekkaleisthai*, is the normal verb for making a challenge; I still follow Louis Robert, *Hellenica* 7 (Paris, 1949): 109 n. 2, here and take this as the boast reflecting a bold fighter, not a barrister. For another example of *ekkaleisthai* apparently referring to challenge, see Joachim Ebert, *Stadion* 7.2 (1981): 206–07. *Epexelthon* is translated here as "assaulted," comparing Paus. 5.21.12–15, which describes how a disqualified boxer grew enraged and illicitly struck the victor, an act which cost him a heavy fine. The "irregular contest" seems to me to be the sort of deliberate exchange of blows, like the gory end of the bout of Kreugas and Damoxenos (Paus. 8.40.5) instead of a bout finished in its normal course. Harris sees a reference to a "rerun" contest following an appeal: given the thinness of the evidence it is impossible to choose with certainty.

22. On Asclepiades' membership in Alexandria's Museum, see *OGIS* 714 (= *IGR* I.154); *SEG* 16.595; and Pleket, "Soziologie," 57, 80 n. 4, for further references and discussion.

23. Evidence for Rufus's victory: *IvOl* 54/55 (= *Syll.*³ 1073, = Reinhold Merkelbach, *ZPE* 15 [1974]: 99–104). Cf. Moretti, *Olympionikai*, 808. Walter Ameling, *Epigr. Anatol.* 6 (1985): 30, has noted the technical force of *sebastognostos* as a title of someone who knows Caesar and has convincingly argued that the plural *Sebastous* shows Rufus's acquaintance with the Caesars was long-standing and deep. Dittenberger's comment on *IvOl* 54 suggests that it was quite extraordinary for tie victors to be so honored, but see Kaibel, 939, for another example.

24. On Claudius Apollonius and Claudius Rufus, see *CIG* 5910 (= *IG* 14.1107, = *IGUR* 1.244); Moretti, *Olympionikai*, 890, 924, 927.

25. On Rufus of Perinthus, see Ameling, n. 23, above.

26. Eusebius, *Praep. ev.* 5.34. Healing powers, see Eitrem, *RE* 8.1, 1135.

27. State gratitude, see Eitrem, *RE* 8.1, 1135; fear of Marathon heroes, Paus. 1.32.3.

28. Hesychius, s.v. *kreittonas*.

29. Size of the heroes, Aristotle, *Pol.* 7.14, 1332b, Eitrem, *RE* 8.1, 1118. Fontenrose (n. 12, above), 89–91, gives further examples of athletes whose legends show features of hero cults. Böhringer (n. 12, above) sees elements of the werewolf figure in the hero-athlete: Euthymos's otherworldly protagonist (or his mirror image) wears a wolf-skin, and the boxer Damarchos of Arcadia, according to a legend contemptuously rejected by Pausanias 6.8.2, was changed into a wolf for nine years. Lycanthropy is not the unifying theme of athlete-heroes, of course, but it does illustrate well the liminal aspects of their status in Greek thought.

30. The fundamental works on this topic are Pleket, "Soziologie" and "Ideology," and Young, *Olympic Myth*; on *Olympic Myth*, see also the reviews of Don Kyle, *Classical Views* 29 n.s.4 (1985): 134–42, and M. B. Poliakoff, *AJP* (forthcoming).

31. *Old Oligarch* 1.13; 2.10. On the Old Oligarch 1.13, cf. E. Kalinka, *Die pseudoxenophontische Athenaion Politeia* (Leipzig and Berlin, 1913). The passage is problematical, in that *epitedeuein* refers to pursuing a profession, not to a pastime, and thus it would be atypical of the aristocracy, whose wealth was based on inheritance, not work. Kalinka concludes that the treatise must refer to the guilds of athletes and musicians. Notwithstanding the weight *epitedeuein* in and of itself carries, the context of this passage suggests that the Old Oligarch is referring to the vicissitudes of aristocrats; what does remain clear is the prejudice that serious sport and music are not for the lower classes. Isokrates in the fourth century similarly described sport as a characteristic of people with leisure (7.45), and this belief appears even in the first/second centuries c.e., when Dio Chrysostom writes (*Or.* 3.124–26).

32. Caricature in Theophrastos, *Char.* 27 ("opsimathia"). A grave monument praising a deceased Greek youth reads, "At birth, the gods granted to me excellence in the ways of the Muses and of the palaestra." (*SEG* 2.424, cf. further Richmond Lattimore, *Themes*

in Greek and Roman Epitaphs [Urbana, 1962], 286). These two traditional groups of skills were in no way incompatible.

33. On Timasitheos, see Hdt. 5.72. Young, *Olympic Myth,* 161, suggests that he might be a better example "of the soldier of fortune than of the conservative, old guard, aristocrat," but the strong possibility remains that he was part of the antidemocratic, aristocratic coterie of families struggling against Kleisthenes' reforms. Moretti *IAG* 15, discusses Kallias and the implications of his ostracism. On Chairon, see Athenaeus 11.509; Paus. 7.27.7; on Atyanas, see Cicero, *pro Flacc.* 13.31; Marcus Aurelius in *Script. Hist. Aug.* 4.9; on Flavillianus, see *IGR* 3.500; Louis Robert, *Études Anatoliennes* (Paris, 1937), 131 n. 5. General discussion in Pleket, *Soziologie,* 68–69.

34. Louis Robert, *Rev. Phil.* 41 (1967): 7 ff., 28 ff.

35. Aristotle, *Rhet.* 1365a, 1367b, on which see Don Kyle (n. 30, above), 134–42. Delian Apollonia, (*IG* 11.2, 203, 205, discussed in Th. Klee, *Zur Geschichte der gymnischen Agone an Griechischen Festen* [Leipzig, 1918]). Dream book of Artemidorus 2.20; Zenon in *P Cair. Zen.* 1.59060 (= *Sel. Pap.* 1.88); *P Lond.* 1941; discussion in Poliakoff, *Studies,* 133–34. Slaves in competition, see Gardiner, *AAW* 50, *CR* 43 (1929): 210–12.

36. On Herminos's certificate, see *P Lond.* 1178, esp. lines 84 ff. Herminos's illiteracy, cf. *P Lond.* 1158.6; his older brother's untutored and crudely written signature is in *P Lond.* 941, 946. See further Hans Gerstinger, "Zum Faustkämpferdiplom des Boxers Herminos alias Moros aus Hermopolis Magna aus dem Jahre 194 n. Chr.," *Anzeiger der Österreichischen Akademie der Wissenschaften* (1954), 57–61.

37. Dio Chrys. 66.11 tells how an athlete received the huge sum of five talents "as hire," i.e., merely for his appearance at a festival—a victory would of course bring even more profit.

38. Kallikrates, *MAMA* 8.417 (= Louis Robert, *Hellenica* 13 [Paris, 1965], 134–47). Alfidius, G. E. Bean, *Belleten* 29 (1965): 588–93 n. 2 (= Reinhold Merkelbach, *ZPE* 18 [1975]: 146–48). Aurelius Achilles, see Louis Robert, *Opera Minora Selecta* 1 (Amsterdam, 1969), 614–28.

Chapter VIII

1. Genesis 32 : 25–29 in the new Jewish Publication Society translation. The Hebrew verb *wayeavek* ("wrestle") is unique in the Hebrew Bible, but the context and etymology as well as the translation *palaio* in the Septuagint make its meaning clear. *Wayeavek* is formed from the same stem as a biblical noun meaning "dust," and Fr. Brown, S. R. Driver, C. A. Briggs, *A Hebrew and English Lexicon of the Old Testament* (Oxford, 1953), s.v. *'bq,* note the parallel derivation in Greek of *konio* ("get dusty," in wrestling) from *konis* ("dust"). The etymology connecting the noun *'bq* (= "dust") with the verb *'bq* (= "wrestle") was already extant in Talmudic times, see Ḥullin 91a. Cf. also the version of the story of Jacob's match in Hosea 12 : 5.

2. For examples from cultures world wide, see Weiler, *Agon* 275–84. Christopher Ulf in Weiler, *Sport,* 46–47, records the interesting fact that in Hawaii native leaders led troops of wrestlers against other groups.

3. For a discussion of the folk traditions behind Jacob's encounter, see C. Westerman, *Genesis,* Biblischer Kommentar 1.2 (1977), on these verses.

4. Many scholars have attempted to identify Near Eastern depictions of wrestling with this passage from the Gilgamesh epic, see, *e.g.,* Cyrus Gordon, *Iraq* 6 (1939): 4; A. L. Oppenheim, *Orientalia* 17 (1948): 29–30. This is, however, pure guesswork, as G. Furlani, "Das Gilgamesh Epos," *Das Gilgamesh Epos,* Wege der Forschung 215 (Darmstadt, 1977), 417 ff. has well argued. J. Tigay, *The Evolution of the Gilgamesh Epic* (Philadelphia, 1982), 181–89, argues that sexual oppression of the men of Uruk was not one of Gilgamesh's offenses; Tigay suggests that he may have continually bested the youth of the city in athletic contests, then claimed as the prize the *ius primae noctis.*

5. Alexander Heidel, *The Gilgamesh Epic and Old Testament Parallels* (Chicago, 1946), 32 with n. 57, argues that Gilgamesh won, as does Oppenheim (n. 4, above). Furlani (n. 4), 379, says Enkidu.

6. Gratianne Offner, "Jeux corporels en Sumer," *Revue d'Assyriologie* 56 (1962): 31–38, argues that when Gilgamesh bends over with his foot on the ground it signals a formal winning tactic: "La tactique de l'athlète expérimenté est d'avoir assez de souplesse et de maîtrise de soi pour garder les pieds sur le sol quels que soient l'attaque et le déplacement du centre de gravité du corps."

7. Ibn Ishaq, *Sirat Rasul Allah*, 258, trans. A. Guillaume (Oxford, 1955), 178–79, noted and discussed in J. M. Sasson, *Orientalia* 43 (1974): 404.

8. Cf. B.127 ff. and C.128 ff. in G. R. Castellino, *Two Shulgi Hymns*, Studi Semitici 42 (1972): 40–43, 257–59.

9. On the wrestling imagery of Aeschylus, *Oresteia*, see M. B. Poliakoff, "The Third Fall in the *Oresteia*," *AJP* 101 (1980): 251–59. On Zeus and Kronos, see further, Weiler, *Agon*, 173–74. The myth of Zeus wrestling Kronos and Apollo's role as a boxer are ancient, appearing in Aeschylus and Homer, respectively. Much later texts play fancifully with the theme of gods and heroes as athletes, e.g., Nonn. 10.375–77 has Zeus lightheartedly wrestling with and yielding to Herakles. Eventually, the two great athletic heroes Herakles and Theseus must wrestle each other. Photius *Bibl*. 190. 151a, a Byzantine work, tells how they wrestled to a draw, with Theseus gaining the sobriquet "another Herakles."

10. See Paus. 1.39.3; Apollod. ep. 1.3; Schol. Pl. *Laws* 796a; Weiler, *Agon*, 153–56. Weiler, *Agon*, 154, argues that the stories as we have them reflect an early version in which Kerkyon is no ogre but a local hero of Eleusis, renowned for his wrestling skill, removed from his place in mythology when Theseus became the great national hero of Athens and the region surrounding it.

11. On Antaios, see Pindar, *Isthm*. 4.56–61; Pl. *Theaet*. 169b; Philostr. Im. 2.21; Lucan 4.589–660, further Weiler, *Agon*, 129–39. For portrayals of the Antaios legend as pankration, see *BM* B196 (*LIMC* I.3); *BM* B 322 (*LIMC* I.6); Naples 2519 (*LIMC* I.9); Paris, Mus. Rodin 954 (*LIMC* I.11); Munich 1710 (*LIMC* I.14); Varsovie 142.330 (*LIMC* I.27); Vienna 3692 (*LIMC* I.28); F. Brommer, *Herakles II* (Darmstadt, 1984), pl. 18 (ex coll.). Pl. *Lg* 7.796a credits Antaios with having invented certain wrestling tricks (which Plato finds unacceptable for the wrestling of his ideal state because they are the tactics of "worthless brawling"); of all literary sources, only Diod. 4.17.4 explicitly writes that the giant had wrestling skill.

12. The antiquity of the notion that Antaios could perish only when lifted off the earth is a much disputed question. W. H. Roscher, *Ausführliches Lexicon der griechischen und römischen Mythologie* (Leipzig, 1884–86), I.362, argued that since Gaia (Earth) appears on classical vase paintings, the legend must antedate the Hellenistic Age. But Olmos and Balmaseda in *LIMC* point out that the identification of the female figure with Gaia and the male with Poseidon is most uncertain. A papyrus fragment, probably part of a Hellenistic tragedy, seems to portray Antaios getting renewed power and protection (*P Oxy*. 27.2454, lines 11–13, cf. also H. Lloyd-Jones, *Gnomon* 35 [1963]: 438); this is the earliest literary witness, but the damaged text does not tell how Antaios got this renewed power. Professor Merkelbach has suggested (by letter) that the myth of Antaios's vulnerability when lifted from the earth derives from the wrestler's observation of the power and advantage that the waistlock held (see p. 40). A wrestler is in great danger of losing when lifted from the ground; it would be fitting for the son of Earth to perish off the ground. Cf. further F. Brommer, *Herakles II* (Darmstadt, 1984), 38–41. A good, balanced discussion appears in Weiler, *Agon*, 129–39.

13. Eryx in Apollod. 2.5.10; Paus. 3.16.4; Diod. 4.23.2; Vergil, *Aen*. 5.410–14; further Weiler, *Agon*, 146–49. Menoites, Apollod. 2.5.12.

14. On Ptolemaic use of Greek and Egyptian themes in propaganda, see Ludwig Koenen in *Egypt and the Hellenistic World*, ed. Sanders, Van T. Dack, Verbeke, Studia Hellenistica 27 (Leiden, 1983), 170–71. Theokritos *Herakliskos* (XXIV) tells of young Herakles, on which see Ludwig Koenen, "Eine agonistische Inschrift aus Agypten und frühptolemäische Königsfeste," *Beiträge zur Klassischen Philologie* 56 (1977). On the bronzes, cf. H. Kyrieleis, *Antike Plastik* 12 (Berlin, 1973): 133–47; Kyrieleis in his n. 11, p. 136, takes note of G. Grimm's arguments for the early dating to Ptolemy II. Some of the distinctive features Kyrieleis notes are the lotus leaves in the victor's hair, the Egyptian braiding,

in some examples a crown. Of the eight existing copies, five were found in Egypt; it seems almost certain that they are miniature copies of a massive statue which stood in Hellenistic times. See also Ludwig Koenen and D. B. Thompson, *BASP* 21.1–4 (1984): 115–18. Kallimachos, *Hymn IV* (Delos), 185–87, "[Apollo claims some Gallic shields as his trophies], The others will be hung as a multitude of trophies for the hardworking king [Ptolemy], after they have watched the soldiers who once bore them gasp out their lives in the flames." On this poem, see Ludwig Koenen, *Chronique d'Égypte* 34 (1959): 110–11.

15. Theophanes Continuatus 5.12 (229–30 Bekker). Other accounts of Basil as an athlete are John Scylitzes 123.3–124.31 (Thurn), Genesius 4.26 and 4.39–40. On Basil I, and the Byzantine histories about him, see Poliakoff, *Studies*, 149–60.

16. Pythagoras on undesirability of victory in Porphyr. *Vit. Pyth.* 15.

17. Aristotle, *Nichomachean Ethics* III. 12, 1117b 2. On the agon in Stoic and Cynic thought, cf. V. Pfitzner, *Paul and the Agon Motif* (Leiden, 1967), 23–35.

18. See the excellent discussion by Reinhold Merkelbach, "Herakles und der Pankratiast," *ZPE* 6 (1970): 47–49.

19. Isokrates 4.1 (*Panegyrikos*).

20. On Diogenes, see Dio Chrysostom, *Orations* 8 and 9; 8.12–13 (quoted).

21. Epiktetos 3.22.58; Epiktetos 1.18.20.

22. Note what Philo says in *de migr.* 89 f. on the absolute necessity of rigorous adherence to the Laws of Moses; this is admirably discussed in E. R. Goodenough, *An Introduction to Philo Judaeus* (Oxford, 1962), 75–90.

23. See Harris, *Greek Athletics and the Jews* (Cardiff, 1976), 69–70, for further references and discussion.

24. One text of Jewish origin, *The Testament of Job*, presents Job as a wrestler, though some scholarly opinion holds that in its present form it is the work of Christian reediting, cf. Montague Rhodes James, *Apocrypha Anecdota*, Texts and Studies 5.1 (Cambridge, 1897). Outside of this text, all mention of Job as a wrestler does come from clearly Christian sources. Chrysostom: Epist. 6 (*PG* 52.599.35ff.).

25. Clement, *Paid* 3.49–51 (*Die griechischen christlichen Schriftsteller der ersten drei Jahrhunderte* 12.1, 264–66); it must be observed, however, that he relies heavily on Plato, *Laws* 796a, in this passage. Apostolic Constitution 8.29–30 (*PG* 1.1131–32). Novatian, *On the Spectacles* 2 (*PL* 4.811–12). An excellent study of church attitudes toward sport is Alois Koch, "Leibesübungen im Frühchristentum und in der beginnenden Völkwanderungszeit," *Geschichte der Leibesübungen* 2 ed. H. Überhorst (Berlin–Munich–Frankfurt, 1978), 312–40.

26. Tertullian, *On the Public Shows* 18.

27. Commentary on Psalm 1 : 1 in Tosleftah *Avodah Zarah* 2:5–6, cf. also Babylonian Talmud *Avodah Zarah* 18b, which adds that even if there is no idolatry in the stadia, camps, and mimes, one must avoid them since they are still "the seat of the scornful." The definitive discussion of Mishna *Shabbat* 22 : 6 is in Saul Lieberman, *Greek in Jewish Palestine* (New York, 1942), 92–97; the translation of the passage is also Lieberman's. Ms. variants between *kordima* and *peeloma* (here translated as "wrestling area") make clear that there was a Palestinian version of the text with the latter form.

28. Ephebic club, see *Corpus Inscriptionum Judaicarum* 755. On Alexandria, see *P Lond.* 1912 (= V. Tcherikover and A. Fuks, *Corpus Papyrorum Judaicarum* [Cambridge, 1960], no. 153; note, however, the dissenting interpretation of A. Kasher, *American Journal of Ancient History* 1/3 (1976): 148–61. Further texts and discussion in R. R. Chambers, "Greek Athletics and the Jews" (diss., Miami University, 1980), 150–54. On athletics in the Diaspora, see L. H. Feldman, *Jewish Social Studies* 22 (1960): 224–28.

29. Philo as eyewitness, *Every Good Man is Free (Quod. Prob.)* 26; *Providence* 58; education of children, *Special Laws* 2.229–30.

Appendix

1. On the thirst of the dead for blood, see J. G. Frazer, *Golden Bough*, pt. 3, *The Dying God* (London, 1911), 97. Eitrem, *RE* 8.1 1123. See also Erwin Rohde, *Psyche* (London,

1925), 36–38; Roscher I.2, 2505; Walter Burkert, *Greek Religion* (Oxford, 1985), 59–60, 194. Rohde suggests that some of the graves of the Mycenaean Greeks had funnel-shaped openings so that the pious might pour offerings to the deceased; on the thirsty dead, see Emily Vermeule, *Aspects of Death in Early Greek Art and Poetry* (Berkeley, 1979), 57–58. On the blood offerings to Patroklos, see the note of Walter Leaf, *The Iliad*[2] II (London, 1902), 473, 619–20 (*kotuleruton ereen haima*).

2. M. Andronikos, *Totenkult*, Archaeologica Homerica IIIw (Göttingen, 1968), 82–84, collects and discusses evidence for human sacrifices in Greek burials from the Mycenaean to the Geometric periods, c.1700–800 B.C.E. Many of the skeletons initially reported as sacrificial victims prove upon closer examination to be quite ambiguous evidence, but a few cases seem fairly convincing. A royal grave at Dendra in Cyprus, c. 1000 B.C.E. yielded human bones mixed with those of animals, suggesting a practice of simultaneous animal and human sacrifice not unlike that of Achilleus. Some later Cypriot graves contain skeletons which appear to have been buried with hands and feet bound; see further, Vassos Karageorghis, *BCH* 87 (1963): 373 ff. G. E. Mylonas, *AJA* 52 (1948): 60, argues that Achilleus's sacrifice is purely an act of vengeance without cultic implications: I still feel persuaded by Rohde (n. 1, above), 13–14, that Achilleus's emphasis that the sacrifice is "for you" (Patroklos) in 23.20 ff. and 23.180 ff. compels the reader to see cult at work here. See also Walter Burkert (n. 1, above), 60.

3. Albert Henrich in his important article "Human Sacrifice in Greek Religion: Three Case Studies," *Le Sacrifice dans l'antiquité*, Entretiens sur l'antiquité classique 27 (Geneva, 1981), 195–242, argues that "the Greeks clearly preferred the fiction of human sacrifice to its reality," and that most mythical and legendary reports are narrative personifications of rituals involving animal sacrifice: Greeks had a strong tendency to identify human sacrifice with either their mythical and distant past or, more often, with barbarous nations.

4. Alexander, in Iustin. 11.2.1; Philopoimen in Plut. *Philop.* 21. Death of Hephaistion, Plut. *Alex.* 72. See Ludolf Malten, "Leichenspiel und Totenkult," *Mitteilungen des Deutschen Archaeolog. Instituts Röm. Abt.* 38/39 (1923–24): 300–40.

5. See G. Ville, *La Gladiature en occident des origines à la mort de Domitien*, Bibliothèque des écoles françaises d'Athènes et de Rome 245 (Paris, 1982), 9–14, on the different motives for human sacrifice.

6. *Maschalismos*, the murderer's practice of dismembering and binding his victim, with the intention, it seems, of hindering the ghost from taking its revenge, is a vivid glimpse into Greek superstitions about the angry dead; see Rohde (n. 1, above), 582–86.

7. Meuli, *Agon*, esp. 30–34, 56–57. Aborigine practice, Lucien Lévy-Bruhl, *Les fonctions mentales dans les sociétés inférieures*[5] (Paris, 1922), 326.

8. On the Mycenaean *larnax*, see the excellent discussion of Wolfgang Decker, *Stadion* 8/9 (1982–83): 1–24. Games for Oedipus, *Il.* 23.679–80, for Achilleus, *Od.* 24.85–97, for Amarynkeus, *Il.* 23.630–44; others, cf. *Il.* 22.162–64.

9. Cf. Malten (n. 4, above), 308 ff.; L. E. Roller, "Funeral Games in Greek Literature, Art, and Life" (diss., Univ. of Pennsylvania, 1977). On demanding dead, see Frazer (n. 1, above), 93–103, noting particularly the accounts in Hdt. 1.167 (Agylla), and Plut. *de sera numine* 17 (*Mor.* 560 b–f).

10. Cf. G. S. Kirk, *The Songs of Homer* (Cambridge, 1962), 124–25, on Homer's misconceptions concerning the military use of the chariot, and 190 ff. on confusion over the types of shields and spears used in battle; further, P. .A. L. Greenhalgh, *Historia* 22 (1972): 532–33. New discoveries in West Semitic epigraphy suggest the Greeks knew writing much earlier than the mid eighth century, when our earliest examples occur, cf. Jonah Naveh, *The Early History of the Alphabet* (Jerusalem and Leiden, 1982), 175–86: there is every reason for Mycenaean relics to find their way into Homer.

11. Meuli, *Agon*, 60, notes with candor that he cannot explain the sense of events like discus, chariot race, and archery contest but maintains that the analogies with other peoples' practices make the origin of sport undoubtedly funeral practice. In "Ursprung," 203, however, he suggests that when the ritual duel and other rites diminished grief, certain cultures, prompted by their *Lust am Wettkampf*, instituted annual

games in honor of the deceased which were not tied to combat. I have argued, of course, that *Lust am Wettkampf* deserves a primary, not secondary, role in the origin of sporting festivals.

12. The Tanagra *larnax*, as Decker (n. 8, above) points out, shows a particularly brutal combat, since the participants wear no armor. This would, perhaps, suggest that funeral games indeed had a primitive and savage origin, and we can observe a lessening of this cruelty between the thirteenth century, when the *larnax* was made, and the armed combat which Homer describes. It is problematic, however, that the *solos* event that Homer describes also finds archaeological support in the thirteenth century; as Decker persuasively argues, the *solos* event, in which the "discus" and the prize are the same items, is paralleled by the discus-shaped lumps of metal recently recovered from a thirteenth-century B.C.E. ship's cargo found off the Turkish coast. The discus/ *solos* event seems to be as old as the bloody human combat.

13. On the authenticity of the Olympic register, see J. P. Mahaffy, *JHS* 2 (1881): 164–78. Alfred Körte, *Hermes* 39 (1904): 224–43. Rewards at the Panatheneia *IG* II.2² 2311. Plutarch's mention of lethal Olympic sport is in *Quaest. Conv.* 5.2 (= *Mor.* 675c–d). Meuli, *Agon*, 45 n.1, puts faith in it.

14. On decorum in the games, see M. W. Dickie, "Fair and Foul Play in the Funeral Games in the *Iliad*," *JSH* 11.2 (1984): 8–17; C. W. Macleod, *Homer, Iliad 24* (Cambridge, 1982), 28–31. Ethnographic data in Frazer (n. 1, above), 97; Meuli, *Agon*, 51–57. (Meuli, *Agon*, 52) argues that Plato, *Laws* 830b ff., recommends more dangerous gloves, the *sphairai*. The *sphairai*, however, as Plato makes clear, are *less dangerous* than other thongs, cf. the discussion of these gloves in chap. 5.

15. Textual problems in *Il.* 23.798–810, see Leaf (n. 1, above), 529. On the southern Italian and Roman evidence, see Malten (n. 4, above), 317–31. G. Ville (n. 5, above) is particularly emphatic in calling the explanation found in Servius an "aition, invention d'un érudit hellénistique," noting the tenuous case for human sacrifice in Italian funeral ritual.

16. Malten argues that the presence of a flute player on the British Museum sarcophagus (Malten [n. 4, above], 313–14) establishes the scene as an agon. But the flute player accompanies the hoplites on the Chigi amphora, and there are numerous attestations of its military applications, *e.g.*, Thuc. 5.70; Plut. *Spartan Sayings* (*Mor.* 238b); see further, J. K. Anderson, *Military Theory and Practice in the Age of Xenophon* (Berkeley, 1970), 77–82.

17. Kassander in Diyllos, quoted by Athenaeus 155A (= Jacoby, *FGrHist* 73 F 1); Herodotos 5.8 on Thracians; Xen. *Hellenica* 3.2.5.

18. Quarrel between Attica and Boeotia, Harpokration, s.v. *apatouria* with Dindorff's note (Oxford, 1853), ad loc. for further references (= Ephoros *FrGH* no. 70, fr. 22); Thryeia, Hdt. 1.82; Sigeion, Suda, s.v. Pittakos; Diogenes Laertius 1.74; Plut. *de malign. Herod.* 15 (*Mor.* 858a–b).

19. Hdt. 6.92 and 9.75; Paus. 1.29.5 on Nemean victory. Strabo, 8.3.33 (357C), cited and discussed in G. Glotz, *La solidarité de la famille dans le droit criminel en Grèce* (Paris, 1904), 271–87, which has an extensive discussion on the role of the duel in Greek life. Glotz suggests that dueling was the origin of Greek sport, and the funeral games reflect contests of various degrees of danger and severity for the possessions and power of the deceased. "Le concours gymnique est une forme particulière du duel conventionel, à la fois simplification de la guerre et antecédent du procès criminel" (p. 282). This theory, more than Meuli's, accounts for the great variety of athletic contests attested so early in our records and also gives due weight to the great number of duels which had nothing to do with funerals. But given the fact that both in *Il.* 2.774 ff. and *Od.* 8.110–30 we find people doing sport, just for the sake of sport, I still suggest that sport "originated" in Greece largely for its own sake. On single combat, see further, J. J. Gluck, *Acta Classica* 7 (1964): 25–31.

20. Funeral games as a survival, Meuli, "Ursprung," 190; original form of contest a lethal duel, Meuli, "Ursprung," 192: "Kern dieser Kampfspiele war das, was allen gemeinsam ist, also der Zweikampf, offenbar der blutige, ja wohl ursprünglich der mit dem

Tod des einem Fechters endigende Zweikampf." For contrast M. Bayliss, "The Cult of Dead Kin in Assyria and Babylonia," *Iraq* 35 (1973): 115–25: Mesopotamian dead were very demanding and very unquiet when their needs were not met; moreover the royal cults of the dead might stretch back for many generations. But for all of this, Bayliss, at least, offers no indication that combat or games were part of this cult.

21. Achilleus attaches great importance to *kleos* in *Il.* 9.413–20, valuing it more than life; in *Il.* 7.89–91, Hektor envisions the funeral monument of the Greek who might fall in a duel against him as a source of eternal *kleos*. For a full discussion with bibliography, see Jasper Griffin, *Homer on Life and Death* (Oxford, 1980), 95–102. On fame as a motive for private financing of games and rites, cf. Roller (note 9, above), 23, and B. Laum, *Stiftungen in der griechischen und römischen Antike* (Leipzig, 1914), 49–50. Nonfunerary games in Homer: *Od.* 8.110–30, *Il.* 4.388–90, 11.698–702, cf. Roller (n. 9, above), 48. Apollo's festival, in *Homeric Hymn to Apollo*, 149–50. Weiler, *Sport*, 84–85, offers a balanced discussion of the possible motives for games in Homer.

BIBLIOGRAPHY

Altenmüller, Hartwig. "Letopolis und der Bericht des Herodot über Papremis." *Jaarbericht van het Vooraziatisch-Egyptisch Genootschap "Ex Oriente Lux"* 18 (1964): 271–79.

Ameling, Walter. *Epigraphica Anatolica* 6 (1985): 27–33.

Andronikos, M. *Totenkult.* Archaeologica Homerica III W. Göttingen, 1968.

Burckhardt, Jacob. *Griechische Kulturgeschichte* 4. 1898–1902; new ed. Darmstadt, 1977.

Chambers, R. R. "Greek Athletics and the Jews 165 B.C.–A.D. 70." Diss., Miami University, 1980.

Crowther, N. B. *Studies in Greek Athletics.* Special issue of *Classical World* 78.5 and 79.2 (May–June 1985 and November–December 1985).

Damm, H. *Die Zweikampfspiele, Die gymnastischen Spiele der Indonesier und Südseevölker,* pt. 1. Leipzig, 1922.

Decker, Wolfgang. *Annotierte Bibliographie zum Sport im alten Ägypten.* St. Augustin, 1978. Supplements in *Stadion* 5 (1979): 161–92 and *Stadion* 7 (1981): 153–72.

———. "Das sogennante Agonale und der altägyptische Sport." In *Festschrift Elmar Edel,* ed. M. Görg and E. Pusch, 90–104. Bamberg, 1979.

———. "Neue Aspekte zur Erforschung der altägyptischen Sportgeschichte." *KBSW* 4 (1975): 41–59.

———. "Die mykenische Herkunft des griechischen Totenagons." *Stadion* 8/9 (1982–83): 1–24.

Delorme, J. *Gymnasion.* Bibliothèque des écoles françaises d'Athènes et de Rome 187. Paris, 1960.

Dickie, M. W. "Fair and Foul Play in the Funeral Games in the *Iliad.*" *Journal of Sport History* 11.2 (1984): 8–17.

Ebert, Joachim. *Griechische Epigramme auf Sieger an gymnischen und hippischen Agonen.* Abhandlungen der Sächsischen Akademie der Wissenschaften zu Leipzig 63.2. Berlin, 1972.

Ehrenberg, Victor. *Ost und West.* Brünn and Leipzig, 1935.

Finley, M. I., and H. W. Pleket. *The Olympic Games, The First 1000 Years.* New York, 1976.

Gardiner, E. N. *Greek Athletic Sports and Festivals.* London, 1910.

———. *Athletics of the Ancient World.* Oxford, 1930.

———. "The Pankration and Wrestling." *Journal of Hellenic Studies* 26 (1906): 4–22.

———. "Wrestling." *Journal of Hellenic Studies* 25 (1905): 14–31, 263–93.

Geertz, Clifford. "Deep Play: Notes on the Balinese Cockfight." In *The Interpretation of Cultures*. 412 ff. London, 1975.

Ginouvès, René. *Balaneutike, Recherches sur le bain dans l'antiquité Grecque*. Bibliothèque des écoles françaises d'Athènes et de Rome 200. Paris, 1962.

Harris, H. A. *Greek Athletes and Athletics*. London, 1966.

———. *Greek Athletics and the Jews*. Cardiff, 1976.

———. *Sport in Greece and Rome*. London, 1972.

Hopkins, Keith. *Death and Renewal*. Cambridge, 1983.

Huizinga, Johan. *Homo Ludens*. English ed. Boston, 1950.

Jüthner, Julius. *Antike Turngeräthe*. Abhandlungen des archaeologisch-epigraphischen Seminars der Universität Wien. Vienna, 1896.

———. *Philostratos über Gymnastik*. Leipzig, 1909.

Jüthner, Julius, and Erwin Mehl. *RE* Suppl. 9, 1314–52.

Jüthner, Julius, and F. Brein. *Die athletischen Leibesübungen der Griechen*. Österreichische Akademie der Wissenschaften, philosophisch-historische Klasse, Sitzungsberichte 249, I. Vienna, 1965.

Knab, Rudolph. "Die Periodoniken." Diss, Giessen, 1934.

Koch, Alois. *Die Leibesübungen im Urteil der antiken und frühchristlichen Anthropologie*. Schorndorf / Stuttgart, 1965.

———. "Leibesübungen im Frühchristentum und in der beginnenden Völkswanderungszeit." In *Geschichte der Leibesübungen*, vol. 2, ed. H. Überhorst, 312–40. Berlin–Frankfurt–Munich, 1978.

Krause, J. H. *Gymnastik und Agonistik der Hellenen*. Halle, 1841.

———. *Olympia*. Vienna, 1838.

Kyle, Don. "Directions in Ancient Sport History." *Journal of Sport History* 10.1 (1983): 7–34.

Kyrieleis, Helmut. "Kathaper Hermes kai Horos." *Antike Plastik* 12 (1973): 133–47.

Lieberman, Saul. *Greek in Jewish Palestine*. New York, 1942.

Liermann, Otto. *Analecta epigraphica et agonistica*. Dissertationes Philologicae Halensis. Halle, 1889.

Malten, Ludolph. "Leichenspiele und Totenkult." *Mitteilungen des Deutschen Archaeologischen Instituts, Römische Abteilung* 38/39 (1923–24): 300–40.

Marrou, H. I. *Histoire de l'éducation dans l'antiquité*⁶. Paris, 1965.

Merkelbach, Reinhold. "Der griechische Wortschatz und die Christen." *Zeitschrift für Papyrologie und Epigraphik* 18 (1975): 101–48.

———. "Herakles und der Pankratiast." *Zeitschrift für Papyrologie und Epigraphik* 6 (1970): 47–49.

———. "Die unentschiedene Kampf des Pankratiasten T. Claudius Rufus in Olympia." *Zeitschrift für Papyrologie und Epigraphik* 15 (1974): 99–104.

Meuli, Karl. *Der griechische Agon*. Cologne, 1968.

———. "Der Ursprung der Olympischen Spiele." *Die Antike* 17 (1941): 189–208.

Moretti, Luigi. *Iscrizioni agonistiche greche*. Rome, 1953.

———. *Olympionikai, i vincitori negli antichi agoni olimpici*. Atti della Accademia Nazionale dei Lincei 8. Rome, 1959.

Nadel, Siegfried. *The Nuba*. Oxford, 1947.

Oberhuber, Karl. *Die Kultur des alten Orients*. Handbuch der Kulturgeschichte II. Frankfurt, 1972.

Offner, Gratianne. "Jeux corporels en Sumer." *Revue d'Assyriologie* 56 (1962): 31–38.

❦ Olivová, Vera. *Sports and Games in the Ancient World*. London, 1984.

Pfitzner, V. C. *Paul and the Agon Motif*. Leiden, 1967.

Pleket, H. W. "Zur Soziologie des antiken Sports." *Medelingen van het Nederlands Instituut te Rome* 36 (1974): 57–87.

———. "Games, Prizes, Athletes, and Ideology." *Stadion* 1 (1976): 49–89.

Poliakoff, M. B. *Studies in the Terminology of the Greek Combat Sports*. Second ed. Beiträge zur Klassischen Philologie 146. Meisenheim, 1986.

———. "Jacob, Job, and Other Wrestlers: Reception of Greek Athletics by Jews and Christians in Antiquity." *Journal of Sport History* 11.2 (1984): 48–65.

Robert, Louis. "Les épigrammes satiriques de Lucillius sur les athlètes, parodie et réalités." *L'épigramme grecque*. Entretiens sur l'antiquité classique. Geneva, 1968.

Roller, L. E. "Funeral Games in Greek Literature, Art, and Life." Diss., U. Penn 1977.

———. "Funeral Games for Historical Persons." *Stadion* 7 (1981): 1–17.

Sasson, J. M. "Reflections on an Unusual Practice Reported in ARM X:4." *Orientalia* 43 (1974): 404–11.

Scanlon, T. F. *Greek and Roman Athletics, A Bibliography*. Chicago, 1984.

———. "Greek Boxing Gloves: Terminology and Evolution." *Stadion* 8/9 (1982–83): 31–45.

Schröder, Bruno. *Der Sport im Altertum*. Berlin, 1927.

Segal, Erich. "To Win or to Die of Shame, A Taxonomy of Values." *Journal of Sport History* 11.2 (1984): 25–31.

Sjöberg, Åke. "Trials of Strength, Athletics in Mesopotamia." *Expedition*, The University of Pennsylvania Magazine of Archaeology 27.2 (1985): 7–9.

Stecher, Anton. *Grabgedichte auf Krieger und Athleten*. Commentationes Aenipontanae 27. Innsbruck, 1981.

Touny, A. D., and S. Wenig. *Sport in Ancient Egypt*. Leipzig, Amsterdam, 1970.

Vandier, Jacques. *Manuel d'archéologie égyptienne* IV. Paris, 1968.

Vandier d'Abbadie, J. "Deux nouveaux ostraca figurés." *Annales du Service des Antiquités de l'Égypte, Cairo*, 40 (1940): 467–88.

Ville, G. *La Gladiature en occident des origines à la mort de Domitien*. Bibliothèque des écoles françaises d'Athènes et de Rome 245. Paris, 1981.

Weiler, Ingomar. "Aien Aristeuein." *Stadion* 1.2 (1975): 199–227.

———. *Der Agon im Mythos*. Darmstadt, 1974.

———. *Der Sport bei den Völkern der Alten Welt*. Darmstadt, 1981.

Wilsdorf, Helmut. *Ringkampf im alten Ägypten*. Würzburg, 1939.

Wilson, J. A. "Ceremonial Games of the New Kingdom." *Journal of Egyptian Archaeology* 19 (1931): 211–20.

Young, David C. *The Olympic Myth of Greek Amateur Athletics*. Chicago, 1984.

INDEX

Classical Texts Cited

Aelian, *Var. hist.*:
2.6: 168n24
2.24: 182n1
8.18: 184n12
9.3: 166n14
10.19: 165n6
12.22: 167n20
14.18: 165n6
Aeschines:
Against Timarchos 1.132: 130
Against Ktesiphon 3.183–86: 113–14
Against Ktesiphon 3.206: 83
Aeschylus:
Agamem. 167 ff.: 136, 169n2
Choeph. 338–39: 169n2
Africanus, Sextus Iulius, *Ol.*:
23: 173n13
33: 165n5
Ambrose:
Comm. on Ps. 36 51–55 (*PL* 14.1038–41): 56, 169n4, 170n8, 171n3
Comm. on Ps. 118 21 (*PL* 15.1567): 169n35
Anthologia Palatina:
9.588 (Alkaios): 8, 164n3
7.692 (Philip or Antipater): 171n6
6.256 (Antipater): 165nn5, 8
11.75 (Lucillius): 87
11.77 (Lucillius): 87
11.78 (Lucillius): 73–75
11.81 (Lucillius): 87
16.1 (Damagetos): 165n8
16.2 ([Simonides]): 10, 165nn8, 10; 177n43
Apollodoros:
2.5.10: 187n13
2.5.12: 40, 170n8, 171n16
Ep. 1.3: 187n10
Apollonios of Rhodes:
2.52—ff.: 173nn6, 14
2.90–92: 84
Appian, *BC* 3.68: 169n35
Aristeides, I.2: 168n29
Aristophanes:
Equites:
490–91: 167n18
571–73: 169n3